WHALE ON COPYR[

Fifth Edition

AUSTRALIA
LBC Information Services
Sydney

CANADA AND USA
Carswell
Toronto

NEW ZEALAND
Brooker's
Auckland

SINGAPORE AND MALAYSIA
Thomson Information (S.E. Asia)
Singapore

INTELLECTUAL PROPERTY GUIDES

Whale on Copyright
Fifth Edition

Jeremy J. Phillips
B.A. (Cantab.), Ph.D (Kent)
Intellectual Property Consultant,
Slaughter and May, London

Robyn Durie
B.A. (Sydney), LLM (London)
Linklaters & Paines, London

Ian Karet
M.A. Oxon.
Linklaters & Paines, London

LONDON • SWEET & MAXWELL • 1997

First Edition: 1971 R.F. Whale
Second Edition: 1972 R.F. Whale
Third Edition: 1983 R.F. Whale and J.J. Phillips
Fourth Edition: 1993 J.J. Phillips, R. Durie and I. Karet
Fifth Edition: 1997 J.J. Phillips, R. Durie and I. Karet

Published in 1997 by
Sweet & Maxwell Limited of
100 Avenue Road, Swiss Cottage, London NW3 3PF
Typeset by York House Typographic Ltd, London
Printed and bound in Great Britain by
MPG Books Ltd, Bodmin, Cornwall

No natural forests were destroyed
to make this product; only farmed timber was used and replanted.
A CIP catalogue record for this book is available
from the British Library.

ISBN 0 421 593 806

FOREWORD

In getting on for three decades since the publication of the first edition of Royce Whale's *The Law of Copyright*, the world in which copyright governs the unauthorised use of protected works has changed almost unrecognisably. In 1970 freedom to copy the printed word was limited not just by law but by opportunity: even in most developed countries most people did not have access to a reprographic copier. Recorded music was available in the form of gramophone records, but domestic tape-recording was a clumsy and time-consuming activity which yielded poor quality results. The off-air copying of television broadcasts was still a dream, as was the electronic compilation and dissemination of data by means of computers and modems. Yet then, as now, there was a clearly perceived need for laws to secure a fair balance of interests between creators and users of copyright-protected works. And now, as then, there is a need for a simple guide to the provisions of copyright law which presumes neither a familiarity with the mechanisms of the law nor too great a familiarity with the workings of those many industries which copyright touches on a day-to-day basis.

So much has happened in terms of copyright law in the past four years that a reader might be forgiven for assuming that it is time to start learning the subject afresh. This is not in fact the case for, while the multitudinous detail which in particular characterises British copyright law has undergone major change, the problems addressed by copyright and the principles which it applies in addressing them remain broadly the same. This means that, while there are many textual differences between this edition and its predecessor, the overall framework of the two books remains the same.

In its fifth edition *Whale on Copyright* now welcomes its third publishing imprint, having been published first by Longman and then by ESC. Now it is for Sweet & Maxwell to bring forth this volume in its own name, and to bind its reputation as a first-rate publisher of legal practitioners' works to a title which is read principally by those practitioners' clients. It is suspected that this book has in fact guided more than one practitioner through the tumultuous seas of copyright law and it is hoped that more will continue to derive its benefits. It remains for the triumvirate of authors to thank Sweet & Maxwell for its continued confidence in this title and to acknowledge with gratitude the support and co-operation of the two law firms from which the authors have drawn their encouragement.

Jeremy Phillips
Robyn Durie
Ian Karet
London, September 1997

CONTENTS

Foreword   *v*

Chapter 1 – The Evolution of Copyright   **1**
Introduction   1
"Copyright" through Letters Patent   2
Copyright at Common Law   3
Copyright of the Stationers' Company   3
The Statute of Anne, 1709   4
Common Law Copyright after 1709   7
The Expansion of Copyright, 1814 to 1988   8
Beyond 1988   10
Crisis of Copyright   11

Chapter 2 – Theory of the Author's Right   **12**
Copyright or Author's Right?   12
Is Copyright a Property Right?   14
Copyright as a Moral Right   15
The Author's Right: France and Germany   16
The Copyright System: What is its Foundation?   17

Chapter 3 – Sources of British Copyright Law   **20**
Statute Law   20
Common Law   20
Statute-based Case Law   21
International Treaties   22
European Community Law   22

Chapter 4 – Organisation of the Copyright, Designs and Patents Act   **24**
The Parts   24
The Chapters   24
The Schedules   25

Chapter 5 – Can I Claim the Benefit of Copyright Protection under the Act? **26**
Categories of Work Protected   27
Literary work   28
Dramatic work   29
Musical work   30

      Artistic work   31
      Sound recordings   34
      Films   34
      Broadcasts   35
      Cable programmes   36
      Typographical arrangements of published editions   37
      The requirement of originality   39
      The requirement of fixation   40
   Qualification for Protection   41
      Qualification by authorship   41
      Qualification by country of origin   41
      Permanence of qualification   41
      Absence of qualification   42

Chapter 6 – Duration and Scope of the Copyright in Works   **43**
   General Provisions   43
   Transitional Provisions   44
   Acts Restricted by the Copyright in Works   44
      Issuing copies to the public other than by rental or loan   46
      Renting or lending a work to the public   47
      The performance or showing or playing of a work in public   47
      Broadcasting the work and transmitting it by cable   48
      Making any adaptation of the work   50
      Doing, in relation to an adaptation of the work, any of the acts specified
          in relation to the original work   51
      Publication right   51
   Extended and revived copyright   51
      Extension of term   52
      Revived term   52

Chapter 7 – Ownership of Copyright   **53**
   Basic Provision as to Ownership   53
   Joint and Collective Works   53
   Letters   54
   The Employment Exception   54
   Reversionary Interest   55

Chapter 8 – Moral Rights   **56**
   Scope of Moral Rights   56
   Berne Convention   57
   Purpose of Moral Rights   57
   WIPO Performances and Phonograms Treaty   58
   Introduction of Moral Rights in the U.K.   58
   Right against False Attribution   59
   Right of Paternity   59
   Right to Object to Derogatory Treatment   60
   Right of Disclosure   62

Duration of Moral Rights   62
Joint Ownership   62
Infringement   62
Disposition of Moral Rights   62
Commencement of Moral Rights   63

Chapter 9 – Miscellaneous and Supplementary Provisions   **64**
Assignments and Licences   64
Future Copyrights   65
Bequest by Will of the Copyright in an Unpublished Work   66
Crown and Parliamentary Copyright   66
   Crown copyright   66
   Parliamentary copyright   67
   Crown and parliamentary copyright in practice   68
Copyright Vesting in International Organisations   70
Folklore   70
University Copyright   70
Deliveries of Copies to the British Libraries and Other Libraries   70
Miscellaneous Provisions   71

Chapter 10 – Copyright and Designs   **74**
The Old Law   74
The New Law   76
   Copyright   76
   Design right   76
   Registered designs   78
Licences of Right   78
Transitional Provisions   79
Overlapping Rights   79

Chapter 11 – Extent of Operation of the Act   **80**
Extension of the Act to the Isle of Man, Channel Islands, Colonies and
   Dependencies   80
   Extension provisions   80
   Power to amend the Act in countries to which it extends 82
Application of the Act to Countries to which it does not Extend   82
International Organisations   84
Denial of Copyright to Foreign Works   84

Chapter 12 – Infringement of Copyright   **85**
Primary Infringement   85
Secondary Infringement   85
Exceptions from the Copyright in Works   87
   Introduction   87
   Fair dealing   87
   Non-statutory fair dealing and unfair dealing   89
   Incidental inclusion   90

Educational copying   90
Copying by libraries and archivists   91
Copying by librarians of articles and periodicals and parts of published works 92
Copying by librarians in order to supply copies to other libraries   92
Copying by librarians or archivists to replace copies of works   93
Copying by librarians or archivists of certain unpublished works   93
Lending of copies by libraries and archives   93
Public administration   94
Anonymous or pseudonymous works   94
Public reading and recitation   94
Scientific abstracts   95
Recording of folk songs   95
Artistic works on public display   95
Advertisement of artistic works   95
Copies of artistic works by the artist   95
Public lending of copies of works   96
Use of films where reasonable inquiry fails   96
Use of sound recordings for charitable purposes   96
Incidental recordings from broadcasts or cable programmes   96
Recording by the Independent Television Commission and the BBC   96
Recording for purposes of time-shifting   97
Photographs of television broadcasts or cable programmes   97
Exceptions in relation to showing or retransmission of broadcasts and
* cable programmes*   97

Chapter 13 – Remedies for Infringement of Copyright   **98**
The Plaintiff's Options   98
Action available to the Plaintiff   98
Delivery Up   100
Remedies available to an Exclusive Licensee   101
Introduction   101
The exclusive licensee as plaintiff   102
Licences as of Right   103
Proof of Facts in Copyright Actions   103
Presumption of authority   103
Presumptions of subsistence and ownership where the author is not named   104
Presumption of originality and first publication   104
Criminal Proceedings in respect of Certain Infringements   105
Search Warrants   106
Criminal Offences by Companies   106
Compensation for Copyright Owners in Criminal Cases   107
Restriction of Importation of Printed Copies   107

Chapter 14 – The Copyright Acts of 1911 and 1956   **109**
The Copyright Act 1911   109
Statutory licence to reproduce works for sale   110

Reversion of copyright   110
Extended copyright under the 1911 Act   112
Summary of the 1911 Act's significance   115
The Copyright Act 1956   115
Part I: Copyright in original works   115
Part II: Copyright in derivative works   116
Part III: Remedies for infringement of copyright   116
Part IV: Performing Right Tribunal   116
Part V: Extension of restriction of operation of the Act   116
Part VI: Miscellaneous and supplementary provisions   117
The Schedules   117

Chapter 15 – Copyright and International Law   **118**
The Berne Copyright Union   118
Introduction   118
Legal nature of the Union   118
Revisions of the text   119
The Universal Copyright Convention   122
Relaxations in Favour of the Developing Countries Incorporated in the Paris
1971 Revisions of the Berne and Universal Copyright Conventions   124
Historical background   124
The Paris amendment of 1971   125
The Agreement on Trade Related Aspects of Intellectual Property Rights
(TRIPs)   126
WIPO Copyright Treaty   127
International Convention for the Protection of Performers, Producers of
Phonograms and Broadcasting Organisations   127
Introduction   127
Legal provisions   128
WIPO Performances and Phonograms Treaty   129
European Agreement concerning Programme Exchanges by means of
Television Films   130
European Agreement on the Protection of Television Broadcasts   130
European Agreement for the Prevention of Broadcasts Transmitted from
Stations outside National Territories   131
Convention for the Protection of Producers of Phonograms against
Unauthorised Duplication of their Phonograms   132
Brussels Convention on the Protection of Satellite Transmissions   133
Vienna Agreement for the Protection of Typefaces and their International
Deposit   133
Convention for Avoidance of Double Taxation on Copyright Royalties   134
Treaty of Rome   134
Exploitation of copyright   134
Harmonisation   135

Chapter 16 – Copyright and Information Technology   **136**

Computers and copyright   136
    Computer programs   136
    Electrocopying and electronic publication 137
Electronic mail   138
Database protection under U.K. law   139
Introduction to the new E.U. Database Directive   139
The Directive in brief   140
    What is a database?   140
    What databases are protected?   141
The Directive and copyright protection   141
The Directive and "*sui generis*" protection   143
International considerations   144
    The position of non-E.U. countries   144
    International treaties   144

Chapter 17 – Collective Licensing   **146**
Introduction   146
Practical Considerations   147
How does a Typical Collecting Society Function?   147
What Happens if there is no "Monopolistic" Collecting Society?   148
Rights in Sound Recordings   148
Mechanical Recording Rights in Musical Works   149
Further Development   149

Chapter 18 – Copyright Tribunal   **151**
Introduction   151
Performing Rights in International Law   152
Membership of the Copyright Tribunal   152
Procedure   153
Appeals   154
Costs   154
Jurisdiction of the Tribunal   154
Licensing Schemes   155
Licensing by Licensing Bodies   155
Matters to be Taken in Account by the Copyright Tribunal   156
Photocopying Licences   156
Rental   157
Certification of Licensing Schemes for Educational Establishments   157
Powers Exercisable in Consequence of Competition Reports   157
Inclusion of Sound Recordings in Broadcasts   158
Television and Radio Programmes   158

Chapter 19 – Rights in Performances   **159**
Rights and Performance under the 1988 Act   159

Chapter 20 – Protection outside the Copyright System   **162**
Introduction   162

Public Lending Right   162
Confidential Information   163
Trade Marks   165
   Unregistered marks   165
   Registered marks   166
Breach of Contract   167

Chapter 21 – Copyright Clearance and Practical Advice   **168**

Appendix   **170**
List of Associations   170

Index   **176**

CHAPTER 1

THE EVOLUTION OF COPYRIGHT

INTRODUCTION

The first thing to understand about copyright is that it is not merely the right to prevent copying. The word "copyright" is, therefore, a misnomer. This is unfortunate in that it has obscured the moral basis of the right it designates and has led to misconceptions which, it is suggested, have influenced legislation in a sense unfavourable to those to whom the right attaches, that is authors.

Traffic in goods and services is based on the proposition that they will be obtained only in return for such consideration, if any, as those supplying the goods or services demand. It may be said, therefore, to be relatively easy to conduct such traffic even without the backing of the law. The manufacturer, the manual worker and the performing artist are in a position to assure themselves — before they supply their goods or services — that what they regard as adequate remuneration has been or will be forthcoming. The level of remuneration will be dictated in most cases by considerations of supply and demand, costs of production and transport, economic conditions, and so on.

The problem of protecting authors' interests is much more difficult. It is of the essence of authors' works that they be revealed to the public, where they are exposed to the dangers of plagiarism and piracy. Reproduction of authors' works has been made easy by modern techniques, while the distribution of pirated copies has become almost impossible to control.

It is, however, a vital concern that the interests of authors and publishers should be adequately protected. In nations with developed economies, the livelihood of those who create and distribute the literary, dramatic, musical, artistic, scientific and educational material which is the fabric of their civilisation and the source of their knowledge depends on such protection. In the developing nations too there is an increasing awareness that through the availability of intellectual property-protected products, in particular computer systems and industrial designs, dependency on others can be turned into self-sufficiency.

There is no doubt that the profession of author is extremely ancient, and that throughout recorded history there were persons gainfully employed as artists, sculptors, dramatists and composers. In some cases these authors may have gained their livelihood by providing their services against remuneration. In other cases, the author occupied a post in the household of some ruler or magnate. In return for his services he received board and lodging and perhaps something by way of remuneration. On the other hand, some of the earliest writers of whom we have knowledge, such as biblical prophets and psalmists and the Greek and Roman historians and poets, were moved to record their personal or religious experiences, or were encouraged to use their talents for the edification of patrons and their circles, although no doubt many also hoped for fame.

Dramatists were from earliest times in a special position in that they were able to charge the public for the right to attend performances of their plays, as did such playwrights as Shakespeare and Racine later on (whose works were still without copyright protection) by arrangement with their troupes of performers.

The moral basis for the protection of authors' rights has probably been appreciated for as long as the profession of author has existed; that is to say plagiarism, while widely practised by individuals, has generally been condemned by public opinion. Plagiarism did not, however, in itself present a sufficiently urgent case for the enactment of legislation in protection of authors' rights. The effective protection of such rights throughout the greater part of history was that the copying of authors' works, or at least literary ones, was a long and costly process, while the market for such works was until relatively recent times so restricted that the economic return in respect of the making of unauthorised copies was small. It is for these reasons that the protection of authors' property has been a very late arrival on the legislative scene.

With the advent of the printing process (introduced in England by Caxton in 1476), the manifold reproduction of copies of literary works became relatively easy and the situation was profoundly changed. The increasing demand for copies of literary works led to a business of meeting this demand and to the obvious necessity, if this business was to flourish, of protecting the printer against piracy of his production.

"COPYRIGHT" THROUGH LETTERS PATENT

The first effective steps to grant exclusive legal rights in literary works (and very occasionally in graphic works such as engravings) were the privileges granted by the sovereign of the sole right to reproduce specific works, which were a source of considerable profit to the Crown. These privileges, in the form of a grant of Letters Patent, were generally enjoyed by the printer; but in some instances the beneficiary was the author himself, who in turn transferred his rights to a printer and publisher, naturally for a consideration. The process though which the author's work reached the public was essentially what it is today, requiring the collaboration of author, entrepreneur (publisher) and printer. In earlier times, however, the publisher (bookseller) and printer were very often the same person.

Since the earliest of these privileges generally concerned the right to publish the classic works of antiquity, the need to seek the author's consent or to acquire his manuscript did not arise. The duration for which the privilege was granted was usually quite specific (for example, seven years) but might occasionally be renewable thereafter. Not infrequently the penalties entailed by infringement of the privilege were prescribed in the patent. In his turn the privilege holder would have the obligation to deposit a copy or copies of the work with the royal library.

The system of privileges is not, however, the true ancestor of statutory copyright. Apart from the fact that it was sought and granted almost exclusively in the works of long-dead authors, this privilege attached only to specific works and could not be claimed as of right. Today's copyright, in the U.K. and in most other countries, attaches *automatically* to *every* work falling within defined limits. This copyright in its modern form in the U.K. is derived from two distinct sources: (1) the common law or customary rights recognised by the courts of the time; and (2) the copyright of the Company of Stationers, which was effectively the sole right to publish a specific work.

COPYRIGHT AT COMMON LAW

Common law may be defined as a body of decided cases which serve as precedents, together with customary practice, which the courts recognise as a valid basis for the administration of justice when the case is not one which is subject to statutory enactment (statutory law always overrides common law). After the introduction of printing in England, the dissemination of literary works entailed the danger of unauthorised copying and, side by side with the system of privileges, there arose a concept of something like a property right in literary works which gradually took root in the common law. The provenance of this common law copyright is unclear and is the subject of considerable debate. When the House of Lords reviewed the extent of common law protection for authors in 1769, it clearly conceded that there existed the right of authors to prevent others from publishing their hitherto unpublished works, but there was little evidence of any further copyright protection.

COPYRIGHT OF THE STATIONERS' COMPANY

The earliest of the great landmarks in the history of English copyright is the Star Chamber Decree of 1556, granting the Charter of the Stationers' Company. As might be expected from its origin, the purpose of the constitution was to control the printing and dissemination of printed matter in the interests of church and state, not to encourage literary production by commercially or politically motivated entities. Accordingly it was decreed that no-one should practise the art of printing unless he was a member of the Company, and severe penalties were prescribed for infringing the Decree. The Company of Stationers was one of the livery companies of the City of London; its membership encompassed book-binders, printers and booksellers.

It appears to have been obligatory from the Company's beginnings for its members to enter in the Company's register the work which they claimed the right to copy (not only books, but also ballads, maps, pictures, sermons and so on). The Company had the power to make bylaws and, so long as these bylaws did not infringe statute law, they were regarded as having legal force. As only members of the Company could, except by right of royal privilege, print books at all, it was established that the person making the entry had the exclusive right in perpetuity to copy the work.

The stationers regarded their copyright as limited to the copying and distribution of the work and did not claim any right of initial ownership of the work which they had the right to copy. Indeed they had no need to do so for, by accepting the validity of rights recognised to the authors in the common law, which were in effect the ownership of the work, they were able to acquire by assignment from the author a valid authority to copy the work. This right could be further assigned by the copyright owner in accordance with the Company's regulations.

What the statute regulated, in the interest of censorship, was the printing and importation of copies, which could be done only by members of the Company, but it was the Company itself which established the exclusive right in perpetuity of a specific person (as indicated in its register) to make copies of a specific work. The government did not concern itself with the ownership of the copyright; its concern was with censorship, which it exercised through the medium of the Company.

The position of the Stationers' Company was strengthened by later Decrees of the Star Chamber, in particular that of 1637, which provided that every book should be licensed and entered in the register book of the Company of Stationers, and further that:

> "... no person within this Kingdom or elsewhere shall imprint or import ... any copy ... which the said Company of Stationers, or any other person or persons, hath or shall have, by any letters patent, order or entrance in their register-book, or otherwise, the right, privilege, authority or allowance solely to print, nor shall put to sale the same."

It is known that not all books were in fact entered on the stationers' register. In these cases publication may have been licensed by the Company, but for some reason no entry was made. It is possible also that these books were not entered because of resentment of the Company's monopoly or through unwillingness to pay the registration fee.

The Star Chamber was abolished in 1640 and its Decrees, including those in favour of the Stationers' Company, lost their validity. In 1643 the Long Parliament adopted an "Act for Redressing Disorders in Printing" which provided that, under pain of various penalties:

> "No book shall be printed unless the same shall be licensed and entered in the register-book of the Company of Stationers, according to ancient custom;

> no person shall hereafter print any book lawfully licensed and entered in the registers of the said Company for any particular members thereof without the license and consent of the owner or owners thereof; nor yet import any such book formerly printed here from beyond the seas ... "

Further Acts and Ordinances followed, both before and after the Restoration. The regulation of printing for political purposes was still the main concern of the legislation, but the monopoly of the right to copy, vested in the Stationers' Company, was an essential part of the system and the Company's copyright was specifically confirmed.

The last of these Acts, the Licensing Act of 1662, expired in 1694, and with it expired the statutory regulation of the printing right on which the stationers' prerogatives were based, as well as the censorship. Those whom the statute had recognised as owners of the copyright were left without the protection summarily enforceable by penalties and seizure of copies which they had hitherto enjoyed; now they had to be content with such redress as they could obtain under the common law.

The Stationers' Company endeavoured to fill the legislative gap by strengthening its bylaws which were, however, applicable only to its own members. Meanwhile it attempted to obtain the adoption of new legislation.

The Statute of Anne, 1709

The next major development of copyright was effected neither through evolution of the common law nor through the activities of the Stationers' Company, but through Parliament, in the form of the Copyright Statute of Anne, 1709, which placed in an entirely different perspective the interrelationship of authorship, printing and publishing. In summary, since 1556 the state, for reasons totally unconnected with any intention to protect the rights of authors, had decreed that only members of the Company of Stationers might print and import books. The Company, through its regulations, had established that those who were registered as the owners of the copies of the published work had a right in perpetuity to restrain publication by others of those works. The right itself had not been created by statute. The owner was, at least in theory, always a member of the Company and the author, unless entitled to membership of the Company, could not own the copyright, although he enjoyed certain rights (based on the act of creation and deemed natural rights) recognised in the common law. These rights included the right, subject to the censorship, to publish. This right was deemed to be included in the sale of the manuscript to the bookseller or other prospective owner of the copyright.

In view of the difficulties created by the statutory void, the stationers repeatedly prayed Parliament for protection of their "copies". The object of these petitions was not the *creation* of a property right in their "copies", for they already conceived of themselves as having this right under the common law by assignment from the authors. What they wanted was effective *statutory protection* of that right. This protection was recognised by Parliament but, to the consternation of the stationers, it was not they who enjoyed its benefit.

The material parts of the Act of 1709 are as follows:

> *"Title*
> An Act for the Encouragement of Learning by vesting the Copies of printed Books in the Authors or Purchasers of such Copies during the Times herein mentioned.
>
> *Preamble*
> Whereas Printers etc ... have of late frequently taken the Liberty of printing, reprinting and republishing Books without the Consent of the Authors or Proprietors of such Books ... for preventing such Practice and for the Encouragement of Learned Men to compose and write useful Books, be it enacted that ...
>
> *Section I*
> ... the Author of any Book or Books already printed, who hath not transferred to any other the Copy or Copies of such Book ... or the Bookseller or Booksellers, Printer or Printers, or other Person or Persons, who hath or have purchased or acquired the Copy or Copies of any Book or Books, shall have the sole Right and Liberty of printing such Book or Books for the term of twenty-one Years to commence from the 10th April [1710], and no longer ...
>
> and
>
> ... the Author of any Book or Books not yet printed ... and his Assignee or Assigns, shall have the sole Liberty of printing and reprinting such Book or Books for the Term of fourteen years from the date of Publication thereof ... and no longer.
>
> *Section XI*
> Provided always, That after the Expiration of the said Term of fourteen Years the

> sole Right of printing or disposing of Copies shall return to the Authors thereof if they are then living, for another Term of fourteen Years."

The Act further provided that literary pirates were to forfeit their copies to the proprietor of the copy, who was to make waste paper of them, and that the pirate was to pay to the owner one halfpenny, and to the Queen another halfpenny, for every infringing sheet found in the pirate's possession. These sums, while apparently small, provided a far greater deterrent against unauthorised copying than the equivalent provisions today.

Section II of the Act provide that no-one should be subject to forfeitures or penalties in respect of books published after the Act came into force unless the title to the copy of the book had, before such publication, been entered in the register book of the Company of Stationers. It was not obligatory, however, for such entry to be made in favour of a member of the Company. It could be made in favour of the author or any other person entitled under the Act; in other words, copyright was no longer the privilege of the Stationers' Company.

The entry in the register had to be accompanied by the deposit of nine printed copies for the use of universities and libraries. Default in delivery of these copies entailed penalties. The publishers considered this requirement to be an unjustifiable burden on their business and therefore resisted it. Indeed, the requirement to deliver copies to the British Library (formerly the British Museum) and certain libraries has been maintained to the present day,[1] in spite of continued complaints by publishers. The Universities Copyright Act 1775 strengthened the provisions of the Statute of Anne both as to deposit and registration, which were expressly made conditions of suit of infringement. The Act of 1775 did not, however, make either requirement an express condition of securing copyright. In *Beckford v. Hood* (1798) the court ruled that the essential purpose of registration was to serve as notice and warning to the public, who might otherwise infringe unknowingly. It is interesting to note that even in the U.S. today, where registration has ceased to be a requirement of securing copyright only since March 1, 1989, that practice is still recommended on a voluntary basis for exactly the same reason.

To sum up, after *Beckford v. Hood* it was clearly established that the statutory copyright in published books was secured by publication, independently of any formality. The failure to register prevented an action for penalties against an infringer (although other remedies were available, such as an injunction to prevent further infringement), but did not affect the copyright. This principle, protection without the obligation to comply with formalities, has remained basic to copyright legislation in most countries of the world and to the international copyright conventions. The copyright system took another road in the U.S., where formalities, including deposit of copies and registration, became an obligatory requirement for securing copyright in published works, with profound consequences for the international protection of such works.

The essential difference between the Statute of Anne and the earlier legislation regulating the printing, publishing and importation of books, apart from the dropping of the censorship provisions, was that the right was now granted by the state, not derived from the bylaws of the Stationers' Company, and that this right was now available to

---

[1] British Library Act 1972, s. 4.

anyone, because neither the author nor his assignee had to be a member of the Company in order to enjoy the Act's protection.

COMMON LAW COPYRIGHT AFTER 1709

Although it was the stationers who had solicited the new legislation, they did not greatly benefit from it. They lost the exclusive right to claim copyright and, in place of the copyright in perpetuity which they had enjoyed under their byelaws, they received merely the sole right to print and sell those previously monopolised works for a further period of 21 years. This right was coupled to a further opportunity to acquire copyright for just 14 years, renewable for a similar term, in new works. However, the limitation on the duration of the right was for the moment of minor importance, because the assignees still claimed the perpetual right to copy under assignment from the author of his common law rights. It became, accordingly, important for the stationers to establish that the authors had this perpetual right under the common law.

In the first cases to test the effect of the Statute of Anne it was assumed that the Statute had not suppressed the common law right, but merely added to it. In the case of *Millar v. Taylor* (1769) in particular, it was held that the author had a common law right after publication of his works which had not been displaced by the Statute of Anne and which continued to be enforceable even after the expiry of the statutory copyright period.

In 1774 the question came up again for decision in the great case of *Donaldson v. Beckett*. The judges were asked to give their decisions on a series of questions and in essence decided that the author's rights in his published works expired at the end of the statutory protection period, being exercisable only under and in accordance with the statute. The author's rights at common law in *unpublished* works remained intact.

The merits and demerits of this landmark decision from the point of view of the various groups concerned — that is the authors, the publishers and the general public — can be, and have been, differently contended. It has been argued by Professor Lyman Ray Patterson[2] that the decision has been misunderstood in that it was specifically limited to the effect of the statute on the printing and publishing right — the copyright — and did not purport to hold that the author's common law rights consisted only of that right. The author's common law right had, however, never been clearly defined. Traditionally it was identified as that right which the booksellers purported to acquire from the author and which constituted their copyright, that is the printing and publishing right. Nevertheless, both in the courts and outside them, expression had been given to the view that the creative act established, between the author and his work, rights of a moral or personal nature but that these rights, if they existed, were not comprehended within the Statute, which envisaged only the more limited purpose of regulating the book trade. Historical reasons decided, however, that the author's right and copyright did not preserve separate identities and that the copyright, with its more restricted significance, was to eliminate the former.

The common law right in unpublished works was finally abolished by the Copyright Act 1911, which replaced it with a set of rights carefully defined and delineated by statute.

---

[2] *Copyright in Historical Perspective* (Vanderbilt University Press, 1968).

The Expansion of Copyright, 1814 to 1988

It was argued by the booksellers that the statutory period of protection provided by the Act of 1709 was too short for the effective conduct of their business, but it was not until 1814 that an Act was passed "to afford encouragement to literature". This Act substituted for the previous term of 14 years, with a reversionary 14 years to the author (if then living), a term of 28 years, to begin from the first day of publication and, if the author should be living at the expiration of that term, for the remainder of his life.

The first Bill which may be said to have been sponsored specifically on the basis of justice to literary authors was that of 1837, with which the name of Mr Sarjeant Talfourd, one of the greatest protagonists of authors' rights, will always be honourably associated. The criticism levelled by Talfourd at the existing legislation was, in his own words, that:

" ... the present term of copyright is much too short for the attainment of that justice which society owes to authors, especially those, few though they be, whose reputation is of slow growth and enduring character."

The opposition, however, was bitter, and the battle dragged on for years. In reintroducing his Bill in 1841 Talfourd proposed a copyright of 60 years from the death of the author. The Bill's most eloquent and decisive opponent was the most eminent author of his time, Lord Macaulay, who gave a striking example of a paradox noted during the earlier history of copyright, that authors were seldom active defenders, and were occasionally active opponents, of authors' rights.

The reason for what appears on the surface to be a strange attitude can be appreciated. It lay in a certain pride, and a reluctance to be thought to be inspired by any motive except the expression of a God-given talent and a desire to serve mankind through the exercise of this gift. But of course Macaulay was a very successful lawyer and Government servant, who had ample means of subsistence and was not dependent on earnings from his literary work. A better exposition of the situation of most authors is that of Pierre-Augustin Carron de Beaumarchais, the author of *The Barber of Seville*, who in the eighteenth century observed:

"It is said in the foyers of the theatres that it is ignoble of authors to plead for payment — they who pride themselves on thoughts of fame. This is well said; fame is indeed attractive, but it is forgotten that to enjoy it only for one year nature has condemned us to eat 365 times."

Macaulay argued that there was no natural right to literary property or, if there was, it did not survive the original proprietor. Copyright, he said, was a monopoly, making books dear and thus only to be justified within certain limits by expediency. He urged that extending the term beyond the author's death would not benefit him and that his heirs' expectation of such benefit would not be an inducement to him to labour. He defined copyright as "a tax on readers for the purpose of giving a bounty to writers", and he thought that the descendants of a great author might frequently disapprove on various grounds of the author's works and so injure the public by refusing to republish them.

Macaulay was correct in arguing that the purpose of copyright is to require the users of authors' works to pay a bounty to the author, but the world has come to regard as entirely equitable the contention that authors should be paid by those who enjoy their works. The world indeed is uncomfortably conscious that some of the greatest benefactors of mankind, geniuses in the fields of literature, music and the arts, have been harassed into untimely death by poverty precisely because they were not able to secure a reward based on the public's demand for their works. It has also come to be regarded as equitable that authors, like the owners of real property, should be able to bequeath to their heirs a valuable asset.

It is also the case, as the Gregory Committee acknowledged in its Report in 1951,[3] that copyright no longer operates (if it ever did) to delay the publication of cheap editions of books. The "paperback explosion" of the last 70 years is, arguably, a product of copyright protection rather than a consequence inhibited by it. Thus it can be said that in every respect Macaulay's arguments have been refuted by disinterested opinion and by experience, but they are insidious and are raised in different guises even today.

An amended Bill was introduced in 1842 and, in spite of some criticism from Macaulay, was adopted. It provided a statutory protection period of 42 years from publication, or until seven years from the death of the author, whichever was the longer. This was the Copyright Act 1842, which covered "books" including pamphlets, music sheets, maps and plans. This Act was applicable throughout Her Majesty's dominions.

In the two centuries between the Statute of Anne and the Copyright Act 1911 some 40 Acts enlarging the scope of copyright were adopted. Thus engravings were protected under the Engraving Copyright Act 1734; works of sculpture under the Sculpture Copyright Act of 1814; and paintings, drawings and photographs by the Fine Arts Copyright Act 1862. Musical and dramatic compositions were held to be "books" within the meaning of the 1842 Act. The extension of the scope of copyright concerned not only the category of work but also the acts in relation to the work to which the copyright applied. Thus the right of representation or performance was first recognised by the Dramatic Copyright Act 1833, which protected the performing right in dramatic pieces at places of entertainment. The 1842 Act extended the provisions of the 1833 Act to include the performance of musical works.

These Acts, with the exception of certain provisions, were repealed by the Copyright Act 1911, which codified the statutory law of copyright, abolished common law copyright and rendered it unnecessary to obtain registration at Stationers' Hall as a condition for bringing an infringement action. The passage of the Copyright Act 1911 saw British copyright governed by a single, integrated piece of copyright legislation for the first time since 1709. Since this Act was applied or extended to numerous common law jurisdictions, in some of which it is still of legal effect, its overall importance to the international development of copyright-based trade should not be overlooked.

The Copyright Act 1956, described in detail in the first three editions of this book, provided a revised version of the 1911 Act which, while differing in many individual features, was still recognisably related to its predecessor. The 1956 Act served its purpose well until the early 1970s, when the copyright-related industries underwent an apparently irreversible metamorphosis as a consequence of the discovery and development of new technologies for the reproduction and dissemination of authors' works. The period from August 14, 1973 (the date of establishment of the Whitford Committee on Copyright Law)

---

[3] Cmd. 8662 (October 1952), Para. 22.

to November 14, 1988 — when the Copyright, Designs and Patents Act 1988 received the Royal Assent — can best be described as a period of increasingly frenetic reform activity and piecemeal legislative amendment.

Broadcasting was first specifically protected under the Copyright Act 1956, but had been considered as falling within the scope of public performance under the Copyright Act 1911. By the early 1980s it became apparent that traditional terrestrial television and radio broadcasting was likely to be heavily supplemented, if not overtaken, by the provision of cable programme services and satellite broadcasting systems. The Cable and Broadcasting Act 1984 therefore amended the terms under which broadcasts were protected and established a new right in cable programmes themselves. The complex definition of "cable programme" has led to speculation that the provision of certain types of online information may itself be protected by copyright, a conclusion which, if correct, was certainly not foreseen by Parliament as a likely or expected consequence of this legislation.

Computer programs were not specifically mentioned by the Copyright Act 1956 even though they were in industrial use, admittedly in relatively rudimentary form, from the end of World War II. Legislative amendment by means of the Copyright Amendment (Computer Software) Act 1985 enabled computer programs to be analogised to "literary works", a position made firmer by the more explicit draftsmanship of the 1988 Act.

BEYOND 1988

The Copyright, Designs and Patents Act 1988, being the culmination of nearly a decade and a half of intensive lobbying and legislative activity, was hailed as a new peak of achievement in terms of both the scope of rights protected and the detail with which the balance was reached between the interests of the owners of those rights and of users of the works protected by them. However, what was viewed from below as a peak was seen, once reached, as no more than a base camp from which further heights of protection were to be assaulted. In this further ascent, guidance has come from two international bodies: the Commission of the European Union and what was formerly the United Nations Committee on Trade and Development (UNCTAD).

From the European Commission has come directives (i) defining the interplay of computer software copyright — which prohibits copying — and the need to stimulate competition in the creation of interactive or interoperable software, (ii) extending the term of most U.K. copyright works well beyond the minimum duration required by international conventions, (iii) harmonising rental and lending rights, (iv) recognising additional authors of works such as films and (v) establishing a two-tier system for the protection of databases. From UNCTAD has come the establishment of the World Trade Organisation (WTO) as an international policeman whose "patch" includes the monitoring of the minimum norms of copyright protection required of all nations which have signed the TRIPs (Trade Related Aspects of Intellectual Property Law) Treaty.

Whatever steps are taken by Parliament in the protection of copyright in the future, it is unlikely that they will ever echo the pioneering steps of the 1709 and 1911 Acts. More likely they will simply be taken in conformity with or fulfilment of internationally agreed standards. Indeed, given the increasing globalisation of copyright interests, it is unlikely that any single country will again be in a position to initiate ground-breaking reforms. The future cannot, however, change the past; the British contribution to the development of copyright law, and to the welfare of both copyright owners and users of the works, is one of which this jurisdiction can be justly proud.

CRISIS OF COPYRIGHT

It is not irrelevant to copyright today to recall the contrasting viewpoints expressed so long ago by Macaulay and Beaumarchais because they show that it is in the very nature of copyright to excite controversy, and because this is as true today as it ever was. Today, however, the extent and manner of application of copyright protection have, under the pressure of circumstances that could not have been imagined two centuries ago, become so contentious as to lead to the well-recognised "crisis of copyright."

These pressures come from two sources, the first of which is well illustrated by Article 27 of the Universal Declaration of Human Rights adopted by the United Nations, which reads:

"(1) Everyone has the right freely to participate in the cultural life of the community, to enjoy the arts and to share in scientific advancement and its benefits.
(2) Everyone has the right to the protection of the moral and material interests resulting from any scientific, literary or artistic production of which he is the author."

The pressures for access to sources of information and culture conflict with limitations on the right to such access. This conflict is felt particularly in countries, whether developed or developing, that are overwhelmingly importers of copyright material and exporters of copyright royalties. Moreover, in many countries the government itself, through its control of broadcasting and education, is by far the largest user of authors' works.

Accordingly, over much of the world, it is increasingly the practice to use, whether consciously or not, the sanction of the principle expressed in the first clause of the Article to erode the principle of the second.

The other source of pressure is a communications revolution. This threatens to overwhelm the capacity of the providers and distributors of information and entertainment material to exercise their rights under laws which are themselves often in areas of technological advances.

In this book it is the intention not only to expound copyright as it is now practised, but also to look at ways in which the British Government, its legislative partner and master, the Commission of the European Union, and those concerned on both sides of the conflict are endeavouring to adjust copyright protection to meet this crisis.

CHAPTER 2

THEORY OF THE AUTHOR'S RIGHT

COPYRIGHT OR AUTHOR'S RIGHT?

The author has only the fragile protection of the law against unauthorised use of his work by way of reproduction, publication, public performance or mutilation. Unlike the provider of goods or services, he cannot defend himself against misappropriation by withholding that which he supplies. The legal conception on which the protection of his rights is based is not therefore merely an academic question, either for him or for those who understand that such protection is a vital national interest. Such protection is, of course, also indispensable to the investment of capital and skill in the production and distribution of authors' works.

The word "copyright" itself calls for some comment. At the time when the Statute of Anne was adopted it was not the custom to give a short title to Acts of Parliament, and the title in fact borne by the Act was:

> "An Act for the Encouragement of Learning by vesting the Copies of printed Books in the Authors or Purchasers of such Copies during the Times therein mentioned."

The word "copyright" is nowhere mentioned in the Act, and the first use of this word remains obscure. The literary historian Roy Wiles has recorded what may perhaps be one of the earliest uses of this expression, which occurs in an assignment dated October 2, 1740, of the "copy right".[1]

As outlined in the previous chapter, for some 150 years copyright was quite simply the exclusive right to copy and, except for the implied right to publish, nothing else. It was accordingly not an author's right but a publisher's right; indeed it was the publishers, in the guise of booksellers and printers, who created this right for themselves as a necessary protection for their business. It was this right that the Statute adopted and limited in 1709 and, although under the Statute the author became entitled to hold copyright, the interest protected was still essentially, in its practical effect, the publisher's exclusive right to copy.

In so far as the author had rights independent of the traditional exclusive right to copy, these rights existed only in the common law. "Copyright" was, therefore, an appropriate term for the right granted by the Act of 1709, but as the author's other rights (for example,

---

[1] Reproduced in *Serial Publication in England before 1750* (Cambridge University Press, 1957).

the right to prohibit performance and recitations of his work) were in turn accommodated in the copyright statute, the label "copyright" became increasingly inappropriate.

If the Statute of Anne had carried a short title, this might well have been "Literary Property Act", reflecting a view of the nature of copyright that long prevailed and influenced legislation. That term would not, however, have been appropriate because, as is not generally recognised, the author's right is not properly situated in the sphere of property but has other and more significant sources.

Again, it is right that "learned men" should be encouraged to produce literary, dramatic, musical and artistic works especially at the present time, when the demand for such works is vast. Yet the world need not fear that, even without encouragement, the supply of such works would altogether fail. When the creative urge is strong enough there will be creation, even under the most discouraging conditions. It is submitted, therefore, that such encouragement is not the truest basis for the recognition of the authors' rights. That basis, it may be thought, is rather the moral imperative derived from the act of creation itself.

However, the title "Literary Property Act" might have mitigated some of the unhappy consequences of the historical causes, briefly referred to in the preceding chapter, which decided that the author's right would lose its identity in the concept of the copyright, and not vice versa. One can imagine that as categories of authors' works other than books became the subject of protective legislation, it would have followed that the title "Literary Property Act" would have become the "Authors' Property Act", and that what is now called copyright would have become known as "author's property right". While the latter term would not, for the reason already mentioned, have been ideal, it would have been greatly preferable to copyright, which, it is submitted, has by its semantic character been unfavourable to authors' interests in the countries of the English language. Two reasons may be mentioned in support of this opinion.

First, the word "copyright" is an impersonal one and has, therefore, become dissociated from the author, who is the true repository of the right. The author's assignees, like the author, are copyright owners, but they cannot claim to be authors of the work assigned. The natural sympathy which is felt by most people for the creator of literary, dramatic, musical and artistic works is not always extended to the creator's assignees, but the distinction has been blurred by attributing to both — before the introduction of some special authors' rights under the 1988 Act — much the same status under the law. In this context it is interesting to note that cultures which have adopted more personal terms for copyright (for example, French "droit d'auteur"; Spanish "derecho de autor"; Italian "diritto d'autore"; German "Urheberrecht") have almost instinctively adopted a more sympathetic attitude towards the role of the author as creator and beneficiary of his intellectual produce. Secondly, the term "copyright", precisely because it is impersonal, has now become attached to species of work other than authors' works. This means that such physical entities as sound recordings, pre-recorded video-cassettes and floppy disks, not to mention such metaphysical media as broadcasts and the supply of cable pro- grammes, are works as much protected by copyright as an author's works. Put in cruder terms, the author's right protects the author's message while copyright indiscriminately protects both the message and the medium by which it is disseminated.

Is Copyright a Property Right?

Probably the earliest theory of the legal nature of the author's right is that of a form of property right. At all events, this theory has frequently been applied to explain the copyright system. However, the very nature of copyright — a right to permit or to prevent other people doing certain acts with the author's or owner's work — meant that the effect of regarding copyright as property was to treat it as analogous to land or moveable goods, types of property from which others can be physically excluded.

The truth of the matter is that copyright has two dimensions. The first is that of its transmissibility by the author: he can give his copyright away, he can sell it, he can license others to use it and he can leave it to his heirs, just as if it were a lawnmower or a plot of land; in this sense copyright is easily seen as "property". The second dimension deals with its enforcement against others, and it is in this case that the analogy with property is more difficult to sustain. For example, if copyright is a form of property, it could be questioned why (except to the extent that practical considerations dictate) the possession of that property should be limited in time when the property is incorporeal, and not so limited when it is material. There are indeed many other restrictions on copyright in favour of research, study, education, dissemination of news, and even of entertainment, which are incompatible with the notion of property.

It is understandable, therefore, that both legal theory and practice have made a distinction between the author's rights in his unpublished works and those in works he elects to publish. According to this view the author is entitled to all the legal rights of person and property while his work remains unpublished, but forfeits these rights (or at least those of property) when he makes his work accessible to everyone and must accept the right of the state to afford him only such protection as the state, recognising that it is in the public interest for the author to reveal his work, decides to grant him.

This indeed was the legal position, in imprecise form, as it emerged from *Donaldson v. Beckett*, although not as a conscious application of a principle but accidentally, as a result of the interpretation of the working of the Statute of Anne. A clear dichotomy between private and public interests in an author's work still remains, but the detailed provisions of modern copyright law have all but obscured it. In any case this principle, while it has the merit of rationality, does not in itself lead to any specific concept of the author's right, for at least it needs supplementing by an additional concept of the author's rights in his published works.

For example, if the author consents to the recording of his work on a CD and to the distribution of that disk to the public, is he entitled to make his consent conditional on the recording not being used as in public performance or broadcasting? Can he argue that if hundreds or thousands of people are to hear his work through the medium of a single disk, then the sales of that CD, in which he has an interest, may be prejudiced? It may be objected that the performance or broadcast may in fact promote sales of the CD, but this objection begs the question of principle.

The concept of copyright as a form of property is given colour by the fact that it can be bought, sold or "hired" (licensed). What is concerned here, however, is the right, not the material object in which the work is manifested, which is indisputably a piece of property. The person who owns a picture, sculpture, book or manuscript is not necessarily the owner of the right to publish, reproduce or perform in public the work incorporated into it. In other words, the right must be distinguished from the work itself and from its physical support, if any: and the transfer of the right by the author to another party, along with the physical support, is not necessarily to be regarded as the transfer of the work itself.

On the other hand, the incorporeal nature of the created work demands that it be treated differently from the material object in which it is embodied. For example, a painting may be destroyed by its owner and will thus cease to exist as property, but the right to copy it will not cease. Or again, if a manuscript is stolen from another, he has lost his property utterly; while if it is copied without his permission, it remains in his possession but can be "stolen" by copying many times over.

Accordingly, if copyright is a form of property this form is very different from that of real property; hence the invention and employment of such terms as "intangible property", "intellectual property", "creative property" and "incorporeal property".

The property theory of copyright is all the more unsatisfactory in that the property may be declared to belong to someone other than the author, on the fiction that it is some other person who is its author. For example, under the Copyright Act 1956 the "author" of a photograph was the owner of the film on which it was taken; and in the U.S., a fellow common law jurisdiction, the "work for hire" doctrine even today deems the employer of a creative employee to be not merely the owner of that employee's copyright in works created under the service contract, but indeed the "author".

COPYRIGHT AS A MORAL RIGHT

The copyright system appears to be concerned only with the copyright — that is, the right to do certain acts in relation to the work. When these rights have been transferred, it is not concerned with the fate of the work itself, the emanation of the author's mind and personality. If it is accepted that the work nevertheless exists as an entity which is not identical with its physical support, if any, then it may also be accepted that transferring from the author to another the ownership of the material manifestation of the work (conveying a true property right), together with the right to do certain acts in relation to the work (conveying the copyright), does not necessarily signify that a relationship is established between the work and the new owner of these rights, which is substituted in all respects for the relationship between the work and its author. Some element must, it may be thought, always remain of the latter relationship which the transfer of the property right and the copyright does not convey and is incapable of conveying.

The Copyright, Designs and Patents Act 1988 has recognised the special position of the author with its introduction of a "moral rights" code (described in Chapter 7 below). The moral rights are, in principle, of a non-pecuniary nature; they are not bought or sold by authors or others, but exist specifically to protect the author against the depredations of others and occasionally against his own human weaknesses. Such rights enable their holder to insist that he, and not another, is credited with the authorship of his works and that his works should not be distorted or mutilated by others. In some jurisdictions moral rights go a good deal further.

It is formally acknowledged in the legal systems of some countries that this special relationship exists between the author and his work, which is indissoluble, and which is the concern of legislation on authors' rights; and it is this acknowledgement which distinguishes such a system (called in this book the system of the author's right) from the copyright system. The effects of this formal acknowledgement will be illustrated by a brief reference to the legislation of two countries which practise the system of the author's right.

THE AUTHOR'S RIGHT: FRANCE AND GERMANY

While the theories of the author's right are various, it can be said that in general, and whatever their particular leanings, they see that right as composed of two elements, the first of which is the moral or personal right of the author to assert his creative relationship to his work, the second being the right to put his work to economic purpose; but this basic conception can be worked out in different ways. For example, the German Copyright Law of 1965 defines the scope of the rights it protects in the following general terms:

> "Copyright shall protect the author with respect to his intellectual and personal relations to the work and also with respect to the utilization of the work." (UNESCO translation.)

This definition may be contrasted with that contained in the French Law of 1957:

> "The author of an intellectual work shall, by the mere fact of its creation, enjoy an exclusive incorporeal property right in the work, effective against all persons.
>
> This right includes attributes of an intellectual or moral nature, as well as attributes of an economic nature, as determined by this law." (UNESCO translation.)

There is between them a subtle but decisive difference, which does not depend solely on the much more categorical character of the French statement.

The German definition is based on a monist or unitary theory which, while recognising that the author's right consists of two elements — the right to assert his personal relationship to the work he has created and the right to exploit the economic potentialities of the work — does not find it possible to distinguish the limits of each element, and considers them accordingly as two facets of a single right.

The French definition, however, is based on what is usually called the dualist theory. This recognises in the author's right the elements of two different orders. There is a separation of the author's right to assert his creative relationship to his work and his right to put the work to economic use.

The bond between the author and his work, based on the relationship between the creator and that which he has created, will be indissoluble and unassignable under both definitions, but this necessarily entails different solutions to some questions, for example the important matter of assignment of rights.

Since one element of the author's right is conceived of in the German Law as unassignable, and that element is an integral part of a single right, it follows that the right cannot be assigned (that is, the ownership transferred), although it can pass by testamentary disposition. The German author, therefore, while he can license the exclusive or non-exclusive exploitation of his work, cannot assign the right, but under the French Law the author can assign the economic (patrimonial) element in that right. Thus the formulation of a law on authors' rights in accordance with a specific concept of that right will necessarily and designedly shape that law.

One must not of course suppose that, however strictly a copyright law may be drafted in the light of a basic concept, it will not be vulnerable to some degree of deviation as the result of pressures of one kind or another during its passage through the legislature and afterwards. Nevertheless, where there is such a concept, these pressures will meet with resistance. Where the system of protection is not based on any identifiable concept or principle, as in the countries operating a copyright (as distinct from an author's right) system, resistance to them will be weaker.

THE COPYRIGHT SYSTEM: WHAT IS ITS FOUNDATION?

The true motive of copyright legislation would seem to be that which is discernible in the Title to the Statute of Anne of 1709, and again in the Act of 1842, which begins:

> "Whereas it is expedient to amend the law relating to Copyright and to afford greater Encouragement to the Production of Literary Works of lasting Benefit to the World ... "

that is, it is intended to encourage authors and publishers to produce. Encouragement, however can take surprising forms. As recently as 1967 it was propounded by a writer on copyright that the best "encouragement" that could be given to authors and publishers would be to reduce the level of protection accorded to their works, thus obliging them to produce more to earn the same standard of subsistence.

The probable tendencies of copyright legislation based on the "encouragement motive" are strikingly illustrated in the following passage from the Report of the Canadian Royal Commission on Patents, Copyrights, Trade Marks and Industrial Designs (1957):

> "Copyright is in effect a right to prevent the appropriation of the expressed results of the labours of an author by other persons. ... The right is regarded by some as a 'natural right' on the ground that nothing is more certainly a man's property than the fruit of his brain. It is regarded by others as not a natural right but a right which the state should confer in order to promote and encourage the labours of authors. Generally speaking, those who appeared before us advocating long and strong protection held the first view; those who were in favour of weaker and shorter terms of protection held the second."

Significantly, the Canadian Commission did not think it necessary to choose between these alternatives. The approach to legislation on authors' rights in the countries of the copyright system has always been similarly pragmatic. In the Report of the Gregory Committee the question of the nature of the author's right was not even raised. The Whitford Report (Copyright and Designs Law (1977), hereafter the "Whitford Report")[2] likewise did not consider the question of "moral rights" which are an emanation from the author's right system and indeed an important, nonassignable element of it. The Report likened copyright to "fair play" for authors; but "fair play" is based as much on a code of conduct as it is on the existence of formal legal rules. While the White Paper "Intellectual Property and Innovation" (1986)[3] was prepared to recommend the implementation of

[2] Cmnd. 6732 (March 1977).
[3] Cmnd. 9712 (April 1986).

such rights, its motivation was largely that of raising the level of British copyright protection so as to enable the U.K. to ratify the 1967 Paris text of the Berne Convention.

Article 6*bis*(1) of the Berne Convention states:

> "Independently of the author's economic rights, and even after the transfer of the said rights, the author shall have the right (1) to claim authorship of the work and (2) to object to any distortion, mutilation or other modification of, or (3) other derogatory action in relation to, the said work, which would be prejudicial to his honour or reputation."

It had been argued, in the Whitford Report and elsewhere, that the moral right in the terms defined above would not be appropriately sited in a piece of "economic" legislation such as a U.K. Copyright Act; but there was no reason why the pragmatic approach that characterises our copyright system should have excluded the enunciation of a broad principle to guide the operation of its rules. Such a principle might, it is suggested, be that of the recognition of a personal and economic relationship between an author and his creation, a relationship which the Act purports to protect within the context of the public interest as a whole.

The enunciation of such a principle would not be without practical utility. It would inject into the Act a much needed element of objective sensitivity which is appropriate to the unique nature of the author's creative act, and it would weaken the generally held misapprehension that copyright is, and should be, no more than a property right.

It would of course be wrong to suggest that it is theory, or absence of theory, as the basis of copyright legislation that alone determines whether such legislation is an effective instrument for the protection of authors' rights. In a country such as the U.K., where literature and the arts flourish because creative ability abounds, where they are a source of national pride, where vast production is required to satisfy the needs of a literate population thirsty for entertainment, instruction and intellectual stimulation, where the enjoyment of authorised copyright-protected copies is easily affordable by the majority of the population and where the associations of copyright owners are not without influence, support for copyright will be strong and will be reflected in national legislation.

Nevertheless, inherent in the situation is a disturbing dichotomy. A strong copyright law is necessary to the economic support of the small minority of the population which is intellectually creative; it is therefore in the public interest. A strong copyright law entails restrictions on access to the works of this minority; this is therefore against the public interest. It is this delicate balance of the public interests which it is the task of copyright legislation to resolve.

There is no doubt at all that the great weight of the pressures in support of these two interests is on the side (at the extreme position) of unrestricted access to the author's published works, works which, as it is sometimes put, have been "dedicated to the public", and there is no physical obstacle (short of the author's not revealing his work at all) which can halt these dynamic pressures at a point which will leave the ultimate public interest "in balance". The author's right, however, has none of this dynamism; it rests, in legislation of a purely pragmatic inspiration, on precisely the same proposition as that of the opposing pressures — the public interest. As the Whitford Report commented:

"We recognise too that copyright protection not infrequently involves a conflict between public and private interests and that there is a need in certain cases for the exclusive right of the author to be limited. On the whole, we agree ... that the balance between the rights of the copyright owner ... and the exceptions in favour of copyright users ... is about right, and that no abrupt change in the balance is called for."

What clearer admission of the pragmatic consideration of the balance of competing interests could be found?

The position of the author under such legislation is not, therefore, a strong one and this vulnerability has been strikingly exposed in those countries (including developed countries) where the copyright system has been adopted but where the influences favouring the author's right are weaker than they are in the U.K.

This very brief incursion into the highly complex field of theory on the nature of the author's right is not intended to explore that field. Its purpose is to indicate the dimensions of the subject and to suggest that it is possible to feel some anxiety about the future of the author's right in the countries of the copyright system. This is first because of the tendency under that system to attach copyright on equal footing to subject-matter other than authors' works (and even to give that subject-matter some degree of precedence), and secondly, because the system lacks a principle which offers firm resistance to the enormous pressures to which the author's right is now subject.

It is indeed submitted that no legal system which fails to recognise the moral imperative deriving from the creative act will adequately defend the author's interests. That imperative will command respect for the creative relationship between the author and his work and, while not excluding the principle of "fair use", will be reluctant to encroach on the author's enjoyment of his work's economic potentialities.

This imperative is strongly reinforced by the fact that authors are required to accept the statutory limitation on the period during which they and their heirs may exercise their rights, and that the public has the enjoyment of the vast public domain constituted by authors' works which have fallen out of copyright at the end of this period.

CHAPTER 3

SOURCES OF BRITISH COPYRIGHT LAW

The law which nowadays confers copyright protection on works of authors and others in the U.K. and which determines the extent of that protection is derived from a variety of sources. In order to understand fully how copyright protection works — and why so prima facie simple a notion as copyright protection has become so convoluted a subject — each of these sources needs to be examined.

STATUTE LAW

The principal source of copyright law as enforced in U.K. courts today is the Copyright, Designs and Patents Act 1988, together with its many Schedules, Rules, Orders, transitional provisions which govern the legal status of works created before August 1, 1989, the date on which that Act came into force, and subsequent statutory amendments. This Act (hereafter simply "the Act") is the longest copyright law in the world. Part I of the Act, which deals with "traditional" areas of copyright like books, films and records, covers no fewer than 179 sections, many of which are themselves lengthy and complex. A further 33 sections in Part II govern rights in performances, while the unregistered design right found in Part III contains a further 52. By way of comparison, the Copyright Act 1956 contained just 51 sections in its entirety.

The Act, and corresponding legislation in other countries with a common law tradition, differs in style from copyright laws of the civil law "droit d'auteur" countries. The Anglo-American drafting technique aims to state the law with the utmost clarity and particularity so that the words of any of the Act's provisions can be affirmed to be selected specifically in order to convey one particular meaning. The words used by Parliament are interpreted literally, although there are "canons of interpretation" which mitigate absurdities (but not anomalies) in the law. What Parliament says, Parliament means; what Parliament does not say, Parliament is taken to have intended to omit. For this reason, the Act is detailed in its form. In contrast, copyright rules of civil law jurisdictions (for example, France, Germany, Latin America and Scandinavia) are expressed in terms of relatively broad principles which the courts are called on to apply and interpret in accordance with their general tenor and spirit. This is why the laws of civil law countries may appear to the U.K. lawyer to lack precision. As noted above, the development of U.K. copyright law is now partly in the hands of the Commission of the European Community. There is a feeling amongst English judges that when Parliament brings into English law European provisions, it should do so using the original "European" language; so the strict reliance on literal interpretation may, in time and as the law develops, begin to wane.

COMMON LAW

In addition to the statute law, the decisions of the courts are often shaped into legal doctrines which have a vital force as powerful as statute law itself, even though no legislative authority has discussed or approved them. These decisions form a body of law known as common law. As each new year brings a fresh crop of statutes, the area governed by common law principles shrinks like an Amazonian rain forest before the developers, but some important areas of copyright law and practice are still governed by the common law. These include the rules for making contracts, which determine when copyright licences and assignments have been made and what their force will be. Common law also covers the doctrine of "restraint of trade", which prevents, for example, music publishers securing exclusive rights to publish music by composers while those same publishers have no duty to make an effort to publish and promote the composers' works. A further area of common law influence is the principle, found nowhere within the Act but treated with the force of statute, that obscene publications do not enjoy the protection of the law of copyright.

The legal cases which, like accretions of tiny organisms, build up the massive coral reef of common law, are subject to a number of common law rules which determine their significance. For example, there are three strata of English courts which decide copyright cases; they are, in ascending order of importance, the High Court, the Court of Appeal and the House of Lords. A higher court's decision is binding on a lower court, but not vice versa. However, as a matter of respect and judicial comity, a higher court will rarely depart from a reasoned decision of a lower court without itself giving detailed reasons for doing so. Once the House of Lords has ruled on a decision, the point before it becomes well-nigh immutable (although the House of Lords is not bound by its own decisions) and is unlikely to be changed except through an Act of Parliament. Appeals to the Court of Appeal are relatively uncommon and quite expensive; appeals from the Court of Appeal to the House of Lords are quite rare. Appeals are unlikely even to be entertained unless an important point of law is at stake or there are pressing commercial reasons for them. When, as in the case of copyright law over the last decade, the proportion of copyright litigation determined by appeal courts rises, that is either a sign that existing law no longer adequately governs its sphere of operation or an indication of the substantial resources available to copyright owners and their opponents in court.

STATUTE-BASED CASE LAW

Halfway between statute law and common law is a body of law which behaves as though it were common law although its very existence is referable to statute law. This is the corpus of case law which interprets and elucidates provisions of an Act of Parliament. In the case of the Act, there is still very little reported case law to interpret provisions for which two or more distinct applications can be found. However, under the Copyright Act 1956 the volume of case law was considerable.

Like the common law decisions, cases involving the interpretation of statutes are subject to the rules which make a higher court's decision a binding precedent which lower courts must follow; likewise, a court will not willingly depart from a non-binding precedent without giving a good reason for so doing. There is, however, an extra dimension of interpretation which governs these cases yet which is lacking from the common law. That extra dimension is the fact that the intention of the legislature when it passed an Act must be taken into account and given the fullest effect.

In practice the intention of Parliament is usually respected by courts interpreting the words of an Act quite literally, on the basis that Parliament must have intended to use the words which it actually incorporated into a text which has been discussed in three Readings before Parliament and in a more analytical "committee stage". Sometimes there may also be extraneous matter ("travaux préparatoires") which preceded the drafting and the passage of the legislation in question, and which can be said to have indicated what Parliament was seeking to achieve. The admission of such extraneous material — even if it is as distinguished and influential as, say, one of the major international copyright conventions to which Her Majesty's Government is party — was, until recently, rigorously opposed, but now takes place with increasing frequency as more statute law is based on European Directives and less statute law is capable of convincingly cogent interpretation in the absence of recourse to *Hansard* reports of Parliamentary proceedings.

INTERNATIONAL TREATIES

For more than a century countries which respect copyright have entered into agreements and treaties with each other. Some of these treaties are designed to establish worldwide standards of acceptability for national copyright laws; others are designed to enable the inhabitants of one country to enforce their rights in another; others again endeavour to ensure that copyright royalties paid by one person in country A to another in country B are not the subject of taxation in both countries A and B. These treaties are not directly enforceable in the courts of the U.K. unless there is a specific provision in a U.K. statute which dictates to the contrary. Accordingly, an author or publisher who feels that U.K. laws are in breach of the country's treaty obligations under international law cannot sue in the U.K. courts for any redress.

EUROPEAN COMMUNITY LAW

In 1973 the U.K. became a member of the European Economic Community, now the European Union (E.U.). Under the European Communities Act 1972 the Treaty of Rome and its subordinate legislation was given the full force of law in Britain. Indeed, where British law and Community law are in conflict, it is the latter which is to prevail over the former. So far as copyright is concerned, the main effect of this is that an owner of copyright in a work cannot divide up the territories of the Common Market, giving a different licensee in each one the exclusive right to exploit his copyright within his own "patch". He can however enjoy copyright in one Member State even if his copyright in the same work was never recognised in one or more of the other Member States.

European Community law normally takes the form of Regulations and Directives. Regulations are directly enforceable in each E.U. Member State without the need for Parliamentary intervention, while Directives impose upon each Member State a duty to see that certain laws are enacted but leaves to the discretion of each Member State the means by which this is to be done. If the U.K., or indeed any other Member State, fails wholly or in part to implement a Directive (for example, by providing insufficient protection for a copyright owner or user), that injured party may, in some circumstances, be able to sue the U.K. Government and secure compensation for its loss.

Apart from the Treaty of Rome and its subordinate legislation, there is also a body of interpretative case law from the European Court of Justice and its subordinate court, the Court of First Instance. Decisions of the European Court of Justice are always expressed in terms of principle, and in many cases take the form of responses to hypothetical questions put to it on references made from national courts. These expressions of principle are generally respected as having the full force of national law in all Member States.

CHAPTER 4

ORGANISATION OF THE COPYRIGHT, DESIGNS AND PATENTS ACT

Since the main part of this book is given over to an account of the law as laid down in the Act, it is appropriate to explain at this point how that Act is organised. Its length and complexity do not make it immediately accessible to the casual reader, although it should be said that a good deal of its text is couched in language which is less difficult to understand than that of its predecessor.

THE PARTS

The Act is divided into seven Parts, each encompassing a particular topic. The seven Parts are:

- Part I, dealing with copyright;
- Part II, which establishes rights in performances;
- Part III, creating a design right which may be enjoyed without the formality of registration;
- Part IV, amending existing legislation on registered designs law;
- Parts V and VI, which concern patents, trade marks and those who practise in those disciplines (these Parts have no relevance to copyright law and are not discussed in this book);
- Part VII, which touches on a miscellany of uncategorised matters.

THE CHAPTERS

Parts I and III of the Act are divided into Chapters for ease of reference. The fact that a particular topic is dealt with in one Chapter rather than another can be of legal significance, since the meaning or scope of a particular provision which is ambiguous or unclear can be elicited from its general context and from the substance of those provisions which surround it.

The 10 Chapters of Part I cover the subsistence of copyright, the nature of the owner's rights in it, the many exceptions to the owner's rights, "moral rights" which are enjoyed by a work's creator rather than by the copyright owner, assignments and licences, infringement, licensing schemes, the Copyright Tribunal, and which works and which authors qualify for protection, as well as the usual collection of miscellaneous provisions which do not conveniently fit within any of the previous chapters listed.

Part III of the Act is divided into five Chapters. These deal with, respectively, the design right in original designs, the rights of the design owner, exceptions to the design owner's rights, and the jurisdiction of courts and of the Comptroller-General of Patents, Trade Marks and Designs in design right cases, followed by miscellaneous provisions.

THE SCHEDULES

Following the Act there are eight Schedules. These are rather like appendices, enjoying the force of law by virtue of the relevant sections of the Act itself which explicitly refer to them.

The Schedules to the Act are as follows:

- Schedule 1, covering the transitional provisions which are inevitable when one set of intellectual property laws is superseded by another;
- Schedule 2 lists "permitted acts" which may be done without infringing the rights in performances granted under Part II of the Act;
- Schedules 3 and 4 deal with the Registered Designs Act 1949: the first of these Schedules amends it, the second contains a version of the fully revised text;
- Schedule 5, to which no further reference will be made, covers patents;
- Schedule 6 provides the details of special provisions made in favour of the Hospital for Sick Children (Great Ormond Street, London);
- Schedules 7 and 8 contain lists of consequential amendments which changes in the law have forced on other statutes, and a table of Acts repealed in whole or part by the 1988 Act.

Although the contents of the Schedules are no less important than the contents of the main body of the Act, in practice they do not always receive the attention due to them. In part this is because they are perceived, quite wrongly, to be merely ancillary to the statute proper; and in part it is because they are presented in a less user-friendly manner and printed in smaller type.

The Act has been amended on a number of occasions, most notably by the Broadcasting Acts of 1990 and 1996, and by regulations implementing European Directives, notably the Duration of Copyright and Rights in Performances Regulations 1995 and the Copyright and Related Rights Regulations 1996 (to which a set of Copyright and Rights in Databases Regulations 1997 should soon be added).

CHAPTER 5

CAN I CLAIM THE BENEFIT OF COPYRIGHT PROTECTION UNDER THE ACT?

In order to answer the question posed by the title of this chapter, it is necessary to address first a number of subsidiary issues. In logical form they are as follows:

(1) Is my work the sort of work which the Act is capable of protecting?

Even if I work very hard for my living, not everything I do is a "work" within the meaning of the Act. If I sit down and write a book or make a tape-recording of the birds singing in my garden I have made a "work" within the meaning of the copyright legislation. If instead I unload a consignment of bricks into a tidy pile, then — notwithstanding the opinions of the purchasing authorities in the Tate Gallery — my work is not such a "work". Between these two fairly simple examples there are many things I can do which may or may not be a "work", depending on how the definitions of works contained in the Act are actually interpreted.

(2) Do I as an author have appropriate status — or does my work have appropriate "domicile" — to qualify for protection?

Not every person's work can claim to enjoy the protection of the Act. In principle, works by British subjects or residents and which are first published in the U.K. will be protected; if however the author's link with the U.K. is slight or non-existent, or the work is first published abroad, protection will be accorded only if (as is most often the case) the U.K. has entered into treaty relationships with the country of the author's or the work's origin, under which reciprocity of protection is achieved. This topic is discussed in more detail later in this chapter.

(3) Does the jurisdiction of the U.K. courts extend to the areas where my rights are endangered?

This question is one which is asked by lawyers in almost every area of law, but it causes particular problems in all areas of property law, of which copyright is one. In another guise the problem may be put like this. If a Mexican steals an apple which has been grown by an Italian in an orchard in Mazurka, people in the U.K. would be most surprised if the theft trial ever came to court in England. There is a piece of U.K. law, the Theft Act, which makes it illegal to steal apples, but one's normal and reasonable expectation is that it will be the law of Mazurka, not U.K. law, which will enable the thief to be brought to justice. If, however, the stolen apple is imported into England, problems may multiply. The Mexican may say that the apple belongs to him; that he took it from the Italian by force, but that (a) the laws of Mazurka do not accord growing plants the status of property; (b) he gave the Italian sufficient payment to cover the value of the apple, which would constitute a defence under Mazurkan law to any action based on an interference with property rights; and (c) Italians are not a recognised category of person entitled to the protection of the law of Mazurka, a state which has no diplomatic or other relations with Italy. An English court would be forced, with some reluctance, to make reference to complicated areas of Mazurkan law before it could determine the Mexican's entitlement to retain possession of the apple.

Had the dispute involved copyright law, the likelihood of such difficult issues having to be determined by U.K. courts would be very much greater. This is because many infringements of copyright are committed outside the copyright owner's country, to take advantage of cheap labour or raw materials costs or lax law enforcement, while infringing products are then imported into the copyright owner's country where consumer goods fetch higher prices.

Increasingly, a copyright owner will discover that his copyright has been infringed simultaneously in a large number of countries, for example, where counterfeit CDs made in one of Europe's developing economies are then sold unlawfully in a number of countries with strong currencies and well-established markets. This may seem detrimental to the copyright owner, but, paradoxically, come as a blessing in disguise. If the same person or persons are infringing the same copyright in several countries, the copyright owner can go "forum shopping", that is to say that he can choose the country whose laws and courts suit him best and do most or all of his suing there.

Once infringing goods are in the U.K. the jurisdiction of the courts to apply the Act is unquestioned, even though the actual infringements may have taken place abroad (and even though the acts complained of in the U.K. are in breach of U.K. law but are not against the law in the country where they are performed). Rights under the Act may be weaker in respect of infringing works made abroad than if the infringement had taken place here. For example, infringement will take place only if it is in the course of trade. Importing an article for personal use, when its making may have been an infringement in the country of making, will not be an infringement of U.K. copyright. The copyright owner's protection may indeed be wider than the U.K. alone, since there are several jurisdictions outside the U.K. to which the provisions of the Act may be extended. This matter is discussed in Chapter 11 below.

So, to sum up, if the work is the sort of work which copyright is capable of protecting *and* if neither the author's domicile or citizenship nor the work's country of first publication constitute an impediment *and* if the circumstances of an infringement are such that the Act can be applied to it, U.K. law will be applied.

CATEGORIES OF WORK PROTECTED

The copyright protection offered by the Act is not uniform. Different types of work are protected in different ways and for different lengths of time. The headings under which works are protected are laid out in section 1(1) of the Act as follows:

"Copyright is a property right which subsists ... in the following descriptions of work —

    (a)   original literary, dramatic, musical or artistic works,

> (b)   sound recordings, films, broadcasts or cable programmes, and
> (c)   the typographical arrangement of published editions."

An understanding of this provision is not of itself sufficient to enable the reader to understand what is meant by each of these terms. Accordingly, the Act goes to great lengths to flesh out these "descriptions" of works with further elements of explanation or definition. Case law too has given some of these terms an extra dimension by interpreting them in a particular manner. Further problems are added by the inclusion in the section of the word "original"; these too will require explanation. Let us now examine in greater depth, therefore, the "descriptions" of works listed in section 1(1).

Literary work

Section 3(1) defines what is meant by a "literary work". It reads:

> "'Literary work' means any work, other than a dramatic or musical work, which is written, spoken or sung, and accordingly includes —
>
> > (a)   a table or compilation, and
> > (b)   a computer program."

This definition is a far cry from the notion of "book" which permeated the 1709 Statute of Anne. It includes all forms of written and recorded word-based works, including newspapers, slogans, advertisements, mathematical formulae, codes, tables and, as can be seen from the quoted section, even computer programs (whether they can be read by humans or only by machines).

The term "literary" is not to be taken as a term of approbation as to the content of the work, since the literal meaning of the word "literary" is "of or pertaining to letters". Any work made up of letters, whether written or spoken, is deemed to be "literary", for example, an advertising slogan, a code, a list of football fixtures or a shopping list.

A controversial change made by the 1988 Act was to recognise that spoken words themselves are capable of constituting a "literary work". This recognition gives rise to some difficulty in that we all potentially speak literary works without knowing it. We can intuitively discern that there is a difference between:

> "We shall defend our island whatever the cost may be, we shall fight on the beaches, we shall fight on the landing grounds, we shall fight in the fields and in the streets, we shall fight in the hills; we shall never surrender." (Winston Churchill, speech to the House of Commons, June 4, 1940).

and

> "Yeah, well, we've got a two-goal start from the away leg. What we got to do is to keep them out, hold on to the ball a bit and make them come at us, Brian. They've got to really come at us, like, in the first 20 minutes and pull one [goal] back. But we're doing it all in front of our crowd, like, and they'll really be rooting for the lads. They're worth an extra goal." (English footballer interviewed on television, April 1983).

Once written down, both the above quotations constitute literary works, irrespective of their quality. Before they are written down, it seems difficult to distinguish them in law but hard to equate them in fact. They are not in fact distinguishable under the Act.

An old maxim of the law is *de minimis non curat lex* ("the law is not concerned with mere trifles"). The *de minimis* principle will not be found in the Act or any of its predecessors, but its spirit is apparent in the interpretation given by the courts to copyright statutes. Thus the term "original literary work" in the Copyright Act 1956 was held not to cover the single word "Exxon" even though that word was "original" (having been specially coined by Standard Oil of New Jersey), "literary" (consisting of letters) and a "work" (it took much effort to decide on the nature and the suitability of the word in question). There is no clear guideline as to how brief and inconsequential a work must be before it loses the status of a literary work, but the *Exxon* case has itself affirmed a guideline suggested by courts in previous cases, that a literary work must normally be expected to contain some element of information, instruction or entertainment. If it does not, then the likelihood of it being protected by the courts against unauthorised copying is slight.

The definition of "literary work" does not expressly exclude new typefaces, fonts and alphanumeric designs, but these are not literary works, even though they are "works" in the sense that they are derived from effort and "literary" in the sense of being made up of letters. Typefaces are in fact protected by copyright as being "artistic works" (discussed on pages 31 to 34 below).

The term "compilation" has attracted little by way of judicial interpretation, though its meaning is presumed to be wide enough to include not only compilations of other works (*e.g.* encyclopaedias consisting of literary and artistic entries), but also compilations of bare facts, each of which could not of itself enjoy copyright protection, (*e.g.* alphabetical list of telephone subscribers). (The protection of literary works compromising compilations of non-authorised items is discussed below in Chapter 16, in the discussion of databases).

Dramatic work

The legal layman, bewildered at the range of subjects which fit within the category of "literary work", believes himself better able to judge what constitutes a "dramatic work". Drama, in the eyes of the theatre-going public, might conjure up such elements as the plays of Ibsen or the musicals of Andrew Lloyd Webber. In legal terms, however, the matter is not so simple.

The Act, by section 3(1), stipulates (as noted above) that a literary work is any work "other than a dramatic work", from which it is reasonable to conclude that literary works and dramatic works constitute mutually exclusive categories of work. The same section continues:

"'dramatic work' includes a work of dance or mime."

This indicates that any sequence of actions, even in the absence of sound, which has been recorded in a medium from which it may be retrieved and copied *does* constitute a dramatic work. This includes choreography of ballet, mime and dumb-shows. Would it, however, also cover laser shows, firework displays, aeronautical display by the Red

Arrows and *son et lumière*, where there is no direct human activity to be seen and copied (unlike dance or mime) but where, colloquially, one would not abuse vocabulary by describing a repeatable sequence of events or illusions as being "dramatic"? The matter awaits resolution.

The next problem is what to do about plays (the problem arises because the Act does not use the word "play" to describe a category of protectable work). Take Tom Stoppard's *Travesties* for instance. It has two dimensions, one purely verbal (the dialogue) and one dramatic (the instructions given to the actors by the playwright). One could say that such a work was thus both literary and dramatic, were it not for section 3(1)'s insistence that literary work and dramatic work are mutually exclusive categories.

On one level it may not matter whether *Travesties* is a literary work or a dramatic one, since the Act generally treats literary and dramatic works the same way. But in Part II of the Act (which protects rights in performances) "performance" is defined by section 180(2) as meaning:

"(a)   a dramatic performance (which includes dance and mime),
(b)   ...
(c)   a reading or recitation of a literary work."

If *Travesties* is a literary work, then a performer's recitation of it will be protected against the making of unauthorised recordings. If it is a dramatic work, it *cannot* be also a literary work, which means that a performer's recitation will be protected only if it can be described as a "dramatic performance". Readings and recitations *per se* are generally regarded, at least colloquially, as being non-dramatic performances. If, however, this were so, and the reading of passages of *Travesties* were not protected against unauthorised copying, there would be a travesty of justice; yet if the only way of gaining protection is to assert that *Travesties* is a literary work and not a dramatic one, then some may feel that this is a travesty of vocabulary.

Leaving these difficulties aside, the *de minimis* principle discussed above should be briefly considered. It is not yet known how brief or insubstantial a sequence of dramatic actions needs to be before it loses the protection of the law and ceases to be a "dramatic work". It is however submitted that a single action or sequence of closely related actions — for example the "Fosbury flop" in high-jump technique or a sequence of pikes and tucks in high diving — is unlikely to be regarded as a fit subject for the law's protection, no matter how detailed and explicit the instructions for its replication.

Musical work

Following the example of earlier statutes, the Copyright Acts of 1911 and 1956 contained no definition of "music" or "musical work". In the nineteenth century and earlier there was no pressing need to define "music" since there was a relatively clear-cut consensus as to what was, or was *not*, music. By the twentieth century this consensus was already starting to become eroded, as three things happened: (1) music was regarded by many people as more a branch of physics than an area of aesthetics; (2) the frontiers of aesthetic acceptability were themselves gradually rolled back by *avant garde* compositions and by techniques of minimalist and atonal music-writing; and (3) new technologies of performance and recording blurred the previously rigid barrier between "music" and "sound".

The 1988 Act has sought to remove itself from the arena of contentious definition by providing an account of the meaning of the words "musical work" which invites judicial interpretation. Section 3(1) of the Act defines the words as meaning:

"a work consisting of music, exclusive of any words or action intended to be sung, spoken or performed with the music."

From this it is clear that "musical work" inherently excludes both "literary work" (being "exclusive of any word ... intended to be spoken, sung or performed") and "dramatic work" (being "exclusive of any ... action intended to be ... performed"). This exclusivity is necessarily mutual, since "literary work" is defined as excluding a "musical work". Curiously, though, the definition of "dramatic work", which includes "a work of dance or mime", does not explicitly exclude a "musical work".

But what is "music"? Beyond doubt any conventional and repeatable inscription or record of vocal or instrumental expertise which contains the recognisable elements of tone, pitch and rhythm will be regarded as music. Instructions to musicians to make *extempore* performances based on particular musical themes or conventions, on personal meditations or even on spur-of-the-moment inspiration do not, it is submitted, fall within the acceptable understanding of what music is. However, such instructions will be literary works in their own right. The significance of this distinction is that a person who copies a sheet of music and a person who copies a sheet of instructions to a musician will equally be liable as copyright infringers; a pianist who plays the sheet of music will be performing it and thus, if he does so without permission, infringing musical copyright, while the pianist who follows the instructions of the composer to play *extempore* in a particular manner will not be "performing" the literary work in which copyright subsists.

Artistic work

Anything which consists of words or letters has a strong claim to being considered "literary"; anything which consists of musical notation or phrases played by musical instruments stands a good chance of qualifying for the epithet "musical"; but what does an item have to consist of if it is to be regarded as "artistic"? This book will not attempt even to begin to answer this question, but the reader who reflects on it will soon see why the Act's definition of "artistic work" is more an attempt to identify those elements which are inherently part of anything which is "artistic". The world of art is a world governed by subjective perceptions and intellectual positions which do not readily submit to legal application.

To illustrate this point one need look no further, by way of example, than a tin of baked beans on a supermarket shelf. The inscriptions on the label, bearing details of ingredients, manufacture and origin, are mundane and unexciting enough, but every lawyer in the land will agree that they constitute a literary work. The label itself, however, bears a simple arrangement of commonplace shapes and colours. Is it an artistic work? No, says one critic, it is merely a mass-produced strip of printed paper arranged so as to distinguish the beans from other goods in the eyes of a shopper and to enable the printing on the label to be legible; it is not even a product in its own right. Yes, says a second critic, it is the product of skilled intellectual thought and effort, designed to attract the shopper's attention. Why should the fact that it is commonplace, that it is mass-produced, or that it is not a product in its own right, disqualify it from protection as a work of copyright? Most popular songs are comprised wholly or partly of commonplaces, the works of Günther Grass are mass-produced, and the lettering on the label is also not a product in its own right, but *they* are all protected by copyright. The first critic then responds with a *reductio ad absurdum*: if the label on a tin of beans is an "artistic work", is the tin itself not an "artistic work"? Like the label, it too is the product of intellectual thought and effort, and has a certain physical attractiveness of its own. How do you distinguish the label from the tin? These questions — and the determination of Parliament to minimise the necessity of discussing them in court proceedings — lie at the heart of the Act's approach to the protection of the physical appearance of two- and three-dimensional objects.

"Artistic work" is defined within the Act in a particularly cumbersome manner. First, section 4(1) explains what three different things are meant by the words "artistic work"; then section 4(2) defines four of the words used in the definition. Sections 51(1) and 54(1) then add incidental information as to types of work contained within the section 4(1) definition.

The three different categories of work protected under section 4(1) as artistic works are:

> "(a)   a graphic work, photograph, sculpture or collage, irrespective of artistic quality,
> (b)   a work of architecture being a building or a model for a building, or
> (c)   a work of artistic craftsmanship."

Note that the words "irrespective of artistic quality", which serve to "neutralise" the potentially laudatory connotations of the word "artistic", qualify only the first category of works. From this it has been inferred by the House of Lords in *Hensher v. Restawile Upholstery*[1] that works of artistic craftsmanship must therefore have an artistic quality. This inference sheds no light on the level of artistic quality, if any, required for works of architecture, although such works are generally agreed to be artistic *per se*, and without the need for them to fulfil any artistic criteria.

Section 4(2) adds flesh to the bare bones of section 4(1) by defining the words "building", "graphic work", "photograph" and "sculpture". Of these the definition of "graphic work" is most wide-ranging. Such a work includes:

> "(a)   any painting, drawing, diagram, map, chart or plan, and
> (b)   any engraving, etching, lithograph, woodcut or similar work."

The concept of "sculpture" is qualified in two different ways. First, for the avoidance of doubt, the word is taken to include not only the finished product but also, by section 4(2):

> "a cast or model made for the purposes of sculpture."

This is curious. No-one would think that a writer's rough jottings or a painter's preliminary sketchings would be deprived of their status as copyright-protected works simply because

---

[1] [1976] A.C. 64.

they were made as the means to achieve a particular end. However, the notion of "sculpture" in colloquial parlance is so closely associated with the end-product, the perfectly formed object which is exhibited in museums or public places, that it was felt necessary to put the word's meaning beyond dispute. The second curiosity involves the inclusion next to the word "sculpture" of the word "collage" in section 4(1). Since, in literal (but not colloquial) terms, "sculpture" is that which is sculpted or hewn from a single unit of wood or stone, the assembly of a three-dimensional art work made of numerous components or diverse substances would not be a sculpture and could therefore claim copyright protection only as a work of artistic craftsmanship. So, could it be that the word "collage" is added, for the first time in a British copyright statute, to ensure beyond doubt that such a work will fall within the scope of the Act?

Another interesting qualification of "artistic work" lies in the definition of "photo-graph" in section 4(2):

> "a recording of light or other radiation on any medium on which an image is produced or from which an image may by any means be produced, and which is not part of a film."

This definition is wide enough to cover not only X-rays but also photocopies and images recorded by means of desktop publishing scanners, which "read" works fed into them and record them on a computer disk for subsequent use. Indeed, the definition includes interesting markings on the human body which are caused by suntanning. It does not, however, include holograms which fall within the definition of a film.

Leaving now the provisions of section 4, it is important to note sections 51(1) and 54(1). Neither of these sections deals with the subsistence of copyright in a work; each deals instead with exceptions to the law of infringement. The provisions read as follows:

> "51.—(1) It is not an infringement of any copyright in a design document or model recording or embodying a design for anything other than an artistic work or a typeface to make an article to the design or to copy an article made to the design.
> 54.—(1) It is not an infringement of copyright in an artistic work consisting of the design of a typeface [to do various specified acts]."

From this it may be inferred that the following works, in addition to those specifically listed in section 4, are also protected by copyright: (a) a model recording or embodying a design for anything other than an artistic work, and (b) a typeface. Presumably, if such works were not themselves artistic works, it would not be necessary for the Act to list non-infringing acts done in respect of them.

It is unclear how sections 51(1) and 54(1) relate to section 4(1). Only one of the three categories of artistic work described in section 4(1) would seem to include a "model recording or embodying a design for something other than an artistic work" and that is the work of architecture, which is a building or a "model for a building". A model from which a work of artistic craftsmanship, a sculpture or a collage is made cannot be referred to by section 51(1) since the words "recording or embodying a design *for something other than an artistic work*" rule out such a connection. Yet if section 51(1) means "architectural work" — which is unlikely if one examines the overall context of the provision — why does it say "model recording or embodying a design"?

The situation with regard to typefaces, that are implicitly "artistic works" under sections 51(1) and 54(1), is less difficult even if it remains unsatisfactory. The definition of "artistic work" under section 4(1) includes a "graphic work". If a new design for the letters of the alphabet is executed in the form of drawings or sketches of those letters, it is a "graphic work" because "graphic work" includes drawings and the like. If, however, the set of letters is crafted in three-dimensional form by being cut into wood or metal, it will presumably still be a "graphic work", because "graphic work" includes engravings, etchings and so on.

Sound recordings

In addition to the copyright protection of literary, dramatic and musical works, the Act also provides for the protection of a "sound recording". In practical parlance we are talking here of recorded compact discs, audio tapes, gramophone records, the cylinders of mechanical musical toys and the operative punched-card mechanism of fairground organs — any physical object from which recorded sound can be replayed. It also includes the soundtrack of a film, regardless of its form.

A definition of "sound recording" is provided by section 5(1) of the Act. As understood by the draftsmen, "sound recording" means:

"(a)   a recording of sounds, from which the sounds may be reproduced, or
(b)   a recording of the whole or any part of a literary, dramatic or musical work, from which sounds reproducing the work or part may be produced,

regardless of the medium on which the recording is made or the method by which the sounds are reproduced or produced."

The two-part definition, covering both sounds *per se* and recordings of literary, dramatic and musical works, is important to note. From the first leg of the alternative it is clear that not only recordings of authors' works but recordings of bird-song and sound effects such as gunfire, steam locomotive noises and chanting crowds of demonstrators all fall within the scope of the Act's protection.

Films

In addition to the copyright which vests in a photograph, a separate copyright vests in a film. In the old days of silent celluloid films, a film was nothing other than a rapid sequence of photographs. If a single photograph was protected by copyright, a sequence of photographs needed no extra protection. However, as technology became more complex, the introduction of accompanying soundtracks, the practicalities of film release and distribution, and the advent of videotape recording all necessitated further amendments to the law as it originally applied to photographs to the extent that, in the U.K. at any rate, the copyright in a photograph and the copyright in a film have very little in common.

The definition of "film" contained in section 5(1) of the Act replaces that of "cinematograph film" under section 13 of the Copyright Act 1956. The old terminology was felt to be clumsy and pedantic and the old definition, too, was in need of an overhaul since it did not clearly indicate that a sequence of motion pictures recorded on a videotape constituted a "cinematograph film" and was thus entitled to copyright protection.

The new definition is shorter, broader and less ambiguous than its predecessor. "Film" means:

"a recording on any medium from which a moving image may by any means be produced."

This definition applies not only to motion sequences as recorded on celluloid or videotape, but also to cinematographic devices of less technological sophistication, such as "flick-books" — where a sequence of drawings are printed on consecutive leaves of a book, and when flicked through from front to back, convey the illusion of motion — and rapidly rotating illustrated drums which, in the nineteenth century, were popularly used for simulating the motion of a galloping horse.

Note that the definition requires that the image which is recorded must be a "moving" one, not a "changing" one. If I set up a video camera in a picturesque setting so that I can record the changes which appear through dawn, sunrise, daylight, dusk and sunset, I have not made a film since there has been no "motion". Such a work, if it is not a film, is however entitled to enjoy a greater degree of protection than many a film, since it qualifies for protection as a "photograph" (the degree of protection accorded to different types of work is discussed in the next chapter). Nothing in the definition requires that the moving image be an image recorded from the real world. Accordingly the images produced by video games may be regarded as films.

Broadcasts

A broadcast is not an "author's work" in respect of which an individual's creative labour and expertise is protected against unfair and unremunerated exploitation. It is however protected by copyright on account of its great commercial value. In earlier times, when all British broadcasting was in the hands of a monopoly (the British Broadcasting Corporation) or a closely-controlled duopoly, the ownership of copyright in a broadcast was a matter of little significance. It did, however, lead to definitional problems. In copyright terms only the BBC or the Independent Broadcasting Authority could own the copyright in broadcasts under the 1956 Act. Strictly speaking, only those two organisations would then need to obtain permissions to "broadcast" other works. This was clearly not intended. Now that British broadcasting has been partially decentralised and to some extent deregulated, and now too that the European Union has decided to afford copyright-type protection to broadcasts and has considered control of retransmission, the ability to control the further use of material which has been broadcast is increasingly important.

Section 6(1) defines "broadcast" as meaning:

"a transmission by wireless telegraphy of visual images, sounds or other information which —

(a)   is capable of being lawfully received by members of the public, or

(b)   is transmitted for presentation to members of the public."

For the benefit of those whose grasp of physics is weak (including much of the country and the legal profession), "wireless telegraphy" is defined in section 178(1) as:

"the sending of electro-magnetic energy over paths not provided by a material substance constructed or arranged for that purpose."

So the beaming of programmes by satellite, the transmission of programmes by terrestrial over-the-air transmitters and the constant conversation between policemen and their police station on a high frequency wave-band are all examples of "wireless telegraphy"; but they are not "broadcasts" unless they are capable of being lawfully received by the public (which police messages are not) or are transmitted for presentation to members of the public (which climatic information beamed to the Meteorological Office from weather satellites is not). An encrypted broadcast is capable of being lawfully received by members of the public even if they have to pay to obtain the means of "de-scrambling" the encrypted signal. All members of the public who pay are capable of receiving the broadcast. This accords with international telecommunications law and practice.

Cable programmes

The Cable and Broadcasting Act 1984 amended the Copyright Act 1956 by bringing within the ambit of copyright protection a new species of subject-matter, the cable programme. During the early 1980s the government was earnestly advocating the wide-scale operation of local or regional cable television systems, which would be funded by advertising and either by subscriptions or on a pay-per-view basis, as a means of enhancing competition between programme providers. At that time it was thought that cable systems based on the new fibre optic technologies or on traditional coaxial cabling would represent an attractive investment and that a successful, consumer-led television system would replace the supply-led duopoly of the British Broadcasting Corporation and the companies under the umbrella of the Independent Broadcasting Authority.

The introduction of a cable programme right was designed to confer, in respect of the providers of cable programmes, a set of rights to guard against commercial and unauthorised use of their services in a form which was analogous to that granted in respect of broadcasts. Despite the grant of the right cable systems have not yet prospered, the investment having been delayed by the slowness and expense of digging up the streets and telephony having proved more popular than cable television.

The definition of "cable programme" under section 7(1) is "any item included in a cable programme service". Consequently, the term "cable programme service" has to be understood before it is possible to determine what a "cable programme" is. The same section defines "cable programme service" as meaning a service which consists wholly or mainly in sending visual images, sounds and other information:

"(i)   by means of a telecommunications system; and
 (ii) if the sending is done otherwise than by wireless telegraphy; and
 (iii) if the service is for reception at two or more places *or* for reception by the public; and
 (iv) if the service is not specifically excluded by section 7(2)."

Each of these four qualifications needs to be considered in turn.

First, the cable programme service must send programmes by means of a telecommunications system. The words "telecommunications system" are defined by section 178 as meaning "a system for conveying visual images, sounds or other information by electronic means".

Secondly, the sending must be substantially otherwise than by wireless telegraphy. This means that wireless telegraphy may be used for a minor part of the transmission. The definition of "telecommunications system" as can be seen, is functional rather than descriptive; that is, it regards something as being a "telecommunications system" if it performs the tasks designated within the definition, making no attempt to base the definition on the description of a cable system typical of the sort which we might be using today. Instead it uses a definition appropriate to telecommunications regulation, which does not depend on the means of transmission. Its very functionality makes the definition wider than Parliament felt to be desirable, so the qualification in section 7(1) that such a system must achieve its ends "other than by wireless telegraphy" was necessary if the definition of "cable programme" was not to overlap with that of "broadcast".

Thirdly, the service must be intended to be received at a minimum of two places or to be presented to members of the public. This qualification excludes purely private tele-communication services from the ambit of the definition, but even a number of manifestly non-private telecommunication services are excluded from the definition under the next paragraph.

Fourthly, the service must not fall within the explicit exclusions of section 7(2). There are five such exclusions at present, relating to the following: some interactive cable services (where the "audience" is a participant in the service provided or is able to interrogate the provider as in databases); business information systems which operate solely for the purposes of a business and have no connection with any other tele-communications system; services run and controlled by a single individual for his own domestic purposes; self-contained services which are located in (or connect) premises under single occupation; and finally, "services which are, or to the extent that they are, run for persons providing broadcasting or cable programme services or providing pro-grammes for such services". Neither the intention behind the quoted words, nor their meaning, are known to the authors of this book. Under section 7(3), the Secretary of State may add, amend or subtract exceptions under section 7(2) by placing an order before Parliament.

Once an item is included in a "cable programme service", it constitutes a "cable programme" and is thus entitled to copyright protection. There is no apparent *de minimis* level below which protection will not be granted. Thus not only scheduled programmes but any item included in a cable programme service including, it would seem, subliminal messages which the human receiver fails to detect, will be accorded legal protection, as will the retrieval of information via the internet.

Typographical arrangements of published editions

In addition to the copyright which subsists in literary works, a further copyright exists in respect of the published editions of works. This second stratum of legal rights protects the publisher's investment in the production of a "finished version", a commercially viable product which incorporates an author's work. Originally introduced into English law when the typesetting of works was an expensive and labour-intensive activity, the right in published editions has become no less valuable now that both typesetting and facsimile reproduction have become commonplace functions of the electronic publisher of the 1990s. Accessibility has added to this value, now that photocopying is available to all.

The restriction of protection to published works alone now seems arbitrary and in principle unfair, although there has been scarcely a word of criticism for it. The same amount of time and effort may go into the establishment of the text and lay-out of an unpublished work as a published one; indeed, every published work is likely to have started life as an unpublished one, unless at its very inception and creation it can be said to be "published".

Section 175(1) defines "publication" as being the issue of copies of a work to the public, as well as the making of a work available by means of an electronic retrieval system. This definition is not supposed to apply to published editions of works. If it did, we would now have the anomaly that the typographical arrangement of a conventional book would enjoy no protection until copies of that book are sold in the shops, while the typographical arrangement of a law report within the LEXIS database would enjoy protection from the moment it could be retrieved by subscribers to that database, even though those same subscribers may have no idea that the text of that case has become available and may never even seek to access it. Instead, there is the paradox that a work may be "published" without there ever having been a "published edition" of it. If this is too difficult for the law to accept, we may find that the courts will conclude that, notwithstanding the words of section 175(1)(a), the typographical version of a work sitting in a computer database is also a "published edition".

The statutory definition of "published edition" contained in section 8 of the Act explains that it is:

> "in the context of copyright in the typographical arrangement of a published edition, a published edition of the whole or any part of one or more literary, dramatic or musical works."

The precise significance of the qualification which precedes the definition is hard to fathom, since the words "published edition" are not used in any other context in the Act.

The words "typographical arrangement" are not defined within the Act, but their meaning would seem to suggest arrangement of printed letters and symbols", since the word "typography" always suggests the techniques of printing but not the skills of calligraphy. If this is so, the published edition of a facsimile of an ancient and hand-created illuminated manuscript will not qualify for protection as a "typographical arrangement", while such trivial and ephemeral matter as the literary text which appears on a tin of baked beans will be so protected.

The definition thus makes it plain that it is insufficient for there to be a published edition of a literary, musical or dramatic work; there must be a published edition of a typographical arrangement of a literary, dramatic or musical work. A recording of a musical work can be a musical work within the meaning of section 3(1) of the Act, but it is not a typographical arrangement of it under section 8; by playing the tape or disc on which the music is recorded, one can listen to the music but one will gain no idea whatever as to its typographical lay-out. A computer tape or disk, in contrast, may be designed to enable its user to see text on a screen; he not only derives information from the literary work embodied on the tape or disk but derives the visual gratification of seeing its typographical arrangement. It would thus appear to follow that, while section 8 does not protect an audio tape, it will protect a tape containing, for example, a computer game which contains a literary element.

The requirement of originality

An element of originality is requisite in all of the species of work listed above. In some instances this requirement is explicit, in others merely alluded to. The concept of originality is a fertile breeding ground for legal misconceptions, not just among lawyers but among the public at large.

Section 1 declares that copyright vests in, among other things, "original" literary, dramatic, musical and artistic works. The word "original" is not defined by the Act, but it has been extensively discussed by judges in cases decided under the Copyright Acts of 1911 and 1956. The concept of originality has even been considered in the context of cases decided under the pre-1911 law, which did not explicitly require that a work be "original". From the absence of a definition of "original" in the Act, it is reasonable to assume that Parliament intended guidance to be drawn from existing case law.

The main thrust of existing case law is that "original" does *not* mean "new", either in terms of intellectual creativity or of absolute physical novelty. What it does mean is that there is a direct connection between the intellectual and creative activities of the author, on the one hand, and the ultimate generation of the work, on the other.

To explain in more practical terms: if a tourist takes a photograph of the well-known and photogenic tower which houses Big Ben, he knows that there is no novelty in the idea of taking such a photograph — the same idea occurs to hundreds of other tourists daily. He also knows that there is a fair chance that many photographers who had the same idea would have stood on much the same spot in order to take pictures that are effectively identical or highly similar to his own. Neither the tourist's want of intellectual novelty nor his inability to generate an objectively verifiable "new" photograph prevents his work from being "original"; but what makes it original is the fact that he took it himself, using his own judgment and without drawing directly on a photograph taken by anyone else.

In this sense, literary, dramatic and musical works, and all other artistic works than photographs, must be "original". This requirement does *not* however lead one to conclude that "originality" is merely a physical and causative link between a creator and the physical object created. If, for example, I dictate a letter to a secretary who writes it down *verbatim*, the secretary is the party who has established the letter's physical existence — but I am the party who has "originated" it. Both the secretary's effort and mine are required before the work is protectable by copyright; I provide the "originality" element in the letter, while the secretary provides the distinctive and equally vital element of "fixation" discussed under the next sub-heading below.

Where is the requirement of originality with regard to other types of work? With regard to sound recordings and films it is necessary to examine section 5(2), which reads:

> "Copyright does not subsist in a sound recording or film which is, or to the extent that it is, a copy taken from a previous sound recording or film."

Similar provisions in sections 6(6), 7(6) and 8(2) impose a *de facto* originality requirement on broadcasts, cable programmes and typographical editions of published works and prevent the extension of the duration of copyright by mere technical adjustment. This was considered necessary to prevent extension by mere alteration of sound levels or varying of intensity, as occurs when a record is remixed. With colourisation of films the issue is a little less clear — is there sufficient originality in attributing natural colours to a black and white scene in a film?

The requirement of fixation

Ever since the first copyright legislation was promulgated, nearly three centuries ago, it has always been clear that copyright — though described as an "intangible right" — vests in only those works which have a tangible dimension to them. Comments such as "you can copy an idea but you can't copy the form it's expressed in", or "there's no copyright in information but there is copyright in the form in which information is written", exemplify what many experts term the "content/form dichotomy". Copyright does not protect the *content* of a man's thoughts, but it does protect the *form* in which he expresses them.

To the proposition that an idea can be freely copied, but that the words (or other fixed form of expression) which embody it cannot, there is a corollary: nothing can be protected if it is not "fixed" in some tangible or retrievable, hence copiable, form. Thus it would seem that every category of work described above must be "fixed" in an appropriate form before the protection of the law can be given to it.

In terms of what we might call "legal reality", this is not quite the case. For example, a literary work might be "fixed" in the form of a book, a menu, a graffito or a computer disk, but a broadcast — a wireless transmission from one party to another — cannot mean-ingfully be said to be "fixed" in any form at all. A film or other medium embodying the broadcast work is not a "broadcast", not is it necessarily evidence of anything having been broadcast, and the airspace through which the broadcast travels bears no trace of its swift and undulating passage. Similarly a cable programme is not physically fixed in any form, so the law allows for its protection even without there being any demand for it to be fixed in any particular form.

Other types of work must be recorded. So far as literary, musical and dramatic works are concerned, section 3(2) is quite explicit:

> "Copyright does not subsist in a literary, dramatic or musical work unless and until it is recorded, in writing or otherwise ... "

Artistic works are not subject to the same explicit provision, but the concept of an artistic work as defined in the Act is incapable of being understood or applied in the absence of a tangible fixation. Likewise, sound recordings and films, as indicated by the vocabulary which gives rise to their very definition, must be recorded; the sequence of sounds and images which comprise a sound recording or film enjoy no legal status until they have been recorded. Once recorded, however, those sounds are protected by copyright even if they follow the same sequence of sounds which has previously been recorded by someone else. Finally, typographical arrangements of published editions are protected only on the presumption that there has been a "publication", which section 175 of the Act defines as meaning the issue of (physically existing) copies to the public or the making available of a work to the public by means of an electronic retrieval system, for which, at least in terms of today's technology, some form of fixation is required in order for the work to be accessed by the would-be retriever.

QUALIFICATION FOR PROTECTION

Even if a work fits within the categories of protectable work listed above, it must still qualify for copyright protection under British law. The only works which do not need to qualify for copyright protection are those which are governed by Crown or parliamentary copyright (discussed in Chapter 7 below) and those works generated by international organisations such as the United Nations and its agencies.

Chapter IX of the Act determines qualification for protection by reference to criteria relating to the author, the country in which the work was first published and (in relation to broadcasts and cable programmes only) the country from which the work was first sent.

Qualification by authorship

Under section 154(1) a work qualifies for protection if its author is a human being who (i) is a British citizen or enjoys one of five different categories of second-class status which make him British without being a citizen; or (ii) lives or is domiciled in the U.K. If the author is a body incorporated under British law, it too will be pleased to learn that its works qualify for copyright protection.

There is, however, one further distinction which should not be overlooked: that between published and unpublished works. If a work is unpublished, it is the author's status at the time the work was made (or during the time that most of it was made) which is crucial; but where the work is published, the author's status at (i) the time of publication, or in the case of posthumous publication, (ii) the time of his death, determines the status of the work.

Where a work is jointly authored by two or more authors, not all of whom are qualified under section 154, the work will still enjoy copyright protection. For all other purposes, such as the ownership of copyright or the calculation of the duration of copyright, the "unqualified" author is treated as if he never existed.

Qualification by country of origin

If a work qualifies for protection under section 154, its origin is utterly irrelevant. If, however, there is a defect in the status of the author which renders him incapable of conferring copyright protection on his created offspring, his work may still obtain copyright protection under section 155. By this provision any work other than a broadcast or cable programme will enjoy copyright protection if it is *first published* (*not* written or otherwise created) in (i) the U.K., or (ii) any other country to which the Act extends. For the purpose of this provision, the words "first published" mean "published within thirty days in another country", the second (British) publication being fictitiously regarded as taking place simultaneously with the first (foreign) one.

Permanence of qualification

Once a work is deemed to qualify for copyright protection, its status as a protectable work becomes permanent. If the British author of a work later becomes a citizen of a territory to which the Act neither applies nor extends, his work will remain the subject of U.K. copyright law. Likewise, if a work originates from the Isle of Man, to which British copyright legislation extends, but that unfortunate island is later forcibly seized by the inhabitants of Mazurka, a state which has no copyright treaty relations at all, the work will remain copyright-protected even though the legal status of its geographical origin has altered.

Absence of qualification

It is obvious that most works created in the world today do not qualify for protection under the Act. This does not mean, however, that they are not protected under the Act. How can this apparent contradiction be explained?

The answer lies in section 159, which explains that the Act's protection can still be applied to countries to which it does not extend. The effect of this is that a parliamentary Order in Council can declare that another country's authors and published works should be treated in the U.K. just as if they were authors of works qualified under U.K. law. In this way the U.K. has applied its copyright protection to most of the countries of the world. This nationality treatment is required under the two major copyright conventions to which the U.K. is a party: the Berne Convention and the Universal Copyright Convention. It is also required in respect of countries which are not members of the Berne Union but which, as members of the World Trade Organisation, are required to extend the basic norms of Berne Convention protection to other World Trade Organisation countries (the U.K. is a founder member of the WTO). Among the countries whose authors' published works do not automatically enjoy the Act's protection are North Korea, Vietnam, Iran, Syria, Vanuatu and Burundi.

CHAPTER 6

DURATION AND SCOPE OF THE COPYRIGHT IN WORKS

GENERAL PROVISIONS

The duration of copyright in literary, dramatic, musical or artistic works is a period of 70 years from the end of the calendar year in which the author dies. There are exceptions to this general rule in section 12 of the Act in relation to works of unknown authorship, computer-generated works and works of joint authorship. Copyright in works of unknown authorship expires at the end of the period of 70 years from the end of the calendar year in which the work is first made available to the public. Copyright does not revive even if the identity of the author becomes known after the end of that period. "Making available to the public" includes public performance, broadcasting and exhibition in public provided that act is not done without the consent of the copyright owner. Copyright in computer-generated works expires at the end of a period of 50 years from the end of the calendar year in which they are made. The duration of copyright in works of joint authorship is 70 years from the end of the calendar year in which the last or the last known author dies.

Where a film has an identifiable principal director, author of the dialogue or screenplay or composer of "music specially created for and used in the film", section 13B provides that the copyright in the film expires 70 years from the end of the calendar year in which such a person, or the last of more than one such persons, dies. This is the case, irrespective of the duration of the copyright in any literary, artistic or other work which may be written for or used in the film.

Under the provisions of the Duration of Copyright and Rights in Performances Regulations 1995 ("the 1995 Regulations"), copyright works of identifiable personal authorship are divided into two categories. There are those which were still protected by copyright on January 1, 1996 and which were entitled to the benefit of the extension of their copyright term on that date to the current "life plus 70 year" term from the previous "life plus 50" (or, in the case of works by pseudonymous and anonymous authors, from a 50 year to a 70 year post-publication duration of protection). These works are termed "extended works", for obvious reasons. In contrast with extended works are those works which had fallen into the public domain upon the expiry of the previous shorter term of copyright, but which were brought back into U.K. copyright protection by virtue of that the fact that on July 31, 1995, they were still protected by copyright in another jurisdiction which was a Member State of the European Economic Area ("EEA"). Since the duration of copyright for such works in Germany was already "life plus 70", all works which enjoyed German copyright protection on July 31, 1995 began to enjoy the same duration of copyright as that conferred by the Germans. These works fell back into copyright protection in the U.K. on January 1, 1996, for periods which ranged from a retrospective period of five months (for works whose authors died in 1925) to as much as 20 years (for works whose authors died in 1945 and which, under the former U.K. law, effectively fell out of copyright protection on December 31, 1995). To distinguish them from works in which the duration of copyright was merely extended, this second category of works is described as attracting "revived" copyright.

Copyright subsists in sound recordings and films which lack an identifiable personal author of the kind listed in the previous paragraph for 50 years from the end of the calendar year in which they are made or 50 years from the date of release, if that release takes place within 50 years from the date on which they are made. "Released" is defined by section 13 as the first lawful publication, broadcasting or inclusion in a cable programme service, or first public exhibition in the case of a film. Copyright in a broadcast or cable programme expires 50 years from the end of the year in which the broadcast was made or the programme included in the cable programme service and no separate copyright arises in respect of repeats of the broadcast or cable programme.

The copyright in the typographical arrangement of published editions expires 25 years from the end of the calendar year in which the edition was first published.

TRANSITIONAL PROVISIONS

Under the transitional provisions of the 1988 Act, the provisions of the 1956 Act continued to apply to a number of literary, dramatic or musical works first published after the death of the author, to engravings published after the death of the author, to published photographs and photographs taken before June 1, 1957, to published sound recordings made before June, 1 1957 and to published films and films falling within the Film Registration Act. Copyright in published anonymous and pseudonymous literary, dramatic, musical or artistic works (other than photographs) continued in accordance with the 1956 Act. These provisions are contained in paragraph 12 of Schedule 1 to the Act.

The transitional provisions ended the pre-existing perpetual copyright in unpublished photographs and engravings. The term of copyright in all photographs was extended from 50 years from the year of first publication and is the same as for other types of artistic works.

Under the 1995 Regulations the present duration of copyright protection applies to all works, whether originally created before or after the 1956 and 1988 Acts, but with one exception: where the term of copyright in an existing copyright work would have been longer under the transitional provisions of the 1988 Act than would be the case under the 1995 Regulations, that work will continue to enjoy the later expiry date which the earlier law conferred upon it.

ACTS RESTRICTED BY THE COPYRIGHT IN WORKS

The acts restricted by copyright are the exclusive bundle of rights given to copyright owners. Unlike the 1956 Act, which differentiated between the rights given to owners of copyright in literary, musical, dramatic and artistic works and those in sound recordings, broadcasts, films and typographical arrangements of printed works, the Act provides a standard list of rights. This list in section 16 is subject to a number of exceptions. Section 16 restricts the right of anyone other than the copyright owner, without due authorisation:

> "(a)   to copy the work;
> (b)   to issue copies of the work to the public;
> (ba)   to rent or lend the work to the public;
> (c)   to perform, show or play the work in public;
> (d)   to broadcast the work or include it in a cable programme service; and
> (e)   to make an adaptation of the work or do any of the above in relation to an adaptation."

Copyright is infringed by anyone who either directly or indirectly does any of these restricted acts in relation to the whole or a substantial part of a copyright work, or who authorises another to do so.

"Copying" in relation to literary, dramatic, musical or artistic works is defined as reproduction of the work in any material form, including storage by an electronic means. The copyright in a two-dimensional work includes the making of a three-dimensional copy and vice versa. The copying of a film, television broadcast or cable programme includes making a photograph of the whole or a substantial part of the images forming part of those works, other than photographs made for private and domestic use. Although the Act does not say so, it also includes reproduction of the work in any material form. The copying of a typographical arrangement or published edition means making a facsimile copy. In all cases copying includes the making of transient or incidental copies, such as are produced by computers and by the transmission or downloading of materials from email notice-boards and internet websites.

The interpretation of the phrase "substantial part of a work" may present difficulty and has been considered on a number of occasions by the courts. "Substantial" refers to the importance or quality of the part copied rather than solely to its quantity in relation to the whole work. Thus eight bars of a musical work or one page of a book could be held to be substantial parts of the work even though they are relatively short excerpts.

Copyright is extremely flexible. Each of the acts restricted by copyright may be separately assigned or licensed and an assignment of copyright without any qualification means an assignment of all the rights. This is made clear by section 90(2), which provides that assignments may be limited by reference to restricted acts and to the term of those restricted acts. Accordingly, rights assigned or licensed should be carefully specified if they are not to include the entire copyright and the specification should, if possible, conform to the wording used in the Act. An assignment or licence of the "film rights" or the "dramatic rights" will not have precise significance because there are no such rights under the Act and the interpretation of those expressions can lead to disputes, for example as to whether the licensing of a "film right" entitles the licensee to incorporate a work in an interactive multimedia product. An assignment of the "right to reproduce the work in the form of a film" is potentially ambiguous, as is the use of non-legal terms such as the "synchronisation right" (the right to record a sound track of a film) or the "mechanical right" (the reproduction of musical works in sound recordings), since these are merely aspects of what the Act designates as copying the work.

Moreover, the component parts of the copyright can each be limited by contract. Thus the right to adapt a book for stage performance need not extend to an adaptation of the same book for television.

In contracts concerning rights for particular countries or groups of countries, care should be taken to define correctly the territory in view. Loose and indefinite expressions such as "Scandinavia", "the English-speaking countries", or indeed "the former Soviet Union", should be avoided as they may lead to dispute. In contracts drafted by foreigners, the names "England" and "Britain" are frequently used where "the United Kingdom" is meant.

Each of the restricted acts will be considered separately below.

The right to copy most author works will initially be controlled by the person whose name appears next to the © copyright notice, if such notice is attached to them. The mechanical reproduction right (the right to make sound recordings) of most musical works is controlled by the Mechanical-Copyright Protection Society, 41 Streatham High Road, London SW16 1ER.

The Act provides a number of grounds upon which a person can without permission copy or use a work in which someone else owns the copyright. Colloquially they are referred to by many people as "defences". These defences or permissions are known in the Act as "exceptions" and are considered below under the heading of "exceptions from the copyright in works".

Issuing copies to the public other than by rental or loan

The 1956 Act referred to the right of publication of a work. This expression had been considered by the courts on a number of occasions. To clarify the extent of this right, the Act now refers to the right to issue to the public copies of the work. This is defined by section 18 of the 1988 Act as putting into circulation copies not previously put into circulation in the EEA or elsewhere; it does not apply to the subsequent distribution or importation of such copies.

"Publication" is defined in section 175 as issuing copies to the public and includes, in the case of literary, dramatic, musical or artistic works, making them available by means of an electronic retrieval system. There is a definition of "commercial publication" which is used in relation to the exceptions to infringement proceedings in the Act and which means the issuing of copies to the public at a time when copies made in advance of the receipt of orders are generally available to the public, or making a work available by means of an electronic retrieval system.

Building a building to architectural plans and incorporating an artistic work in a building are treated as publication of that work. Section 175(4), however, contains a list of examples which do not constitute publication for the purposes of copyright infringement. In the case of a literary, dramatic or musical work these include performance, broadcasting or inclusion in a cable programme service (other than an electronic retrieval system), and, in the case of an artistic work, exhibition or the issue to the public, issue to the public of copies of works of architecture in the form of buildings or models, sculpture or works of artistic craftsmanship, issue to the public of copies of a film including a work or broadcasting or inclusion of the work in a cable programme service (other than for the purposes of an electronic retrieval system). In the case of a sound recording or film, publication does not include a work being played or shown in public or its inclusion in a broadcast or a cable programme service. References to a publication or to commercial publication do not include a token publication which is merely colourable and which is not intended to satisfy the reasonable requirements of the public.

Renting or lending a work to the public

A new section 18A of the Act gives the owner of copyright the right to restrict the rental or lending of his work to the public. This right, by section 18A(6), applies not only to the rental or lending of copies of a work but to the original version of it too. It does not however apply to all types of work. Literary, dramatic and musical works, films and sound recordings benefit from the new right, as do most artistic works — but buildings, models for buildings and "works of applied art" do not.

What do the terms "rental" and "lending" mean? For the purposes of this right, rental is defined by section 18A(2) as making a copy of a work avaliable for use, on terms that it will or may be returned, for direct or indirect economic or commercial advantage. Lending is defined in similar fashion, except that (i) the work lent will or may be returned other than for direct or indirect economic or commercial advantage (although the operating costs of the lending establishment may be recouped) and (ii) the lending (but not the borrowing) is done by "an establishment which is accessible to the public". By section 18A(3) it is neither an act of rental nor of lending to make a work available for "on-the-spot reference", to exhibit it in public or to make it available for public performance.

This right does not affect the lending of books by educational establishments (section 36A) or by public libraries (section 40A), so long as the book is capable of benefiting from registration under the public lending right scheme introduced under the Public Lending Right Act 1979 (see Chapter 20 below), whether the book is so registered or not.

Film producers should note that their interest in being able to produce copies of films for rental purposes is protected under a new section 93A of the Act. By this provision, where a film production agreement is concluded between an author and a film producer, the film's producer is not merely permitted to rent out copies of the film without infringing the author's rental right but it is presumed — unless the contract provides to the contrary — that the author has transferred his rental right to the producer. This is an unusual example of a copyright being assigned without the requirement of the author's assenting signature. In return for the presumed assignment of his rental right under section 93A, the author (who for this purpose includes the principal director of a film) is entitled under section 93B to the right to equitable remuneration in respect of the rental. This right to equitable remuneration must however be exercised collectively, by a collecting society.

The performance or showing or playing of a work in public

Performance of a literary, dramatic or musical work in public is an act restricted by the copyright in such works. Section 19 provides that this includes delivery of lectures, speeches and sermons and any mode of visual or acoustic presentation such as presentation by means of a sound recording, film broadcast or cable programme. The playing or showing of a sound recording, film broadcast or cable programme in public is one of the restricted acts in those works.

Where copyright is infringed by a public performance or by the playing or showing of a work in public by means of some apparatus such as a television set, the person actually sending the visual images or sounds and the performers are not regarded as being responsible for the infringement — but the person providing the television set is. It is the display of visual images or sounds which is the performance and not the act of broadcasting or otherwise providing the means for the performing.

Section 26 deals with secondary infringement by means of public performance or playing or showing a work in public. The person supplying apparatus for such infringement is liable if he knows, or has reason to believe, that the apparatus is likely to be used to infringe copyright, or if it is apparatus of the normal use of which involves public performance and he does not believe on reasonable grounds that it would not be so used to infringe copyright. A common example would be someone hiring out karaoke or disco equipment. The onus is on the hirer of equipment to make sure that his customers hold the necessary copyright licences — a change in the law introduced at the request of the copyright collecting societies. In addition, a person supplying a copy of a sound recording or film used to infringe copyright is liable if he knows, or has reason to believe, that the copy he supplied or a copy made from it would also be used to infringe copyright.

As with the 1956 Act, there is no definition of "public performance" in the Act. Case law says that it is necessary to refer to the nature of the audience: if it is domestic or of a quasi-domestic nature then it is in the private sphere; but a performance of music to workers in a factory by means of a radio has been held to be a performance in public, as has a dramatic performance to a Women's Institute. The test is thus whether the performance takes place within or outside the domestic circle.

The right to stage a play, while vesting initially in the author, will in practice usually be controlled by the publisher or by the author's agent. The Association of Authors' Agents (see Appendix for details) is a useful starting-point for anyone seeking permission to stage a play in the U.K. The right to perform music in a non-dramatic form is, in nearly every case, controlled by the Performing Right Society Limited, (see Appendix for details) which either grants blanket licences for the public performance of its repertoire generally or permits the public performance of individual copyright works. The PRS controls not only rights to most U.K. music but also a large proportion of foreign copyright music.

Exceptions to the public performance right are considered under the heading "exceptions from the copyright in works" below.

Broadcasting the work and transmitting it by cable

The copyright in literary, dramatic, musical and artistic works, sound recordings, films, broadcasts and cable programmes includes the right to broadcast the work or include it in a cable programme service. The right to transmit a work by means of a cable programme service was widened in 1996 by a new section 144A of the Act. This provision enables the copyright owner, through the collective exercise of rights, to grant or refuse authorisation for the retransmission of a broadcast of his work from any other EEA state in which that work is included.

The definitions of "broadcasts" and "cable programmes" in sections 6 and 7 of the Act apply to the provisions of section 20 which define what constitutes infringement through broadcasting and inclusion in a cable programme in the same manner to which they apply in defining a particular type of copyright work. Exceptions to the right to broadcast and include works in cable programmes are dealt with under the heading "exceptions from the copyright in works". The broadcasting rights and rights to include works in cable programmes will be licensed by the same agencies as those referred to under the heading "performing or showing the work in public" below.

The operator of a cable programme service is exempted from copyright liability under the Broadcasting Act 1990 in respect of broadcasts by the BBC, Channel 3 licensees and Channel 4 and local radio broadcasters, and under the Broadcasting Act 1996 in respect of digital TV services – so Channel 5 analogue needs a licence, but not Channel 5 simulcast. Section 73 of the Broadcasting Act 1990 deems the operator of a cable programme service to be in a position of having a licence from the copyright owner to transmit such services, and the copyright owner can proceed only against the primary broadcaster. This rebroadcasting right does not apply to other broadcasts, including satellite transmissions. The fact that a broadcast has been retransmitted in a cable programme service can, however, be taken into account in assessing the damages for infringement in any proceedings against the initial broadcaster. The reasoning behind the so-called "must carry" rule is that cable programme service providers are facilitating the distribution of the BBC and ITV programmes and there should not be double liability to the copyright owner in respect of the same programme. Nonetheless it may be considered unreasonable that a commercial operator who makes an unauthorised use of authors' works should be exempted from copyright liability. Of course if cable programme operators originate their own programmes, they may become liable to copyright owners in respect of any infringements committed by them if they fail to secure the necessary licences. Also, as mentioned above, European Commission legislation in the area of cable retransmission and satellite distribution favour collective, as opposed to individual, licensing of all programmes, whether originating with terrestrial broadcasters or otherwise.

The free public showing of a broadcast or cable programme does not infringe any copyright in that broadcast or cable programme or any sound recording in it, but section 72 does provide that the fact that the programme or broadcast was seen in public shall be taken into account in assessing any damages for infringement of copyright. Free public showing means that there is no charge for admission and the price for goods or services supplied does not include prices substantially attributable to the facilities afforded for seeing or hearing the broadcast or programme. Hotel guests are not regarded as having paid for admission, nor are members of a society or club where payment is only for membership and not for the provision of facilities for seeing or hearing a broadcast or cable programmes, and is only incidental to the main purpose of the club under section 72(3).

The making of copies of broadcasts or cable programmes only for the purpose of enabling them to be viewed or listened to at a more convenient time is not an infringement of the copyright in the broadcast or cable programme or any work included in the broadcast or cable programme, provided such making is for private and domestic use only. This "time shifting defence" in section 70 was included after much debate in the Act as to how it should be defined.

Bodies may be designated for providing subtitled copies of broadcasts or cable programmes under section 74. Any copying of broadcasts or cable programmes and the supply of such copies to the public is not an infringement. Section 74 is not applicable if there is a certified licence scheme relating to subtitling.

Section 75 contains an exception for the recording for archival purposes of broadcasting or cable programmes. Certain bodies have been designated as archives for the purposes of the Act, namely the British Film Institute, the British Library, the Music Performance Research Centre and the Scottish Film Council.

Making any adaptation of the work

It is an infringement of copyright to make an adaptation of an original literary, dramatic or musical work. It is not an infringement of copyright in respect of all other types of works.

"Adaptation" is defined in section 21(3) as:

(a) In relation to a literary or dramatic work, means —
(i) a translation of the work;
(ii) a version of a dramatic work in which it is converted into a non-dramatic work or, as the case may be, a non-dramatic work in which it is converted into a dramatic work;
(iii) a version of the work in which the story or action is conveyed wholly or mainly by means of pictures in a form suitable for reproduction in a book, a newspaper, magazine or similar periodical;
(b) In relation to a musical work, means an arrangement or transcription of the work."

In relation to computer programs, translation includes versions of the programs converted into or out of languages or codes other than incidentally in the course of running a program. Section 21(1) provides that an adaptation is made when it is recorded, whether in writing or in some tangible form.

The definition of "adaptation" is somewhat limited and does not accord with the word's colloquial meaning. A film is not a dramatic work and thus the rendering of a literary work directly into a film will not constitute an adaptation. However, a scenario or script for a film would appear to be a dramatic work and thus an adaptation of the original literary work. An adaptation may be made of a musical or other work which is in the public domain and subject to provisions of the Act and copyright will subsist in that adaptation as an original work. Thus there are many versions of "Greensleeves" which are the subject of copyright and Sir Neville Marriner was able to earn substantial royalties from his adaptation of Mozart's works in the film *Amadeus* even though the authors of those works are long dead and anyone is entitled to play, publish or otherwise use the original versions without threat of legal sanction. Section 5(2) confirms that the adaptation right does not exist in sound recordings or films, by providing that copyright does not subsist in sound recordings or films to the extent that they are copies of other sound recordings or films.

Difficult questions may arise in respect of burlesque or parody, which are not mentioned in the Act. While cartoons are clearly covered in the definition of "adaptation", the burlesque or parody of a work may be effected without recourse to any of the substance of the work. If, on the other hand, they closely borrow from the plot or other incidents of the original work, then they may be held to infringe the copyright in the work either as copies or adaptations. In either case it is a matter of fact, for a court to decide, as to whether an infringement has taken place or not.

Doing, in relation to an adaptation of the work, any of the acts specified in relation to the original work

Section 21(2) provides that all the acts restricted by copyright apply equally to adaptations and to original works. The same test of substantiality appearing in section 16(3) of the Act applies to adaptation. Similarly, section 76 provides that where acts are permitted in relation to a work, they are permitted in relation to adaptations of that work.

Publication right

A peculiar feature of the Copyright and Related Rights Regulations 1996 is that, by Regulation 16(1), they establish a new right which is not in fact a copyright and which is not incorporated into the text of the Act. This is the publication right, which vests in any author's work which (i) was unpublished at the time when any copyright in it had expired, (ii) which was not a work in which Crown or Parliamentary copyright subsisted, (iii) which is subsequently published in the EEA by a person who is a national of an EEA State, (iv) so long as the publication does not take place in consequence of any act which is unauthorised in the sense that it lacks the consent of the person who owns the physical medium upon which the work is recorded or embodied.

By Regulation 16(6) this right lasts for a period of 25 years from the end of the calendar year in which the first publication takes place. The rights included within its scope are listed under Regulation 16(2) as being, in particular, the rights to issue copies to the public, to make the work available by means of an electronic retrieval system, to rent or lend copies to the public, to perform or exhibit the work in public, to broadcast it or to include it in a cable programme service.

Extended and Revived Copyright

Although the extension or revival of copyright term has been referred to in passing elsewhere in this book, it is helpful to address it directly since it has given rise to some uncertainty on the part of both copyright owners and would-be copyright users.

The European Union has sought to establish not merely in principle but in practice that the territories of the 15 Member States together constitute a single "internal market", within which goods may be moved, bought and sold under conditions which do not restrict the ability of traders to compete with one another. The European Union's Directive on the Duration of Copyright Term sought to eliminate the anomalies and confusions which can result within a single market when a work, protected by copyright in one part of that market, is in the public domain in another. Although most E.U. Member States had a standard duration of life plus 50 years for authors' works (the Berne Union norm), Germany and Spain provided longer *post mortem* periods. It was, therefore, agreed that Member States would harmonise the duration of their copyright at the longer level of protection, taking into account the fact that author' heirs live longer than they did when the "life-plus-50" formula was conceived.

The Directive required member states (i) to extend protection to "life-plus-70" in respect of those works which were still protected under their domestic copyright law and (ii) to revive domestic copyright in those works which, having fallen into the public domain under domestic copyright law, nonetheless enjoyed copyright protection in another E.U. Member State by virtue of its longer copyright law. Following the decision of the European Court of Justice in the *Phil Collins* case (1993), which concluded that Member States were obliged under the Treaty of Rome to offer their own level of copyright protection to works emanating from other Member States where a lower level of protection was provided, this effectively meant that every work which was protected in Germany for life plus 70 years, but in respect of which copyright had expired under domestic law, was brought back into copyright protection for a period which ranged from just six months to a maximum of 20 years, depending upon the date of the author's death.

Extension of term

The 1995 Regulations came into force on January 1, 1996. They extend copyright term in all works which (i) are created after that date, (ii) were created before that date but first qualified for copyright protection after that date and (iii) works in which copyright subsisted immediately before that date. The extended portion of the copyright belongs to the owner of the copyright immediately before commencement. In respect of any reversionary interest, the extension falls within the reversionary period and belongs to its owner. Assignments and licences of copyright remain in force with regard to the "windfall" terms

Revived term

Any work in which copyright under the Act had expired before December 31, 1995, but which was on July 1, 1995 still protected by the copyright law of another EEA state, is entitled to enjoy a revival in the U.K. of its copyright under the Act. The copyright owner is the person who owned it immediately before its revival, subject to the following conditions: (i) if that owner has died or (in the case of a company) ceased to exist, copyright will vest in the author or his personal representative; (ii) in the case of a film, where the owner dies or ceased to exist, copyright reverts to the principal director. Licences and assignments of copyright are effectively revived too. Third parties who do anything which is an infringement of the revived copyright are not liable as infringers in respect of any act which was done in pursuance of arrangements made before January 1, 1995; nor is it an infringement to issue to the public copies of any work which were made before July 1, 1995. Upon the revival of copyright, those acts which are defined in the Act as "restricted acts" shall be treated as having been licensed by the copyright owner, subject only to the payment of a reasonable royalty or other remuneration, so long as the person intending to do those acts gives reasonable notice to the copyright owner of his intention to do them. If he does not give such notice, he will be treated as an infringer and not as a licensee.

CHAPTER 7

OWNERSHIP OF COPYRIGHT

BASIC PROVISION AS TO OWNERSHIP

The basic rule as to ownership in section 11 of the Act is that the author of a work is the first owner of any copyright in it, subject to certain exceptions mentioned below.

The question of whether, and if so to what extent, it is ever justifiable to vest the copyright initially in anyone other than the author, except by express agreement, is obviously fundamental to the protection of authors' rights. Under the 1956 Act there were a number of exceptions to the general rule, but under the Act there is only one main exception. If the author of a literary, dramatic, musical or artistic work makes that work in the course of his employment his employer is the first owner of any copyright in that work, subject to agreement to the contrary. There are also more limited exceptions in relation to Crown and parliamentary copyright and the copyright of certain international organisations (dealt with in Chapter 9 below).

Section 9 of the Act defines the term "author". The basic definition is the person who creates the work. This said, the Act then recognises a number of instances where the author for the purposes of the Act is the person who has the economic interest in the creation of the work rather than being directly concerned in its creation. The author of a sound recording or film is the producer, the person by whom the arrangements necessary for the making of the sound recording or film are undertaken. In addition, the director of a film is now regarded as its author. In the case of a broadcast it is the person making the broadcast, and in the case of reception and immediate transmission of a broadcast it is the person making the original broadcast. In the case of a cable programme the author is the person providing the cable programme service in which the programme is included and, in the case of a typographical arrangement of a published work, the publisher. As for computer-generated works, the author is the person who made the necessary arrangements for the creation of a work.

In some cases the Act recognises that the author of a work cannot be ascertained. For a work to be of unknown authorship the identity of all authors must be unknown. Identity of authors is unknown if it is not possible to ascertain identity by reasonable enquiry.

JOINT AND COLLECTIVE WORKS

Section 10 provides that a work of joint authorship is one produced by the collaboration of two or more authors where the contribution of each author is not distinct from that of the others. If one or more of the joint authors is not qualified for copyright protection within section 153, then any authors who are so qualified for protection would be entitled to the copyright in the whole work.

"Collective works" are to be distinguished from joint works. The expression "collective work" is not defined in the Act, but was defined in the 1911 Act. It means works such as encyclopaedias, anthologies, reviews and newspapers, that is any work which comprises a number of contributions from different authors. For such purposes a song is not a collective work because the contribution of a lyric writer is to a legal category of work different from that of the composer; the lyricist pens a literary work, the composer a musical one.

So far as collective works are concerned, there can be a number of separate copyrights. There is copyright in a collective work as such, which belongs to the editorial compiler who is the author of the collective work, and copyright in each separate contribution, which belongs to the contributor.

LETTERS

It must not be overlooked that letters are literary works and that copyright may subsist in them. The author of the letter is the copyright owner and the recipient does not usually obtain any rights in it. The exception is in the case of letters to a newspaper where the writer clearly intends to grant the newspaper proprietor a non-exclusive licence to publish it. It is generally accepted in such cases that the newspaper has the right to edit the letter, but not in such a way as to amount to false attribution of authorship and subject to the author's entitlement to complain to the Press Complaints Commission in respect of unfair editing.

THE EMPLOYMENT EXCEPTION

As mentioned above, the most important exception to the general rule that the author is the owner of copyright is in the case of employment. That exception applies only to literary, dramatic, musical or artistic works, and not to other types of copyright works. Those works must be made by the employee in the "course of his employment". Those words are repeated from section 4 of the 1956 Act. This means that even the copyright in a work made by the employee in his spare time will belong to the employer if the work was made for the employer's benefit and if it falls within the scope of the employee's duties to make it.

As a matter of common law a person is an employee if he is engaged under a contract of service. The principal facts to be ascertained in deciding whether a person is or is not engaged under a contract of service, as distinguished from a contract for services, are the degree of control over the making of the work exercised by the employer and the extent to which the person doing the work is integrated into the business of the person for whom he does it. On the other hand, a "contract for services" is one between a person and an independent contractor who undertakes to perform specified services for that person. Whether a particular arrangement is a contract of service or contract for services is often a complex question.

Clearly, articles written by a journalist on a newspaper on a subject prescribed by the editor are works made under a contract of service. A contract for services would be that of an independent author commissioned to write a review of a book, the author being left the free exercise of his talents as he thinks fit. A borderline case would be that of a researcher working on a series of one-year contracts for a television company, where the researcher is regarded as self-employed for tax purposes, but receives some benefits of employment from the television company, such as a pension or a staff car. In those cases criteria other than those concerning an author's intellectual creation determine whether or not he is an employee or an independent contractor.

It is always open to the contracting parties to agree between themselves as to how they wish to allocate copyright.

Under the 1956 Act there were further exceptions to the general rule as to copyright ownership in respect of journalists, commissioned artworks or photographs. The transitional provisions of the Act make it clear that the question of who is the first owner of copyright is determined in accordance with the law in force at the time of making the work. Thus, if a work was commissioned before the Act came into force, then the provisions of the 1956 Act apply and the person who commissioned the work would be entitled to any copyright.

Reversionary Interest

The Act continues the provisions of the proviso of section 5(2) of the 1911 Act, which must with the passing of time be of decreasing relevance. Under that proviso, any assignment made by the author as first owner of copyright is to run for 25 years only from the death of the author; thereafter the reversionary interest devolves on the author's legal personal representatives. This reversionary provision does not apply to collective works. The principle applies only to assignments or licences before June 1957, when the 1956 Act came into force. As far as joint works are concerned, it appears that a period of 25 years is calculated from the date of death of the author who dies last.

Reversion is automatic and does not have to be claimed in order to become effective. The utilisation by another of a work in respect of which the author's heirs are entitled to the reversion is an infringement of copyright, actionable in the same way as any other infringement.

CHAPTER 8

MORAL RIGHTS

SCOPE OF MORAL RIGHTS

The question of moral rights was touched on earlier when dealing with authors' rights. This chapter expands on that discussion and explains the types of moral rights included in the Act. Four moral rights are generally accepted in civil law tradition as applying to both authors of works and directors of films. These rights may be seen as relating to authors' creativity rather than the economic aspects of U.K. copyright law, as they relate to honour and integrity rather than to the investment of money. The fifth, the *droit de suite*, is the right of an author who has sold a painting, sculpture or other object embodying his work to receive a proportion of the proceeds of any subsequent resale of that item. This right is regarded in the U.K. as impinging more on economic matters, and has been firmly rejected here. The authors of this book think that it will be introduced only if the U.K. is forced to do so as part of a European Union harmonisation of moral rights.

An example of the split between economic and moral rights is a film. Copyright ownership vests in the producer of a film, who is normally regarded as the person seen to have the economic interest in the project. In response to this, the law recognises the director as having the "artistic" interest in the film. Sometimes an author's creative power will impinge on other types of work for which no moral right is accorded, such as broadcasts, sound recordings and computer-generated works. In the Act, where specifically mentioned in relation to moral rights, the expression "the author of a work" is intended to cover the director of a film. Elsewhere the same expression covers the producer, not the director (though the duration of copyright term is also governed by the notion of the director being an author).

The four generally accepted moral rights are:

— the right of paternity, which is the right of an author of a copyright work to be identified as such;
— the right of integrity, which is the right of an author to prevent or object to derogatory treatment of his work;
— the right of disclosure, which is the right of an author to withhold his work from publication; and
— the right of non-attribution — the right not to have a work falsely attributed to an author.

While ownership of these rights is independent of copyright ownership, they do not arise if there is no copyright in a work. All but the right of disclosure exist independently of copyright ownership and vest only in authors of works.

Three of these moral rights are now specifically incorporated into U.K. law in Chapter IV of the Act. The Act also introduced a limited privacy right in section 16(1)(a). This is part of the right of disclosure, which is not yet fully recognised in U.K. law, other than in the economic right to issue the work to the public. The disclosure right is contained in part in the right to issue copies of works to the public. This economic right applies to all works, including broadcasts and sound recordings which do not have moral rights, and is alienable in the same manner as other copyright rights. It is also limited to the first issue to the public of a work, so authors cannot withdraw their works from the public in reliance on this right once they have been published, unless they have had the foresight to contract for this right and to ensure that it continues to bind subsequent purchasers. A limited privacy right applies to commissioned paintings and photographs under section 85 of the Act.

BERNE CONVENTION

Article 6 *bis* of the Berne Convention provides for the incorporation into national law of the rights of paternity and integrity. It also gives rights in respect of other unauthorised action in relation to a work which would be prejudicial to the author's honour or reputation. It provides that such rights must exist at least as long as copyright and be transmissible by will. The Convention leaves the exercise of the rights to national legislation, including whether such legislation provides for the waiver of moral rights and the method of their enforcement. Article 6 *bis* has been in the Berne Convention since 1928, but it took until 1988 for the U.K. to incorporate moral rights specifically into its copyright law. Before that time a mixture of the laws of passing-off, false trade descriptions, contract, the right against false attribution (which was contained in the 1956 Act) and defamation were relied on as constituting the U.K.'s compliance with its international obligations. This attitude was consistent with that of other common law countries. The USA likewise did not feel that it was required to legislate for moral rights immediately on joining the Berne Convention in 1989, although it has subsequently revised this opinion to a limited extent. Criticism for failure to enact adequate moral rights protection is not however the prerogative only of the common law countries. Even in France, the cradle of moral rights, eyebrows were raised when the extension of copyright law so as to cover the protection of computer programs did not provide for a similar extension of the author's moral rights so as to cover the rights of computer programmers.

PURPOSE OF MORAL RIGHTS

The existence of moral rights is consistent with the traditional *raison d'être* of copyright: to recognise and encourage the result of intellectual creativity on a level with other forms of property. This has been recognised in such fundamental documents as the United Nations Universal Declaration of Human Rights, Art. 27 (2) of which states that:

> "Everyone has the right to the protection of moral and material interests resulting from any scientific, literary or artistic production of which he is the author."

However, the important distinction between moral rights and the economic rights of copyright lies in the independence of moral rights from the works to which they relate. Until 1988 in the U.K., the idea of creating a right dependent on the relationship between an author and his work was regarded with some scepticism. It was for this reason that, as has been mentioned, the U.K. asserted that it had complied with its obligations under the Berne Convention through other areas of the law and by concepts which possessed a well-established pedigree in common law jurisprudence. Damage to reputation was regarded as something which was quantifiable within the concept of defamation. That meant that there had to be some loss of esteem in the eyes of the author's peers and that he should feel that there had been sufficient damage to his reputation to justify the risk and expense of a jury trial.

An action for passing-off provided a remedy for misrepresentations made in the course of trade. While it may not have been necessary to establish financial damage, it was essential that the person making the misrepresentation was in a similar business, or that the injured party enjoyed such a reputation that his goods could be mistaken for those of the wrongdoer. There was no tort equivalent to the right of paternity, so this right could be protected only by contract. This led to some inconsistency, as moral rights are rights of personality and are thus not of their nature assignable.

WIPO PERFORMANCES AND PHONOGRAMS TREATY

While the moral right owes its origin to the concept of the integrity of the author, it is not confined to authors alone. On December 20, 1996 the World Intellectual Property Organization's new Performances and Phonograms Treaty surprised a largely unsuspecting world by providing, in Article 5, that performers of literary and artistic works and folklore would forthwith be entitled (i) to be identified as performers of their performances and (ii) to object to distortions and mutilations of their performances. This Treaty does not come into force until it receives 30 ratifications and accessions. At the time of writing, no country has yet deposited an instrument of accession or ratification.

INTRODUCTION OF MORAL RIGHTS IN THE U.K.

Once the U.K. decided to embrace the concept of moral rights, the first problem was to determine the scope of those rights and the extent of the independence of these rights from copyright. Copyright under the Act is given to a wide class of individuals who are designated somewhat arbitrarily as "authors". It seems that moral rights can exist only where the author and the work are somehow indivisible. For that reason, they have been limited to literary, artistic, musical and dramatic works and films, which are also the types of work protected by the Berne Convention. The distinction between the creative input of the film director and a record producer is perhaps one which is difficult to define, but U.K. law is unlikely to be widened to include sound recordings as a type of work entitled to moral rights.

The rights introduced by the 1988 Act are limited in many ways and the existence of a right to waive or consent to a breach of moral rights is the greatest compromise in the Act. Well advised copyright owners will always secure waivers of moral rights in advance, eliminating the risk of any future liability. This is happening in the publishing and film industries.

RIGHT TO OBJECT TO FALSE ATTRIBUTION

The right against the false attribution of a work is not new to U.K. law, being contained in section 43 of the 1956 Act. It has its antecedents in the Literary Copyright Act of 1886. Section 84 of the Act now provides that a person has the right not to have a literary, dramatic, musical or artistic work falsely attributed to him as author and not to have a film falsely attributed to him as director. Directors were not previously protected. The right does not require the person complaining to be the author of a similar work or indeed of any work at all. No remedy is given to the real author, whose claim to protection might be regarded as stronger. In addition to the primary wrong of issuing or exhibiting works to which a false attribution is applied, there is a secondary wrong in possessing or dealing with a copy of the work in the course of business, where the wrongdoer has, or ought to have, knowledge of the false attribution. False attributions are actionable if false statements are made as to who the author or director is, but dealing with altered works as unaltered is also covered. Thus a false attribution may occur if a copy of a Hockney by Freud is sold as a Hockney or if Zeffirelli's script for "Hamlet" is dealt with as the original by Shakespeare. Where the person who is falsely attributed with authorship of a work has registered his name as a trade mark, the false attribution may also constitute a trade mark infringement. Unlike the right to object to false attribution, which by section 86(2) of the Act expires 20 years after the putative author's death, the rights granted under the Trade Marks Act 1994 are potentially perpetually renewable.

RIGHT OF PATERNITY

The right of paternity, which was introduced by section 77, gives authors of works and the directors of films the right to be identified with their works. The right arises in different circumstances for different works, and may apply when works are published commercially, performed in public, broadcast and shown to the public. The composer of a musical work has no right to be attributed when music is simply performed in public or broadcast, although the right to prevent false attribution will apply to such performance. The rationale for this is presumably that it would be onerous for producers of television and radio programmes to have to give this detail or that it might affect the structure of those programmes. This right to have the title and author of a musical work announced can be, and commonly is, given to the author of a musical work by contract and enforced by collecting societies. Composers are given by the Act the right to be identified on sheet music, records and films. On the other hand, the author of an artistic work does have the right to be identified when his work is shown in public or on film, although he does not have the right to prevent the work from being shown. The right to be identified at public exhibitions goes further than the copyright right in artistic works, which does not provide an exclusive right of public exhibition or performance. The assertion can be of a pseudonym or other form of identification. In the case of an architect, the right of paternity enables him to require his name to be displayed on a building in a manner appropriately visible to persons entering or approaching the building. When more than one building is constructed to the same design, the right applies to the first building constructed. Authors of literary and dramatic works have the right to claim paternity for publication, public performance and broadcasting, including by cable, and when copies of films and records are sold. Directors have paternity rights when a film is shown or broadcast and when copies are sold.

The value of the right given by section 77 is substantially diminished by the requirement under section 78 of the Act that the right be asserted, and by the exceptions and special cases contained in section 79. The assertion of the right to be identified may be general or as part of a copyright assignment or by other written instrument. An oral assertion is allowed by the Act, but is probably not safe as it is hard to prove. In the case of a painting, the signature of the artist on any work will generally be sufficient as an assertion. An assertion made outside an assignment of copyright and not on a painting is binding only if there is actual notice of the assertion. Where it is made in an assignment, its application to third parties depends on the nature of the work. Delay in making an assertion will be taken into account in any proceedings for breach of the right. The other major limitation on the right is the ability of an author to waive his right consensually, as provided for by section 87. When Article 5 of the WIPO Performances and Phonograms Treaty of 1996 is implemented in respect of a performer's right of paternity, Article 20 of the same treaty prohibits the dependence of that right (or indeed any other right granted by the treaty) upon any formality. It is difficult to see how the government could continue to justify the formality of assertion for authors when the same right will be available automatically for performers.

There are a number of other exceptions and special cases. Most importantly, the right does not apply where a work is made by an employee in the course of employment and his employer is the first owner of copyright. This exception includes directors of films who are employed for the purpose of the making of the film. Literary works published in newspapers, magazines, periodicals or reference books do not attract the right. Journalists are regarded as workmen rather than creators. Computer programs, computer-generated works, typefaces and works subject to Crown, parliamentary or international organisational copyright are not covered by the right of paternity; in the case of the last three, the author may assert his paternity only where he has previously been identified on published copies. There are fair dealing exceptions, as for copyright works, together with a blanket denial of the right to any work created for the purpose of reporting current events. This excludes from the moral rights protection the work of cameramen reporting on wars and natural disasters, an established training ground for directors and a source of many dramatic films. Industrial designs and anonymous works are also excluded.

RIGHT TO OBJECT TO DEROGATORY TREATMENT

The right of integrity contained in section 80 of the Act is given to the author of copyright literary, dramatic, musical or artistic works and to the directors of copyright films. The author's right is not to have his work subjected to "derogatory treatment". "Treatment" is defined as any addition to, deletion from, alteration to or adaptation of a work, with the exceptions of translations of literary or dramatic works or the arrangement or transcription of a musical work involving more than a change of key or register. The complete destruction of a work would not appear to be a "treatment" of it.

Treatment is "derogatory" if it amounts to a distortion or mutilation of the work, or is otherwise prejudicial to the honour or reputation of the author or director, tracking the words of Article 6 *bis* of the Berne Convention. This probably means that if a work is published under a pseudonym, such as frequently occurs in the areas of novels concerning crime and romance, the use of the author's real name will not infringe the right since in such a case it would be the knowledge of the identity of the author of the work, rather than any modification to it, which might be derogatory of the author (this may, however, infringe the right of paternity). The question of whether something is derogatory is a question of fact. It is not clear whether or not satire will be treated as an exception, or whether the relevant basis by which treatment will be judged will be subjective or objective. In the case law in Continental countries, which have more experience of moral rights, derogatory treatment is judged by an objective standard.

The right given to authors of literary, musical and dramatic works is to object to derogatory treatment by commercial publication or other such use of a work. The integrity right in artistic works is infringed by the same types of acts, including exhibition in public, and in the case of three-dimensional artistic works, such as works of architecture and sculpture, it includes the publication of graphic works or photographs. The rights of film directors extend to the same acts and also apply to derogatory treatment of the film soundtrack. There is no precondition of assertion, but the right may be waived.

Exceptions exist in relation to computer programs and computer-generated works, reporting of current events and publication of certain works in newspapers, magazines and reference books. There is no similar exception for typefaces. As far as reference books are concerned, the exception appears to prevent freelance journalists or writers from claiming rights. In almost all cases there is no right of integrity in works subject to Crown, parliamentary or international organisation copyright.

For works made in the course of employment or where another person is the copyright owner, an author or film director who is identified at the time of the relevant act may insist only on a "sufficient" disclaimer of association with the act complained of. Outside the exceptions relating to employment there is the added requirement that the author must have already been identified with his work. The BBC also has the power to make alterations in the name of good taste and decency, public feeling and the like. Similar rights do not apply to other broadcasters, who may not feel that they have had such bad experiences in the past that they need to have the right enshrined in statute, or who may not have had the same success in lobbying.

There is no exclusion of the right of integrity for design rights, so that an author of a design may have his right of integrity infringed even though the reproduction of his design may not constitute an infringement of copyright.

There is a secondary wrong committed by a person who possesses or deals with an infringing article in the course of his business, where he knows, or ought to know, that the article infringes the right of integrity. This arises on a regular basis in the insurance salvage business where damaged works of art are "restored" by the insurance company which has acquired them as a condition of paying out under a claim.

The major limitation on the right is that the awarding of an injunction to prevent a breach of section 80 can be prevented by the giving of a "sufficient" disclaimer. Section 103(2) leaves the question of the sufficiency of the disclaimer to the court.

As mentioned previously, accession to the WIPO Performances and Phonograms Treaty 1996 will require the introduction of a right of integrity for the benefit of performers of literary and artistic works within the meaning of the Berne Convention, as well as works of folklore.

RIGHT OF DISCLOSURE

In addition to rights of paternity and integrity, a limited right of privacy has been introduced by the 1988 Act. This right is the first right of privacy to be introduced into English law and is found in section 85. The right is given to a person who commissions a photograph or a film for private and domestic purposes. If that work attracts copyright, then the commissioner has the right to object to the issuing of copies to the public or to the public exhibition or broadcasting of the work. There are exceptions, particularly in relation to incidental inclusion of the work in another. The introduction of this right appears to be some recompense for the removal by the Act of the rights given to the commissioners of such works by the 1956 Act. The Act also removed the rights of those commissioning painted portraits, but no right of privacy is given to them. Perhaps they were thought better able to protect their position, having commissioned an often more expensive work and having possession of the work, without the problem of separate ownership of negatives of photographs.

There are other exceptions to cover parliamentary or judicial proceedings and anonymous works, although the justification for the latter is hard to determine.

DURATION OF MORAL RIGHTS

The rights of paternity, integrity and the right to privacy of private photographs and films exist until the expiry of copyright in the relevant work. The right to prevent false attribution continues for only 20 years after the author's death.

JOINT OWNERSHIP

Joint authors each have independent moral rights and any assertion, waiver or consent must be by each joint author for himself.

INFRINGEMENT

Under section 103, breach of an author's moral rights is punishable as a breach of statutory duty, rather than as an infringement of copyright. The courts are empowered to grant injunctive relief and to award damages. The measure of damages is the amount of money necessary to put the injured party back into the position he would have been in had the breach of statutory duty not been committed. The valuation of this will be hard to estimate. There is no specific provision for the making of an apology, unlike in defamation proceedings. It is presumed, particularly by the provisions relating to disclaimers in the event of infringement of the right of integrity, that breaches are actionable simply because they occur, without there being the usual requirement in statutory duty actions of establishing actual physical or economic damage. This is consistent with the relationship between copyright and moral rights. Infringements of copyright are generally regarded as actionable *per se*.

DISPOSITION OF MORAL RIGHTS

While authors cannot assign their moral rights, which would be inconsistent with their general nature, section 87 of the Act provides that they may waive them or give consent to acts which would otherwise amount to an infringement of such rights. Moral rights may be waived by an instrument in writing signed by the person giving up the right. Waivers can relate to specific works, or be general. They may also relate to future works, be conditional or unconditional or revocable. If a waiver is made in favour of the owner or prospective owner of copyright in the relevant work, it would be presumed to extend to any licensees or assignees in the absence of contrary intention. The operation of the general law of contract or estoppel is expressly reserved, giving very limited protection to the moral right holder. He must either assert his rights regularly, or as required by the Act, or effectively waive such rights. Moral rights are transmissible on death either by a will or to the individual to whom copyright in a work passes. In the absence of either a will or some other form of disposition to a literary executor, the author's personal representative is entitled to exercise the rights.

COMMENCEMENT OF MORAL RIGHTS

The transitional provision in Schedule 1 to the Act provides that any infringing act carried out before August 1, 1989 will not be actionable, although any repetition of such an act may be. Moral rights will not apply to the works of an author dying before that date. The provisions do not apply to any film made before the commencement of the Act; therefore the colourisation of old black and white films will not be actionable as an infringement of moral rights although the colourisation of new black and white films, or the rendering into monochromatic format of new films made in colour, maybe.

The European Commission is studying the area of moral rights as part of its copyright harmonisation programme. This may lead eventually to moral rights which are not as emasculated as those currently in the Act and perhaps to the introduction of the *droit de suite*, or resale right. This would give the author the right to a share in the proceeds of a subsequent sale of his work, when the value may have increased with his fame. Until harmonisation takes place, moral rights will have little practical impact on most areas of copyright law.

CHAPTER 9

MISCELLANEOUS AND SUPPLEMENTARY PROVISIONS

This chapter deals briefly with some miscellaneous sections of the Act; dealings in copyright works (also referred to in Chapter 13 (Remedies) below), Crown and parliamentary copyright and copyright given to universities all of which are contained in the miscellaneous and general provisions of Chapters V and X of the Act.

ASSIGNMENTS AND LICENCES

It is provided in section 90 that copyright is transmissible by assignment, by testamentary disposition or by operation of the law as "personal or movable property". An assignment of copyright is, accordingly, a transfer of the ownership of the copyright and is to be distinguished from a licence, which merely authorises the doing of certain acts. An "agreement to assign" is also to be distinguished from an assignment; such an agreement will pass only "equitable rights", that is, rights valid in equity and which lie within the jurisdiction of the court to recognise, but which are not of themselves legal rights enforceable against infringers.

The section lays down that an assignment of copyright must be in writing, signed by or on behalf of the assignor. Copyright may also be licensed, a licence being a permission to do that which would otherwise be an infringement. The only licence required to be in writing is an exclusive licence. Section 92 defines an exclusive licence as one authorising the licensee to the exclusion of all others, including the copyright owner, to do a particular act. Exclusive licences, like assignments of copyright, can be partial, although an exclusive licence for the term of copyright is likely to be treated as an assignment.

Authors have the greatest interest in understanding the various ways in which assignments and licences may be limited. Thus each of the acts restricted by copyright may be separately assigned; likewise the assignment may be limited to one or more specific countries or smaller areas and to a specific period of time which is not that of the full duration of the copyright. We describe aspects of assignment in greater detail below: the same principles apply to the licencing of copyright in just the same manner as they apply to assignments.

Moreover, limitations may be placed on the assignment of each one of the acts restricted by copyright. Thus an assignment of the right to reproduce a work in the form of a commercial sound recording need not be drawn so as to cover reproduction of the work on the soundtrack of a film; the right to adapt a book for stage performance need not extend to adaptation for television broadcasting; the right to broadcast could be limited to broadcasting either by radio or television. This right to limit an assignment of copyright in such ways is specifically provided in the section, which refers to a number of different types of partial assignment. It follows that assignments of copyright in a work may be made to different persons if the assignments do not conflict as to the acts concerned, territory covered or in any other way. Thus, so far as infringement is concerned, the owner of the copyright is the person who is entitled to the copyright in respect of its application to the doing of the particular act. On the other hand, an assignment of copyright without any limitation may transfer the ownership of the full copyright for all purposes for the full period of copyright and, possibly by implication if not specifically, for all countries where copyright is granted.

The assignment of a right does not in itself impose on the assignee the obligation to exercise the right. If such an obligation is to be a condition of the assignment, then this condition should be written into the contract of assignment. The wording of contracts of assignment or licence is therefore of great importance, and when in doubt authors should consult one of their professional associations or refer the matter to a lawyer.

With respect to assignments made and licences granted before the Act came into force, it is provided in Schedule 1, para. 25(1) that any document which was made or event which occurred before the commencement of the provision — and which had any operation affecting the ownership of copyright or transferring an interest, right or licence in a work — is to have the corresponding operation in relation to the copyright in the work under the Act; of course, this would be only in so far as any period to which the operation of the document was limited extends beyond the commencement of the Act.

However, the same paragraph lays down that this provision is not to apply to future copyrights if the assignment was made before June 1, 1957, so that a purported assignment or licence under the 1911 Act (which did not provide for the assignment or licensing of future copyrights) would be ineffective. The meaning of "future copyright" is considered below.

Paragraph 27 of Schedule 1 provides that section 5(2) of the 1911 Act, which concerns reversion of copyright but has no corresponding provision in the Act, is to remain effective in respect of assignments and licences under the 1911 Act as if it had been re-enacted. This means that 25 years after the death of the author of any literary, dramatic, artistic or musical work assigned or licensed before June 1, 1957 copyright shall cease and in the absence of further assignment vest in the estate of the author. Pre-1911 works continue to be dealt with under the transitional provisions of the 1956 Act. No such transitional provisions are made for films or sound recordings, presumably as it is considered that there are no relevant copyrights.

FUTURE COPYRIGHTS

It was not possible under the 1911 Copyright Act to assign the copyright in a work or other subject-matter yet to be created, but this important faculty was provided in section 37 of the 1956 Act and in section 91 of the Act.

"Future copyright" is defined as:

> "copyright which will or may come into existence in respect of any future work or class of works or on the occurrence of a future event ... "

Section 91(1) provides that if an agreement to assign is made by a prospective owner of copyright, and signed by or on behalf of him, then on that copyright coming into existence the copyright vests in the assignee or his successor in title.

The definition of "future copyright" is worthy of note, since it is not the work but the copyright which will or may come into existence. Thus where a work comes into existence at a future date, no copyright is assigned if that work is one in which copyright does not subsist. It would not appear that the intervening death of the prospective owner will affect an assignment of future copyright.

As related under the preceding heading, a purported assignment or licence of a future copyright made when the 1911 Act was in force will not be effective. Now, under section 91(3) of the Act, a future copyright may be licensed as well as assigned. The provisions of section 101, as described under the heading "Remedies available to an exclusive licensee" (page 101 below), will apply to such a licence. Licences of future copyright are not effective against the interests of bona fide purchasers without actual or constructive notice of such licences, in contrast to assignments which continue to be effective.

Bequest by Will of the Copyright in an Unpublished Work

Under section 93, where under a bequest (whether specific or general) a person is entitled, whether beneficially or otherwise, to the manuscript or other original document recording or embodying a literary, dramatic or musical work, to an artistic work, or to the original material containing a sound recording or film, and the work was not published before the death of the testator, the bequest, unless a contrary intention is indicated in the testator's will, is to be construed as including the copyright in the work insofar as the testator was the owner of the copyright immediately before his death.

Crown and Parliamentary Copyright

The Act witnesses an assertion of Parliament's rights against the Crown. When what were formerly provisions dealing with Crown copyright were divided into Crown and parliamentary copyright (discussed at pages 68 to 69, below), a separate judicial copyright was, fortunately, omitted. The change makes little practical difference, as once a parliamentary Bill receives Royal Assent it ceases to be the subject of parliamentary copyright.

Crown copyright

Sections 163 and 164 contain provisions with respect to copyright in works made by Her Majesty or an officer or servant of the Crown, in the course of his or her duties, such as a civil servant or an employee of a government agency. The effects of these provisions are as follows.

Crown copyright subsists even if the ordinary requirements as to qualification for copyright protection are not met. Thus if the author of a work was not a "qualified person" at the time when the work was made, then the work would still attract copyright by virtue of being so made and that copyright would belong to the Crown. That copyright is still referred to as Crown copyright even if it has been assigned.

Crown copyright in literary, artistic, musical and dramatic works subsists for 125 years from the end of the year in which they were made or, if they were published within 75 years of that date, for 50 years from the end of the year of publication. Otherwise the usual rules as to duration of copyright apply to Crown copyright.

The Crown also has copyright in all Acts of Parliament and Measures of the General Synod of the Church of England. The duration of copyright in Acts is 50 years from the end of the year in which they received Royal Assent. Measures of the General Synod have the same term as other literary works.

Provisions relating to Crown copyright in works created before the commencement of the Act are subject to any agreements entered into before the commencement of the 1956 Act. The duration of copyright in pre-1989 works continues for the terms laid down in the 1956 Act for published literary, dramatic or musical works, artistic works other than unpublished engravings and unpublished photographs taken before June 1, 1957. Similarly the duration provided in the 1956 Act applies to published and other sound recordings made before June 1, 1957 and to published films and films falling within legislation relating to the registration of films. Copyright in unpublished literary, dramatic or musical works continues until the date provided for in the Act or the end of 50 years from the coming into force of the Act, whichever is later. The term of Crown copyright in unpublished engravings and unpublished photographs taken on or after June 1, 1957 continues for 50 years from the coming into force of the Act, as does copyright in unpublished sound recordings made after June 1, 1957 and in unpublished films made after the date. If, however, they are published within that period, the term is then 50 years from the end of the year in which they are published.

Parliamentary copyright

Works made by or under the direction or control of either of the Houses of Parliament are, under the Act, the subject of the new form of copyright, parliamentary copyright. Copyright subsists notwithstanding the ordinary requirements as to qualification for copyright protection.

There are two types of protection: parliamentary copyright owned by the House of Lords and by the House of Commons. Works made under the direction and control of both Houses have joint owners of copyright. Like works of Crown copyright a work originally the subject of parliamentary copyright continues as such, notwithstanding any subsequent assignment. The term of parliamentary copyright for literary, dramatic, musical or artistic work is until the end of 50 years from the end of the calendar year in which the work was made.

Works commissioned by the Houses of Parliament are not regarded as a subject of parliamentary copyright by reason only of being so commissioned, except that any sound recordings, films or broadcasts or cable programmes of the proceedings of either House are the subject of parliamentary copyright.

As with Crown copyright, where only one of the authors is acting under the direction or control of Parliament, then the rules as to parliamentary copyright apply only to that author. Where section 165 does not lay down any special rules, the normal provisions of the Act apply to the other author.

Section 165 provides that parliamentary copyright may be extended to works made by legislative bodies of other countries to which the Act is extended. The only country to which Part 1 of the Act has been extended to date is the Isle of Man.

Copyright in public Bills belongs in the first instance to the House in which the Bill is introduced and, once a Bill has been carried to the other House, copyright belongs to both

Houses jointly. Copyright in private Bills belongs to both Houses jointly and subsists from the time the Bill was first deposited in either House. Copyright in public Bills subsists from the time the Bill was introduced.

Copyright in personal Bills belongs in the first instance to the House of Lords and, once a Bill is carried to the House of Commons, it belongs to both Houses jointly. Such copyright subsists from the time the personal Bill is first read in the House of Lords.

Copyright in parliamentary Bills ceases on Royal Assent, on the withdrawal or rejection of the Bill, or at the end of the session of Parliament in which it was introduced. Such copyright is potentially rather ephemeral. If the Bill is reintroduced, parliamentary copyright again subsists in it. Otherwise no copyright subsists in a parliamentary Bill once it lapses.

Section 167 notionally gives to each House of Parliament the legal capacities of a body corporate on the basis that they continue notwithstanding any prorogation or dissolution. The functions of the House of Commons are exercised by the Speaker or, if there is no Speaker, by the Chairman of Ways and Means, and their rights continue until a new officer is appointed. Functions of the House of Lords are exercised by the Clerk of Parliaments or the Clerk Assistant or Reading Clerk.

The provisions relating to parliamentary copyright apply only to unpublished works to which that copyright would otherwise extend and not otherwise. Private Bills deposited before the commencement of the Act, or personal Bills given a first reading before the commencement of the Act, are not the subject of parliamentary copyright.

In section 171 of the Act, under the heading "Transitional provisions and savings", it is provided that nothing in the Act is to affect any right or privilege of the Crown subsisting otherwise than by virtue of an enactment. The reference here is to certain traditional privileges which are vestiges of the authority exercised by the Crown in the early days of printing over all published matter, and in particular to the sole privilege of authorising the printing of the Authorised Version of the Bible, the Book of Common Prayer, Acts of Parliament and other government publications. These privileges are accordingly "saved" by the Act.

Crown and parliamentary copyright in practice

Her Majesty's Stationery Office (HMSO) administers most Crown copyright and the parliamentary copyright in works published by it. In September 1996 HMSO was reorganised and effectively privatised, although by Letters Patent the Controller of Her Majesty's Stationery Office remained "personally and uniquely" responsible for the administration of Crown copyright and indeed in works of Parliamentary copyright which are published by HMSO. This reorganisation was effected without the need to amend the Act and does not have any bearing upon the legal nature of the copyrights in question. The copyright in other works of parliamentary copyright is administered by the two Houses of Parliament.

As far as Acts and Statutory Instruments are concerned, HMSO permits copying (and republication) of up to 30 per cent of a work during the initial period after the Act has received Royal Assent or a Statutory Instrument has been made. This embargo period ensures a market for HMSO publications. Such copying is in addition to, and in excess of, that permitted by the Act. The embargo period is six months from the date of publication by HMSO for Bills and Acts and three months for Statutory Instruments, Orders and

Rules. Republication must be accompanied by a sufficient acknowledgement. Longer extracts are permitted if accompanied by substantial annotation, as generally occurs with publication of taxation statutes. Hansard, Official Reports and House business papers may be copied and republished without restriction, except in advertising. Only 5 per cent of any other parliamentary papers, such as reports of committees, may be copied and/or republished. Copying of longer extracts requires permission and that is usually not granted within six months of publication by HMSO.

All other Crown and parliamentary copyright material may be copied, in circumstances not otherwise permitted by the Act, only with the permission of the relevant copyright owner, or its delegate. Copying of ordinance survey maps and navigational charts, in particular, requires permission.

The relevant addresses for consent are:

HMSO
Copyright Section (P6)
St Crispins
Duke Street
Norwich NR3 1PD
Tel: 01603 622211
Fax: 01603 723000

The Chief Clerk
Journal Office
House of Lords
London SW1A OPW
Tel: 0171 219 3000
Fax: 0171 219 6715

Clerk of the Journals
Journal Office
House of Commons
London SW1A 0AA
Tel: 0171 219 3000
Fax: 0171 219 6715

Copyright Branch
Ordnance Survey
Romsey Road
Maybush
Southampton SO9 4DH
Tel: 0345 330011

Hydrographic Department
Finance Section
Ministry of Defence
Taunton
Somerset TA1 2DN
Tel: 01823 337900
Fax: 01823 287077

COPYRIGHT VESTING IN INTERNATIONAL ORGANISATIONS

Section 168 provides for copyright to vest in certain international organisations designated by order in a similar manner to Crown copyright. Such copyright subsists for 50 years from the end of the calendar year in which the work was made or such other period as specified from time to time. As far as works of international organisations made before the commencement of the Act are concerned, copyright subsists in such works only if it subsisted under section 33 of the 1956 Act. Copyright in such works continues for the term provided for in the 1956 Act or 50 years from 1989, whichever is the earlier.

FOLKLORE

In accordance with Article 15(4) of the Berne Convention if, in the case of an unpublished literary, dramatic, musical or artistic work of unknown authorship, there is evidence that the maker was a qualifying person by reason of a connection with a country outside the U.K., that fact is presumed and copyright subsists in the work. Any body appointed by another country to protect such copyright may be recognised as having authority by regulation under section 169 (other than to assign the work) and may bring proceedings.

UNIVERSITY COPYRIGHT

From the earliest days of printing, privileges were granted by the Crown to universities. The Copyright Act 1775 granted to the Universities of Oxford, Cambridge, the Scottish Universities of St Andrews, Glasgow, Edinburgh and Aberdeen, together with the colleges of Eton, Westminster and Winchester, the copyright in perpetuity in all books given or bequeathed to them by their authors or their representatives, either before that Act or after it, for the advancement of learning or education.

Although the 1775 Act was repealed by the 1911 Act, section 33 of that Act preserved this copyright, as did section 46 of the 1956 Act. Copyright in these works continues as if it was copyright under the Act but will expire at the end of the year 2039.

Referring to the hitherto perpetual copyright enjoyed by these institutions, the Whitford Committee said that society should, as a matter of principle, have unrestricted use of all works after a stipulated period of protection.

DELIVERIES OF COPIES TO THE BRITISH LIBRARY AND OTHER LIBRARIES

The 1911 Act was in general repealed by the 1956 Act, aside from sections 15, 34 and 37. Those sections continue under the Act. Section 15 of the 1911 Act, continuing and widening a provision of the Copyright Act 1842, requires that publishers, at their expense, deposit a copy of every book published in the U.K. at the British Museum (now the British Library), and also, if written demand is made for it under specified conditions, one copy at the Bodleian Library, Oxford, the University Library, Cambridge, the National Library of Scotland, the National Library of Wales, and the Library of Trinity College, Dublin. A publisher who fails to comply with this requirement is liable on summary conviction to a fine and the value of the book.

For the purposes of these provisions, "book" is defined as including "every part or division of a book, pamphlet, sheet of letterpress, sheet of music, map, plan, chart or table separately published", but is not to include any second or subsequent edition of the book unless such edition contains additions or alterations either in the letterpress or in the maps, prints or other engravings thereto.

However, under the British Museum Act 1932 and regulations made under it, exemption is granted from the obligation to deliver copies unless demand is made for any copy or copies of the following:

> Publications wholly or mainly in the nature of trade advertisements;
> Registers of voters;
> Specifications of inventions;
> Publications wholly or mainly in the nature of timetables of passenger transport services, being publications prepared for local use;
> Publications wholly or mainly in the nature of calendars;
> Publications wholly or mainly in the nature of blank forms of accounts, receipts and so on;
> Wall sheets printed with alphabets, texts or other matter for the purpose of elementary instruction.

Also pursuant to section 15 of the 1911 Act, the National Library of Wales (Delivery of Books) Regulations 1924 exempt certain categories of "books" from the obligation to deliver copies to the National Library of Wales.

It will be observed that this requirement is not limited to books in which copyright subsists, or to books first published in the U.K. The requirement is however limited to books, which would seem to exclude films, sound recording, machine-readable computer programs and the ubiquitous CD-ROMs which are increasingly replacing printed literature in many places of work.

The deposit of books has been criticised as an unfair burden on publishers, especially where there has been a small and expensive print run. The Whitford Committee, while apparently sympathetic to this burden, felt that its weight had been somewhat exaggerated by publishers, and was prepared to alleviate it through tax concessions rather than through copyright law reform. The government Green Paper concluded that current tax concessions were already perfectly adequate for this purpose.

MISCELLANEOUS PROVISIONS

Part VII is the miscellaneous and general section of the Act. It contains four provisions which relate to copyright, as well as administrative parts of the Act dealing with commencement, extent and consequential amendments and repeal.

The first copyright provision in Part VII is section 296, relating to devices designed to circumvent copy-protection. Rights akin to copyright are given to those issuing copies of works in electronic form which are copy-protected. This copyright protection can take the form of encryption with insertion of locks. The rights given are limited to the secondary infringement provisions relating to the making, importing, selling or advertising of devices designed or adapted to circumvent the copy-protection or publishing information to enable this to be done. The person marketing such works also has rights in relation to delivery up and seizure and has the advantage of the presumptions as to copyright and the benefit of the withdrawal against self-incrimination given in cases of copyright infringement by the various rules of court. The section is limited to copy-prevention devices used in relation to copyright works and has not yet been used in the U.K.

Section 296A adds a provision which renders void any contract which prevents the lawful user of a computer program from making any back-up copy which is necessary for him to have for the purposes of the agreed use. Further provisions render void those contract terms which prevent the same lawful user decompiling the program or using any technical means of studying, testing or observing it so as to understand its underlying elements. All three of these provisions were enacted in compliance with the E.U. Software Directive (discussed in greater detail in Chapter 16).

Sections 297 to 299 provide criminal and civil remedies in respect of fraudulent reception of broadcasts or cable programme services. The criminal offence relates to the dishonest reception of a programme. It must be provided from a place within the U.K. and it is necessary to establish the intent to avoid payment of any applicable charge. The civil provisions were amended by the Broadcasting Act 1990 to make it clear that the relevant service need not be one provided from the U.K.; it could be any service provided from the U.K. and directed at any other part of the world, and it is not necessary for any device for unauthorised reception to be made in the U.K. Again the rights are akin to copyright infringement, although it is not necessary to prove knowledge on the part of the infringer. The rights are similar to those for secondary infringement of copyright relating to making, importing, selling or advertising apparatus or devices designed or adapted to enable people to receive programmes if they are not entitled to do so or to publish information which enables this to be done. Rights in relation to delivery up, seizure, and withdrawal of privilege against self-incrimination apply, as does section 97 dealing with innocent infringement of copyright. The provisions of sections 297 and 298 may be extended to programmes provided to countries outside the U.K. on a reciprocal basis. No such order has been made.

The Act was before Parliament at the time that copyright in the play *Peter Pan* by Sir James Matthew Barrie was expiring. Barrie left the copyright in this work to the Hospital for Sick Children, Great Ormond Street, London. At a late stage provision was included in the Bill conferring on the trustees of the Great Ormond Street Hospital a right to receive a royalty in respect of the public performance, commercial publication, broadcasting or inclusion in the cable programme service of that play or any adaptation of it. The copyright was not extended by section 301, so it would have been possible to make television programmes and films of the play, but the commercial exploitation of those programmes and films gives rise to the obligation to pay royalties. The provision was much criticised as being contrary to the spirit of copyright which provides rights for a limited period of time. As it is, the general extension of copyright term which was introduced by statutory instrument in 1995 and which extended the life of the *Peter Pan* copyright until the end of 2007 did not repeal section 301; indeed, it did not mention it at all. The trustees of the Hospital for Sick Children thus presumably enjoy the exercise of the full copyright in *Peter Pan* until it really does expire at the beginning of 2008, whereupon section 301 (and Schedule 7 of the Act which expands upon it) will again be of relevance.

Parts IX and X of the Broadcasting Act 1990 contain various provisions in relation to copyright. The most important provision is section 175, which adds new sections 135A to

135G to the Act. Section 175 provides for a statutory licence for the broadcasting of sound recordings or their inclusion in a cable programme service. The statutory licence may apply when the relevant licensing body, PPL, has refused to grant a licence with either unlimited "needle time" or such needle time as the broadcaster has requested. "Needle time" is an expression used in the broadcasting industry in relation to the air time when recorded (rather than live) music is actually being played. The Copyright Tribunal has jurisdiction to settle the terms of payment. Payment is in accordance with an order of the Copyright Tribunal and, while it is considering the matter, referral to the Tribunal and agreement to pay in accordance with an order made by it is a defence to copyright infringement. In exercising its jurisdiction the Tribunal has to make sure that there is no unreasonable discrimination between licensees. Part IX of the Broadcasting Act also includes a statutory licence for the reproduction of radio and television listings, which is discussed in chapter 18 below dealing with the Copyright Tribunal.

Part X of the Broadcasting Act also inserts a new section 297A into the Act providing a criminal offence in respect of the importation and sale of unauthorised decoders. This section was inserted because of doubts as to the enforceability of section 297 of the Act. It is applicable only to broadcasts and cable programme services.

CHAPTER 10

COPYRIGHT AND DESIGNS

The law governing designs is complex. The 1988 Act made significant changes to the protection given to industrially applied designs in an attempt to sort out the anomalous and highly unsatisfactory situation that had arisen from the courts' interpretation of the 1956 Act and Parliament's attempt to repair the damage. The new law is worded in a technically complex manner which is difficult to comprehend and a detailed discussion of its terms is beyond the scope of this book. Unfortunately, the "old" law still applies to those designs created before August 1, 1989, so both the new and the old law have to be considered. The European Commission is also in the process of trying to harmonise design law throughout the Community, although the agreement, both in terms of detail and in terms of principle, has proved to be enduringly elusive.

The confusion caused by the old law and the changes which the 1988 Act imposes stem from the idea that a design, which is used many times to create similar articles, may be seen as inherently less deserving of protection than an artistic work, which is unique or, at most, part of a limited set of creations. While the idea conforms to the view that new artistic endeavour should be better rewarded than the mere copying of existing items, the legal division has proved far from simple to create.

In this context, "design" means any aspect of the appearance of an article, whether internal or external. The features of a design may be recorded in a permanent record, such as a drawing or a photograph, or electronically. The Act uses the term "design document" to describe such a record.

As well as copyright legislation, the Registered Designs Act 1949 and the Patents Act 1977 also contain provisions covering designs. The Registered Designs Act was substantially amended by the Act, but both its former and its current version also need to be considered. The amended version of the Registered Designs Act 1949 is appended in full as Schedule 4 to the Act.

THE OLD LAW

Rather than trace the unedifying development of the law up until the 1988 Act, it is probably most straightforward to outline the position as it was just before the 1988 Act came into force. The previous statute to amend the law on designs was the Design Copyright Act 1968 and the situation discussed in the following paragraphs lasted for about 20 years. Before this, the 1956 Act had been the controlling statute.

Under the old law, designs could be protected in a number of ways. Some designs were capable of protection under the Registered Designs Act 1949, which allowed the registration of the features of shape, configuration, pattern or ornament applied to an article by any industrial process. In the finished article the features had to appeal to, and were judged solely by, the eye. There was a test of novelty, which was meant to be much stricter than the test of originality applied to copyright works. Some types of design were deliberately excluded from registration. These included methods or principles of construction and features of shape or configuration dictated solely by the function which the article to be made had to perform. The latter exclusion is known as a "must-fit" exception to legal protection, and will be discussed below.

A design was "industrially applied" if it was reproduced or intended to be reproduced in more than 50 articles. This number survives in the new law as the indication of when exploitation is to be considered industrial. The period of protection under the Registered Designs Act was a maximum of 15 years from the date of registration; the right granted was a monopoly which was more similar to a patent than a copyright. For example, there was no requirement to prove copying in infringement proceedings. The proprietor simply had to show that his design (or something not substantially different) had been applied to an article.

Judicial interpretation made it clear that designs which were not intended to appeal to the eye could not be registered. The result was that the manufacturers of a large range of items intended for purely functional tasks could not register their designs and had to rely on copyright protection under the 1956 Act alone. However, many ended up receiving greater protection than Parliament had ever intended, because of the Design Copyright Act 1968. This amended the 1956 Act so as to reduce copyright in designs which could have been registered to a 15-year period, which was of equal length to the protection available for a registered design. The intention was to persuade design owners to apply to register their designs. Owing to the way it was conceived, the 1968 Act amendment reduced copyright only in those designs for which protection could be obtained under the 1949 Act. Since truly functional articles could not be protected in this way, the term of copyright in them was thus not reduced at all. As a result, the full life plus 50 years term applied.

When this anomaly was coupled with the fact that the copyright in a drawing of an unregistrable design could be infringed by a three-dimensional reproduction of the design as shown in the drawing, it became clear that manufacturers of articles based on unregistrable designs had received an extraordinary windfall, because they could stop third parties making items such as spare parts for their products by relying on copyright in the drawing for these items. No-one had expected this result. The courts had attempted to restrict copyright protection in designs rather than expand it. For example, a furniture manufacturer which worked from prototypes rather than design drawings had been told that its crude models were not "works of artistic craftsmanship" under the 1956 Act; thus it seemed that some intention to create an artistic work was required if full copyright protection was going to be given. The use of artistic skills to create an industrial product was not sufficient.

In an attempt to restore some sense to the position, the House of Lords created a so-called "spare parts exemption", which prevented owners of copyright in some unregistrable designs from enforcing their copyright because they were found to have given an implied right to purchasers of their products to repair the goods. The scope of this exemption was never fully tested by the courts, because the 1988 Act changed the law, removing the need for any further works of judicial craftsmanship.

The old law applies to those designs created before August 1, 1989. The transitional provisions are discussed briefly at the end of this chapter.

THE NEW LAW

The provisions of the Act dealing with designs were specifically intended to iron out the old inconsistencies. There were three main changes. First, the enforceability of copyright in artistic works applied industrially was curtailed; second, an entirely new "design right" was introduced; and third, substantial amendments were made to the Registered Designs Act.

Copyright

Copyright will be considered first. As discussed in Chapter 5 above, copyright exists in original artistic works, including drawings which may record a design or the features of a design of a three-dimensional article. Section 51 of the Act restricts this type of artistic copyright by providing that it is not an infringement of any copyright in a design document or model recording or embodying a design, (i) to make an article to the design (that is by reproducing the two-dimensional design in three dimensions), or (ii) to copy an article made to the design (that is infringing indirectly, by copying an article which is itself made to the design). This limitation does not apply to a design document for an artistic work or a typeface. The copyright in a design document still exists, but it is unenforceable where the infringement consists of the design's industrial exploitation.

The first question to consider here is what a "design document" will be. The words will probably be given a fairly broad interpretation. It is still possible that a design might qualify as a work of artistic craftsmanship but, as the old case law applies under the act, this seems unlikely. Drawings of prototypes for furniture will thus be design documents. The prototypes themselves — if they are not regarded as "works of artistic craftsmanship" — may well be sculptures under section 4(1)(a) of the Act, which specifically states that no minimum artistic merit is required to qualify as an artistic work.

Section 52 contains a further restriction on copyright. Where an artistic work has been exploited by or with the licence of a copyright owner for making articles by an industrial process and marketing them, the copyright in that work (rather than in any design document) is restricted to 25 years from the end of the calendar year in which the articles are first marketed. The reference to an "industrial process" means the making of 50 or more copies. As an increasing array of techniques become available for reproducing artistic works, it appears that this provision will restrict rights in large numbers of works.

Design right

Once copyright is no longer enforceable under the Act, the new design right comes into operation. This right was entirely new right which was created in order to deal with the perceived anomalies of the law as it then stood. Few other countries have even felt the need to emulate the U.K.'s approach, which may indicate that the whole area of design is somewhat "over-engineered". The provisions creating this right are set out in sections 213 to 264. The new right is closer to copyright than to registered design right. As with copyright, the design right arises automatically on creation — no registration is needed.

"Design" means the design of any aspects of the "shape or configuration" (whether internal or external) of the whole or part of an article. The design must be "original", which means that it is not commonplace in the design field in question at the time of its creation. This test may introduce a higher hurdle than that applied for copyright in artistic works, but it is certainly less stringent than that applied to registered designs, where designs used or registered in one field can invalidate the registration of a design in another.

There are a number of restrictions on what may qualify for design right protection. Design right will not subsist in a method or principle of construction. Nor does it apply to features of shape or configuration, of an article (1) which enable the article to be connected to, or placed in, around or against, another article so that either article may perform its function (a "must-fit" exception), (2) which are dependent on the appearance of another article of which the article is intended by the designer to form an integral part (a "must-match" exception) or (3) where the design consists of a "controlled representation" within the meaning of the Olympic Symbol, etc., (Protection) Act 1995. A body of case law is now shaping our understanding of the limits of design protection in the many different industries in which the manufacture of designed articles takes place.

The "must-fit" and "must-match" exceptions should prevent manufacturers from establishing a monopoly over spare parts for their products by making them so that only certain items are mechanically functional or aesthetically appropriate. Finally, design right cannot subsist in a surface decoration, which may be protected as a registered design.

The design right lasts a maximum of 15 years from the end of the calendar year in which the design was first recorded in the design document or in which an article was first made to the design, whichever is earlier. However, if articles made to the design are made available for sale or hire anywhere in the world within five years of the first recording or first manufacture, then protection is reduced to 10 years from that later date. The second term will clearly be shorter than the first.

The Act contains detailed provisions as to ownership of designs rights. The designer is the first owner so long as the design is not created under a commission or in the course of the designer's employment. The provision about commissioned designs is anomalous, because it is opposite to that governing commissioned copyright works, where a specific agreement is needed to vest rights in the work in the commissioner.

Design rights are not covered by any of the international conventions dealing with copyright, so the conditions which must be satisfied in order to qualify for design right protection are therefore slightly different from those governing copyright protection in the U.K. Design right applies where the first owner of the design is a citizen of, or a company incorporated or carrying on a substantial business in, the U.K. or another part of the European Union or any other country which provides reciprocal protection to U.K. designs. It remains to be seen how many non-E.U. countries will wish to alter their laws to coincide with those of the U.K.

Design rights may be assigned or licensed, in whole or in part. Section 222 provides that an assignment is not effective unless it is in writing and signed by or on behalf of the assignor. As with copyright, an agreement may be made to assign or to license future design rights.

The unregistered design right gives the design owner the exclusive right to reproduce the design for commercial purposes by making articles to the design or by making a design document recording the design so that articles may be made from it. The design will be reproduced where an exact or substantially similar copy is made. The Act also creates rights to restrain secondary infringements of importing, possessing for commercial purposes or selling or offering for sale, articles where the infringer has reason to believe that the articles are, in fact, infringing. The effect of the infringement provisions is to make "reverse engineering" a primary infringement of the design right. "Reverse engineering" occurs where an infringer (1) takes a product apart to establish how it works or how it is put together, (2) produces his own design drawings from this, and then (3) manufactures his own product from these drawings. It is also an infringement if copies are made without the preparation of intermediate drawings.

Registered designs

The Registered Designs Act was also extended and modified by the Act. Elements of shape and configuration, pattern and ornament are still registrable. Methods or principles of construction and entirely functional features are still excluded, but a new "must-match" exception has been introduced to go with the old "must-fit" provision so as to mirror the unregistered design right exceptions. Section 1(3) of the amended 1949 Act attempts to draw the line more firmly between registered designs and the unregistered design right, providing that a design cannot be registered if the appearance of the article in question is not "material", that is, if aesthetic considerations are not normally taken into account to a "material extent" by people acquiring or using it. The Act introduced a number of other amendments. Under section 1(2) of the 1949 Act a design now merely has to be "new" rather than "new or original" under the old law.

As with design right, the author of a registered design is treated as the owner. The commissioner of a registered design is to be treated as the proprietor. Section 7 of the amended 1949 Act gives a registered proprietor the exclusive right to make or import, sell or offer for sale an article in respect of which the design is registered or one not substantially different from this. The right is infringed by any person who does any of the protected acts without the consent of the proprietor. The amended 1949 Act creates a further infringement where a person does something in relation to a "kit" of components intended to be assembled into an article if treatment of the finished article would have infringed the proprietor's rights.

As a small incentive to designers to try to obtain registered design protection rather than relying on an unregistered design right, the term of protection for registered designs has been increased so that registered designs now have a maximum life of 25 years. The 25-year period is divided into an initial five-year registration with four possible five-year periods following this. Fees are payable for each extension.

It remains to be seen whether Parliament's attempt to encourage registration of designs will work. In the past, the complexities of registry were a strong disincentive to applicants and only a very small number of registrations were applied for. The possibility of obtaining a 25-year monopoly rather than an unknown, unregistered design right with a maximum 15-year term has so far failed to encourage registration. In 1988 the number of registered design applications stood at 8,748, of which 3,894 were from British applicants. By 1995 the corresponding figure had risen to just 9,246, of which only 2,999 were of local provenance.

LICENCES OF RIGHT

Section 237 of the 1988 Act contains an important limitation on the design right, in that any person is entitled as of right to a licence of the design right in the last five years of its life. In default of agreement, the terms will be settled by the Comptroller General of Patents, Designs and Trade Marks, who is head of the Patent Office. Where a design right owner seeks to enforce his rights against an infringer during that five-year period, the defendant can undertake to take such a licence. This severely restricts the remedies available to the proprietor, who is no longer entitled to an injunction or to delivery up of infringing items.

TRANSITIONAL PROVISIONS

The transitional provisions governing old works under the new law appear in Schedule 1 to the 1988 Act. As with all other aspects of designs, they are complex. For designs embodied in design documents or models before commencement of the 1988 Act, the new limited rights provided for by section 51 do not apply for 10 years after commencement. However, during those 10 years, licences of right are available which are similar to those which apply to the new design right. Application may be made to the Patent Office to settle the terms of the rights.

Existing registered designs which would not have been registrable under the amended 1949 Act will expire no later than 10 years from the commencement of the 1988 Act and, in the last five years of their life, licences of right will be obtainable.

OVERLAPPING RIGHTS

It is possible that a designer may be both the proprietor of registered design and the owner of a design right. If this is the case, he will probably try to enforce rights in his registered design rather than the unregistered design right, because the monopoly right should be easier to enforce. There is no need to show copying.

It is also possible that copyright and design right can overlap. On the question of enforcement, section 236 of the 1988 Act provides that where copyright and design rights subsist in a work, it is not an infringement of design right in a design to do anything which is an infringement of the copyright in that work. This means that the proprietor must take action to restrain copyright infringement.

CHAPTER 11

EXTENT OF OPERATION OF THE ACT

EXTENSION OF THE ACT TO THE ISLE OF MAN, CHANNEL ISLANDS, COLONIES AND DEPENDENCIES

This Chapter may seem to the lay reader to be unduly technical, as a result of the regrettably complex nature of the considerations deriving from the relationship of the U.K. to a variety of different territories towards which it has borne, or still bears, responsibilities.

This Chapter deals with "extensions" of the Act and with its "application" to countries to which it does not extend. "Extension" of the Act means that it is given the force of law in jurisdictions other than the U.K.; "application" of the Act means that its benefit is given to works and nationals of another country to which the Act does not extend. To give an example, the law extends to Gibraltar — thus becoming the colony's own copyright law — but it applies to France, giving French authors and works published in France rights in the U.K. similar to those enjoyed by their U.K. counterparts.

Parts I to III of the Act deal with different species of copyright; these are, respectively, ordinary copyright, rights in performances and the unregistered design right. Each of these Parts has different provisions with regard to extension and application of the Act. All three Parts extend the Act so as to cover the four "home jurisdictions" of the U.K.: England, Scotland, Wales and Northern Ireland. Parts I and III of the Act may also be extended, under sections 157(2) and 255(2) respectively, to cover the Channel Islands, the Isle of Man and any colony.

Extension provisions

By a series of Orders the Act has in fact been extended to most of the countries as defined in section 157.

The 1911 Act, unlike the Acts of 1956 and 1988, extended throughout Her Majesty's Dominions except to the self-governing dominions, but these dominions could declare that they adopted it, with or without modifications of a specifically limited character. The purpose was to secure as much uniformity as possible in the copyright legislation of the Commonwealth, and the copyright legislation adopted at that time by the self-governing dominions was essentially that of the 1911 Act. Since then Canada (1921), New Zealand (1962) and Australia (1968) have enacted their own independently conceived copyright laws. These still bear some resemblance to the U.K. legislation, although the passage of time and changing fashions in draftsmanship have done much to diminish areas of common interpretation and application.

The relationship in the copyright field between the U.K. and the independent countries of the Commonwealth does not therefore rest on any common legislative system, or on their special relationship as members of the Commonwealth; instead, like the copyright relationship between the U.K. and countries outside the Commonwealth, it is based on reciprocal protection applied in accordance with international Copyright Conventions to which they are common parties.

Meanwhile some of the more important countries, such as India, Pakistan, Bangladesh, the former African colonies and Malta — to which as part of Her Majesty's Dominions at that time, the 1911 Act extended — have become independent countries; most of them have now adopted copyright legislation of their own devising. Two which have not done so at the time of writing are Jamaica and Trinidad which, it is understood, have continued to regard the 1911 Act as their effective copyright legislation. The position of Hong Kong should also be noted as a jurisdiction which still operates under a copyright system which is strongly influenced by its British past although it has now been subsumed within the control of the People's Republic of China.

There is now, accordingly, throughout the Commonwealth, as elsewhere in the world, a great and inconvenient diversity of copyright legislation, although all of it in the Commonwealth countries and in those of the English language belongs to what has been described in this book as the copyright (rather than the author's right) system.

As a consequence of paragraph 36 of the First Schedule, in so far as the 1956 Act, or any Order made under it, forms part of the law of any country other than the U.K., at a time after that Act has been wholly or partly repealed in the U.K., it is, so long as it forms part of the law of that country, to be construed and to have effect as if that Act has not been repealed. The 1956 Act has of course been repealed in the U.K. by the Act but, in accordance with this provision, that repeal does not affect the Act's continued operation in a country to which it has been extended and of which it has remained the law.

The trappings of copyright are often confused when a country to which British law applies becomes independent. That country needs to know, first, what domestic copyright law governs it and, second, what its rights and obligations are under international copyright conventions. This confusion is partially cleared by section 158, which lays down the rules which are to be followed where a country to which Part I of the Act applies ceases to be a colony. By section 158(2), a former colony's independence date is the date from which the following changes occur: (i) sections 163 and 165 — which take copyright away from the author and give it to the Crown and Parliament respectively — will no longer apply; (ii) if a country to which the Act applies ceases to protect British works adequately, an Order in Council can be made under section 160(2) which will remove the Act's protection in respect of works emanating from that country after a date specified in that Order and which are not created by authors who are citizens or domiciled in any country to which the Act extends; authors from the newly independent colony will no longer be included within this category; (iii) the provisions of sections 154 to 156 relating to "qualified works" and "qualified authors" will continue to govern it until an Order in Council is made, *either* applying the Act instead of extending it *or* declaring that the Act no longer extends to that colony, in consequence of its amendment or repeal there.

Power to amend the Act in countries to which it extends

Under section 157(4) of the Act, the legislature of any country to which any provision of the Act has been extended may modify or add to such provision, as part of the law of that country, provided that no such modification or addition, except insofar as it relates to procedures or remedies or works qualifying for copyright protection, in relation to a work or other subject-matter to which the modification or addition relates, is similar, in relation to that country, to those works in which copyright subsists in the U.K.

For example, the legislature of a country to which the Act has been extended could not modify the Act, except in regard to procedure and remedies, in relation to a work or other subject-matter of which the author or maker was a "qualified person", when the work was made, by virtue of being domiciled or resident in the U.K. at that time; but such legislature could otherwise modify the Act in relation to a work or other subject-matter the author or maker of which was domiciled or resident in that country when the work was made, and who was thus a "qualified person" in relation to that country. The same principle would apply, to cite further examples, in the cases of first publication or the making of a broadcast in that country.

For all practical purposes, however, the Act operates in the countries to which it has been extended to the same effect as it operates in the U.K.

For the purposes of any proceedings under the Act in the U.K., where the proceedings relate to an act done in any country to which the Act (subject to exceptions, modifications or additions) has been extended, the procedure applicable to the proceedings, including the time within which they must be brought and the remedies available, are to be in accordance with the Act as part of U.K. law. However, if the act does not constitute an infringement of copyright under the Act in its operation as part of the law of the country where the act was done, it is not to be treated as constituting an infringement under the Act in the U.K.

APPLICATION OF THE ACT TO COUNTRIES TO WHICH IT DOES NOT EXTEND

Under section 159(1) the Act may be applied by Order in Council in the case of countries to which it does not extend. The effect of this is that the provisions of the Act are made to apply to works which, in relation to the laws of such other country, fulfil the same conditions as those required to attract copyright under the Act, for example, to works whose authors or makers are subjects of that country, or are resident or domiciled there, or which are first published in that country.

The Order may apply the Act subject to exceptions and modifications, and either generally or in relation to such classes of works as may be specified in the Order. However, under section 159(3), no Order is to be made under the section in the case of a country which is not a party to one of the international copyright conventions, unless Her Majesty is satisfied that owners of copyright under the Act will enjoy adequate reciprocal protection in that country. This is on the supposition that a convention to which the U.K. and the other country are parties will ensure by its provisions that adequate reciprocal protection is afforded to each party.

The 1911 Act had, by Orders in Council pursuant to section 29 of that Act, been applied to the foreign countries which, like the U.K., were parties to the international copyright conventions. It was thus necessary to provide that, on the repeal of the 1911 Act by the 1956 Act, the reciprocal protection that had been established was not interrupted. This was done by paragraphs 40(1) and (2) of the Seventh Schedule of the 1956 Act, the effect of which is that where the relevant provisions of the 1911 Act applied immediately before the repeal of that Act to a foreign country, and where no order had been made applying the 1956 Act to the foreign country, the repealed provisions of the 1911 Act were to continue to have effect until, *inter alia*, the making of an Order in Council applying the 1956 Act. Paragraph 4(3) of Schedule 1 of the Act achieves the same end more elegantly by simply declaring:

"Anything done (including subordinate legislation made), or having effect as done, under or for the purposes of a provision repealed by this Act has effect as if done under or for the purposes of the corresponding provision of the new copyright provisions."

The reader is reminded that the two main international copyright conventions are concerned only with literary, dramatic, musical, artistic and cinematographic works (in civil law parlance "authors' works"). Other conventions relate to sound recordings, broadcasts and performers, covering what is referred to in many countries as neighbouring rights. Such conventions have fewer adherents than the main copyright conventions, and are dealt with in Chapter 14 below. So far as other types of work are concerned, the countries with which the U.K. has reciprocal relations are, at present, many fewer in number than those with which it has such relations in the field of authors' works. In addition to the international conventions, E.U. legislation in the area of copyright is of increasing significance. The E.U.'s early experiments in copyright harmonisation, the Computer Software and Rental and Lending Rights Directives, have been followed by Directives on the harmonisation of the term of copyright, copyright protection for satellite and cable broadcasts and protection of databases. The Commission has also been actively considering the areas of reprography, or photocopying, as well as *droit de suite*.

The historical position of the Republic of Ireland should be noted. Works of Irish nationals were protected under the Act of 1911 until the constitution of the Irish Free State in 1921, and thereafter continued to be so protected by virtue of the Irish Free State (Consequential Provisions) Act 1922 and Orders in Council Nos 898 and 899 of 1930. The 1956 Act in turn was applied to the Republic of Ireland by the Copyright (International Conventions) Orders No. 1523 of 1957 and No. 690 of 1964. With the enactment of the Irish Copyright Act in 1963 and accession to the Berne Convention, Rome Convention and Universal Copyright Convention in 1927, 1979 and 1959 respectively, Ireland's special position did not need to be recognised.

Regarding the protection in Ireland of U.K. works, the U.K. Act had been operative in Ireland until the constitution of the Irish Free State. After that the Act was regarded as having continuing effect in the Free State until the enactment by the state of the Industrial and Commercial Property (Protection) Act, effective from August 1, 1927, which practically reproduced the U.K. Act of 1911. Doubts later arose about the legal position in the period between December 6, 1921 and August 1, 1927; the Free State then enacted the Copyright (Foreign Countries) Order 1930, which applied the Irish Act of 1927 to works of nationals of foreign countries which were parties to the Berne Copyright Union, and the Copyright (United Kingdom and British Dominions) Order 1930, applying the provisions of the 1927 Act to the works of U.K. and Dominions nationals. Both these Orders had retrospective effect to December 6, 1921.

The Irish Republic's Copyright Act 1963, in force from October 1, 1964, applies to the works of nationals of the U.K. and other countries which are parties to the International Copyright Conventions. Since 1978 it has also applied to broadcasts, protected for the first time in the 1964 Act, but forgotten about until the Performing Right Society failed to secure damages for copyright infringement in respect of works broadcast in the U.K. but received and transmitted in Ireland by diffusion service. The two Copyright (Foreign Countries) Orders of 1978 now grant the protection of Irish law to all copyright works.

INTERNATIONAL ORGANISATIONS

Provision is made in section 168 for the grant of copyright in original literary, dramatic, musical and artistic works made by or under the control of certain international organisations, where copyright would not subsist apart from that section. These organisations are those of which sovereign powers, or their governments, are members, and which are declared by Order in Council to be organisations to which the section applies. A declaration has been made under the Act in respect of the United Nations.

The section applies to works published by or made by an officer or employee of such an organisation.

DENIAL OF COPYRIGHT TO FOREIGN WORKS

Under section 160 an Order in Council may be made by designating a country as failing to give adequate protection to British works, sound recordings and cinematograph films (being works, recordings or films, the author or maker of which is a "qualified person" for the purpose of the Act).

Such an Order is to provide that copyright under the Act is not to subsist in works, sound recordings and films first published after a date specified in the Order if, at the date of such publication, the author of the work, recording or film was a citizen or subject of the country designated in the Order (but not being at that time domiciled or resident in the U.K. or in another country to which the Act extends) or a body incorporated under the laws of that country.

The section applies only to published works, recordings and films because these could obtain protection as of right under the Act by virtue of first publication in the U.K. or other country to which the Act extends, whereas unpublished works, recordings and films (other than those defined as "British") could obtain protection under the Act only if the author was a subject of, or resident or domiciled in, or a body incorporated under the laws of, a country to which the Act had been specifically made applicable, and such applicability could of course be withdrawn, if it had not been withheld.

No Order has yet been made applying section 160 to any country.

CHAPTER 12

INFRINGEMENT OF COPYRIGHT

Intellectual property rights are essentially negative in character. They only have value which may be exploited by use, assignment or licensing because the proprietor (or in some cases the licensee) can prevent third parties from infringing the right. It is thus most important to understand what may constitute an infringement of copyright and what remedies may be available. There are also numerous exceptions to copyright infringement set out in the act which it will be necessary to consider.

PRIMARY INFRINGEMENT

The copyright in a work is infringed by a person who, without the licence of the copyright owner, does any of the acts restricted by the copyright. As has been said above, such infringing acts may be done either directly or indirectly, or in relation to the work as a whole or to any substantial part of it. Authorising another to infringe copyright must be authorisation to infringe a particular copyright work, and not works in general, such as by the supply of a duplicating machine capable of making more than one copy of any sound recording.

SECONDARY INFRINGEMENT

In addition to primary infringement, copyright may be infringed without doing any of the acts comprised in the copyright but by importation, dealing with infringing copies and providing the means of making infringing copies. There is also secondary infringement in relation to permitting premises to be used for an infringing performance and providing apparatus for an infringing performance.

Section 27 defines an "infringing copy" as one the making of which constituted an infringement of the copyright of the work in question. An article is also an infringing copy if it has been, or is proposed to be, imported into the U.K., and its making in the U.K. would have constituted an infringement of the copyright of the work or an exclusive licence of the copyright in that work. This notional making test clears up previous doubt as to whether the law of the place in which the copy was actually made was relevant for the purposes of U.K. copyright law. The definition of an "infringing copy" is limited by section 27(5); this limits the notional making test by providing that it does not apply to an article which may be lawfully imported into the U.K. by virtue of any enforceable right within the European Communities Act 1972. This adopts or incorporates into U.K. copyright law the European concept of exhaustion of rights.

The owner of the copyright has the right to make, or to authorise others to make, copies of his work. He cannot use national copyright laws and rules relating to secondary infringement to create barriers to inter-state trade within the European Union. This means that if the copyright owner has authorised the printing of a copy of a book in any country in the E.U. he may not prevent its importation and sale in any other Member State. He may, however, use secondary infringement to prevent importation and sale of copies made outside the E.U., when he has not consented to their being imported into the E.U.

It is presumed, until the contrary is proved, that if an article is a copy of a work and copyright has subsisted at any time in that work, then the article was made at a time when copyright subsisted.

Secondary infringement by importing infringing copies is governed by section 22. Infringement takes place when any person, without the licence of the copyright owner, imports into the U.K., other than for private and domestic use, an article which he knows or has reason to believe is an infringing copy of the work. Similarly, by section 23, the copyright is infringed by the person who without the permission of the copyright owner:

(a)   possesses in the course of a business,
(b)   sells or lets for hire, offers or exposes for sale or hire,
(c)   in the course of a business exhibits in public or distributes, or
(d)   distributes otherwise than in the course of a business to such an extent as to affect prejudicially the owner of the copyright an article which he either knows or has reason to believe is an infringing copy.

The making, importation, possession in the course of a business, or the sale or offering for sale or letting for hire of an article specifically designed or adapted to make infringing copies of a work, is also an infringement of copyright if the person doing those acts knows or has reason to believe that those articles are to be used to make infringing copies. The extent of this section is hard to gauge. Presumably the importation of a copy of a film, which can be used for making infringing copies, is not a breach of section 24, whereas the importation of stampers used for the making of vinyl records without the permission of the copyright owner may be.

Section 24 also provides that copyright is infringed by a person who transmits a work by means of a telecommunications system, otherwise than by a broadcast for inclusion in a cable programme service, knowing or having reason to believe that infringing copies of it will be made by means of reception and transmission in the U.K. or elsewhere. Thus, if a person picks up a cable programme elsewhere in Europe which is not intended for reception in the U.K. and transmits it to the U.K. to enable copies of it to be made, then he has infringed the copyright in the works transmitted under section 24(2).

As mentioned above in relation to the performance of, showing or playing a work in public, giving permission for a place to be used for a public performance where literary, dramatic or musical works are performed is an infringement of the copyright in those works unless the person giving the permission believed on reasonable grounds that the performance would not infringe copyright. A "place of public entertainment" is defined in section 25 as including not only buildings usually used for public entertainment but also those which are occasionally made available for hire for purposes of public entertainment such as local or parish halls. This section strengthens the hands of the Performing Right Society in putting the onus on the owner or occupier of such premises to ensure that anyone hiring or using them has the necessary licence.

Section 26 similarly moves the onus in relation to infringement by the provision of apparatus for an infringing performance of a sound recording or a film. Anyone who supplies apparatus or a substantial part of it is liable for infringement if (1) he knew, or had reason to know, that it was likely to be used to infringe copyright or, in the case of apparatus whose normal use involved a public performance, for playing or showing, and (2) he did not believe on reasonable grounds that it would not be so used to infringe copyright. Thus a person supplying large video screens can be liable for infringement if he has reason to believe that a person hiring that screen is likely to use it so as to infringe copyright.

In cases where equipment is normally used for public performance, such as amplification equipment, the person supplying or hiring it has to satisfy the onus to show that he believed it would not be used for infringing purposes. An occupier of premises giving permission for apparatus to be brought on to them is liable for infringement if he knows or has reason to believe that the apparatus is likely to be used to infringe copyright. A person supplying a copy of a sound recording or film used to infringe copyright is liable if, at the time he supplied it, he had reason to believe or knew that it or a copy made directly or indirectly from it would be used to infringe copyright. Thus a video shop which hires a copy of a film to the occupier of a cinema, or to someone who has advertised a public showing of a film, must ensure that if the person hiring the film is not normally in that business they have obtained all necessary licences. The days have passed when video shops could, without hesitation, supply films to organisations such as the Boy Scouts or Women's Institutes without querying what use they would make of the video.

EXCEPTIONS FROM THE COPYRIGHT IN WORKS

Introduction

It is not generally appreciated how far under copyright legislation the authors' "exclusive rights" give way to the public interest in gaining access to his work. It is understood by most people who have no special knowledge of copyright that authors' rights, unlike those in real property, are limited in duration by statute, and that after the termination of the protection period authors' works become public property or, as it is often expressed, fall into the public domain. In the U.K. and in nearly all other countries the author's material interests in the works he has created are extinguished at the end of a specific period, whereupon those works cease to be property at all.

The limitations on copyright and works imposed by the Act, except that of duration, which has already been dealt with, will now be considered and for convenience grouped under the same heading.

Fair dealing

Sections 29 and 30 of the Act are the so-called "fair dealing" provisions. The first fair dealing exception is for research and private study. Section 29 provides that a fair dealing with a literary, dramatic, musical or artistic work for the purposes of research or private study does not infringe any copyright in that work. The fair dealing section also extends to the typographical arrangement of published editions. If the copying for the purposes of fair dealing is not by a researcher or a student, then in the case of a librarian they must comply with the regulations under section 40, dealt with below under the heading "Copying by librarians" or, in the case of any other person, they must state that they do not know or have reason to believe that it will result in copies of substantially the same material being provided to more than one person at substantially the same time and for substantially the same purpose.

This fair dealing exception has to be read together with the library copying and educational copying provisions set out below. The other fair dealing provision, section 30, relates to copying for reporting current events and for criticism and review. It applies to all works and provides that fair dealing for the purpose of criticism or review of a work or a performance of a work does not infringe copyright on condition that it is accompanied by a sufficient acknowledgement. Fair dealing with a work other than a photograph for the purpose of reporting current events again does not infringe copyright if it is accompanied by sufficient acknowledgement. No acknowledgement of ownership is required if the reporting is by means of a sound recording, film, broadcast or cable programme.

"Fair dealing" is not defined in the Act, although "sufficient acknowledgement" is. That expression is defined in section 178 as an acknowledgement identifying the work in question by its title or other description identifying the author, unless the work is published anonymously or if, in the case of an unpublished work, it is not possible to ascertain the identity of the author by reasonable inquiry.

Court decisions have made it clear that fair dealing for the purposes of research or private study means research or study by an individual for his own purposes, but it does not extend to an act done for research or private study by another person. It is not clear what the status is of a copy made for research and private study which is passed on to another person for his or her research and private study.

Whether or not an act constitutes fair dealing depends on the circumstances in each case. The Act nowhere prohibits the copying of the full text of a work from being a fair dealing in it, although it would have been easy for Parliament to do so. Accordingly, it is clear that, if the circumstances are fair, the reproduction of an entire book can constitute a fair dealing, for example when that book is needed for research but is out of print. The Society of Authors and the Publishers Association had jointly agreed, for the convenience of all concerned, what they would regard as fair dealing. This agreement has been withdrawn but is nevertheless a useful guideline. It is uncertain whether it will be given weight in any court of law, although some regard will be given to it.

The two organisations said they would not regard it as unfair if:

(1)   for the purposes of research and private study, a single copy is made of a single extract not exceeding 4,000 words or a series of extracts (of which none exceeds 3,000 words) up to a total of 8,000 words, provided that in no case does the total amount copied exceed 10 per cent of the whole work. Poems, essays and other short literary works must be regarded as whole works in themselves, and not as "parts" of the volumes in which they appear;

(2)   a single extract of up to 400 words, or a series of extracts (of which none exceeds 300 words) up to a total of 800 words, is taken from prose copyright works,

or if any extracts up to a total of 40 lines are taken from a poem, provided that in no case does this extract amount to more than one quarter of the poem.

In some respects these guidelines are fairly generous. Up to 14 or 15 pages may be copied under the guidelines. On the other hand, it is not possible, within the limits suggested, to copy even one couplet of a 14-line sonnet for the purposes of research or private study.

Similar guidelines have been issued by Her Majesty's Stationery Office and these are referred to above in the section dealing with Crown copyright. Licences issued by the Copyright Licensing Agency (see page 174 below) have different limits.

Guidelines perform the useful function of indicating to copyright users what degree of use they might expect to make of a work without taking the trouble to seek permission to make the copy. On the other hand they are unrealistic as far as students and research workers are concerned.

There are now several sets of guidelines, issued by various bodies representing rights owners, which give users of copyright works an indication as to what degree of unauthorised use if likely to be regarded as tolerated (or not) by rights owners. It must be remembered that these guidelines have no legal force and that, while they may be considered to reflect the opinions of copyright owners, there is no guarantee that they will be accepted by the judiciary as accurate reflections on what constitutes a dealing which is "fair".

The problems raised by the institutional copying of literary works are now being tackled by the Copyright Licensing Agency, which is granting blanket licences for photocopying. To date this has been largely confined to the educational sector, but licences have now been negotiated with the Confederation of British Industry and the Law Society. Most licences are on a *per capita* basis to prevent the need for records of copying to be kept.

Non-statutory fair dealing and unfair dealing

Aside from the statutory fair dealing provisions in sections 29 and 30, it is not clear whether the courts can declare that the use of a work is a fair dealing in the absence of express statutory provisions to that effect. This is because fair dealing was before 1911 a common law defence and the Act does not say whether the statutory fair dealing provisions are intended to supersede the old common law or to apply in addition to it. Indeed, section 172 makes it clear that the Act restates and amends copyright law as set out in the 1956 Act only.

It has been suggested judicially that there might be fair dealing defences in the case of public security or safety. It is difficult to see why this should necessarily be so because in most conceivable circumstances it is the content of the work and not the form in which it is expressed which is of vital interest. In any event, in such circumstances it is likely that a section 30(2) defence of fair dealing for the purpose of reporting current events would apply.

The common law does admit a defence of "unfair dealing", although this is not mentioned in the Act. When a work is made which is a copy of another which is itself obscene, immoral, blasphemous or (probably) defamatory, then the owner of the copyright in the original work is powerless to prevent such infringement by copyright law. This is because the courts refuse to do anything which is tantamount to acknowledging the plaintiff's right to control the possession or distribution of any work which is of such an undesirable nature as to be undeserving of the law's protection. Thus, if one man writes an obscene story and another adapts it in the form of an obscene cartoon strip, the law of copyright is powerless to prevent the latter from doing so. On the other hand it may be possible for the author of an otherwise unobjectionable original work to sue for copyright infringement, defamation, slander of goods and passing-off where an obscene infringement of it has been committed.

Incidental inclusion

Section 31 provides that the copyright in a work is not infringed by its incidental inclusion in an artistic work, sound recording, film, broadcast, or cable programme, or the issue to the public of copies of anything whose making is excused under that provision. A musical work is not to be regarded as incidentally included in another work if it is deliberately included. This prevents the practice of what is known as "sampling" of works.

Educational copying

Sections 32 to 36 of the Act lay down permitted acts in relation to copyright works in respect of educational use.

Copyright in a literary, dramatic, musical or artistic work is not infringed if the work is copied in the course of instruction or the preparation for instruction, provided that copying is:

(1)   done by a person giving or receiving instruction; and
(2)   not by means of a reprographic process (that is photocopying or use of an appliance for making multiple copies, but not a film or sound recording).

Also, the copyright in a sound recording, film, broadcast or cable programme will not be infringed if copies are made in the course of instruction or preparation for instruction in the making of films or film sound tracks. Anything done in respect of preparing for, setting, or answering an examination will be a permitted act, with the exception of making reprographic copies of sheet music. It will, however, be a secondary infringement if a copy which was made by virtue of it being "a permitted act" is subsequently dealt with (that is to say, sold, let for hire, offered or exposed for sale or hire).

Short passages may be copied from a published literary or dramatic work in an anthology intended and described as for use in an educational establishment ("educational establishment" is defined as a school and any other such establishment as the Secretary of State may declare) and in advertisements issued by or on behalf of the publisher provided that they contain mainly non-copyright material. However, it is not permitted to use more than two excerpts (by an individual on his own or in collaboration with another) from the same author in anthologies published by the same publisher within a five-year period. There should also be a significant acknowledgement to the author and of the title of the work.

It is not a copyright infringement to perform a literary, dramatic or musical performance in front of an audience of pupils, teachers and others directly connected with the activities of an educational establishment, provided that the performance is by a teacher or pupil in the course of the activities of the establishment or by any other person for the purposes of instruction. Also, the playing of a film or a sound recording or a TV or radio programme at an educational establishment for the purposes of instruction, will not infringe. However, the Act states that a person will not be "directly connected" with an establishment merely because he or she is a parent.

Educational establishments which record television or radio programmes, or make copies of such recordings, will not be deemed to infringe copyright in those works if the copy is made for educational purposes. However, dealing with such recordings or copies amounts to secondary infringement.

This provision will not apply, however, if there is a licensing scheme certified for the purposes of this provision under section 143 of the Act which provides for the grant of such licences. Licensing schemes currently in operation include those operated by the Educational Recording Agency Limited and Open University Educational Enterprises Limited.

Educational establishments may make reprographic copies of passages from published literary, dramatic or musical works for the purposes of instruction without infringing copyright in the work, provided that not more than 1 per cent of any work is copied in any quarter of the year (namely January 1 to March 31, April 1 to June 30, July 1 to September 30 or October 1 to December 31.) If the licensing scheme is in operation and the establishment does not have a licence, then any reprographic copying of copyright works will be deemed to be unauthorised.

The licence cannot restrict the proportion of a work copied within the stipulated period to less than that granted under the Act. Again, a copy which is subsequently dealt with (that is to say, sold or let for hire or offered or exposed for sale or hire) shall be treated as an infringing copy for the purposes of that dealing.

Copying by libraries and archivists

Sections 37 to 44 of the Act and the Copyright (Librarians and Archivists) (Copying of Copyright Material) Regulations 1989 ("the Regulations")[1] deal with copying by libraries and archives.

Prescribed libraries and archives may, under appropriate conditions, undertake copying which would otherwise be infringements of copyright. Under sections 38 and 39 copies may be made of articles in periodicals and parts of published works. Copies may be made to supply to other libraries (section 41) or to replace works in a library or archive's permanent collection (section 42). Copies may also be made of certain unpublished works (section 43). Section 44 allows a copy to be made of an article of "cultural or historical importance" where export restrictions require that a copy is made and deposited in an appropriate archive before it leaves the U.K.

The terms "library" and "archive" are not defined in the Act, which merely refers to "prescribed libraries" and "prescribed archives" being entitled to carry out specific acts of copying. Schedule 1 Part A of the Regulations defines these to include school libraries,

[1] S.I. 1989 No. 1212.

establishments for further education, public libraries, local authority libraries, parliamentary libraries and government departmental libraries, as well as the libraries of any establishment conducted for the purpose of encouraging the study of specified subjects including bibliography, education, fine arts, history, languages, law, medicine and science. Any library in this list not "conducted for profit" is a prescribed library for the purpose of making copies under sections 38 and 39. Regulation 3(5) provides that "conducted for profit" means either directly established or conducted for profit, or part of, or administered by, a body established or conducted for profit. This would include libraries maintained by companies and professional firms.

All libraries in the U.K., irrespective of whether they are conducted for profit or not, are prescribed libraries for the purpose of making copies under sections 41, 42 and 43. Only libraries not conducted for profit, which are either contained in Schedule A or which are foreign libraries conducted wholly or mainly for the purposes of encouraging the study of the various subjects listed above, are prescribed libraries for the purpose of receiving copies made under sections 41 and 42.

Regulation 3(4) provides that all archives in the U.K. are prescribed archives for the purposes of making copies under sections 42 and 43. Only archives not conducted for profit are prescribed archives for the purpose of receiving copies made by other archives.

Copying by librarians of articles and periodicals and parts of published works

Librarians of prescribed libraries may make and supply copies from either periodicals or published editions of literary, dramatic or musical works.

Copies may be supplied only to persons who satisfy the librarian that the copy is required for the purposes of research or private study and will not be used for any other purpose. The mere republication of the copyright work cannot be defended on the grounds that it is intended for private study. Regulation 4(2)(a) provides that a person requesting the copy must supply a written declaration to this effect in form similar to that prescribed in the Regulations. A librarian may rely on such signed declaration unless he is aware that it is false in a material particular. Where a signed declaration is required, the Regulations prohibit copies being made without such a declaration. Where a false declaration is made in order to obtain a copy, the person making the false declaration is liable for infringement of copyright as if he had made the copy himself and the copy he received shall be treated as an infringing copy. This applies whenever a declaration is required by any of the section to allow copying to take place.

A librarian may not supply more than one copy of the same article or material to a single person. Section 38 prohibits the supply of copies of more than one article from the same periodical to one person while section 39 prohibits the supply of more than a "reasonable proportion" of any published work to one individual. A "reasonable proportion" of a work is difficult to define and is likely to be judged by reference to the individual works. The person requesting the copy must pay a sum not less than the cost of production of the copy, including a contribution to the general expenses of the library.

Section 40 of the Act prohibits the production of multiple copies of the same material under sections 38 or 39. A librarian may not supply copies to a person whose requirement is related or similar to the copying requirements of another person. Regulation 4(b) states that requirements are not related if the persons requesting similar amounts of copying do not receive instruction to which the copy is relevant at the same time and place and are not similar if they are not requirements of copies of substantially the same article or part of a work at substantially the same time for substantially the same person.

Copying by librarians in order to supply copies to other libraries

A librarian of a prescribed library may make a copy in order to supply it to another prescribed library. Articles, periodicals or the whole or part of published editions of literary, dramatic or musical works may be copied. Regulation 5(2) sets out the conditions which must be followed. The recipient library must not be given more than one copy of the item. Where the request for copying is of more than one article in an issue of periodical or for a copy of the whole or part of a published edition, the library making the request must supply a written statement that it is a prescribed library and does not know, and could not by reasonable inquiry ascertain, the name and address of a person entitled to authorise the making of the copy. The library making the request must also pay a sum not less than the cost attributable to the production of the copy including a contribution to the general expenses of the library making the copy. This section does not allow copies to be supplied to archives.

There is no restriction as to the proportion of a work which may be copied.

Copying by librarians or archivists to replace copies of works

Under section 42 of the Act, a prescribed library or archive may make a copy of any item in its permanent collection in order to preserve or replace that item or to replace an item in the permanent collection of another prescribed library or archive which has been lost, destroyed or damaged. Regulation 6 provides that the item copied must be part of a permanent collection wholly or mainly maintained for the purposes of reference on the premises of the copying library or archive or available on loan only to other libraries or archives. It must not be reasonably practicable for the librarian or archivist to purchase a copy of the item. If another prescribed library or archive is requesting the copy to replace a lost or damaged item, a written statement must be supplied stating that the requested item has been lost, destroyed or damaged, that it is not reasonably practicable for the requesting library or archive to purchase a copy and, if a copy is supplied, that it will be used only to replace an item in the permanent collection of the requesting library or archive. The requesting library or archive must pay the cost of the copying.

Copying by librarians or archivists of certain unpublished works

Section 43 of the Act allows certain unpublished works deposited with a prescribed library or prescribed archive to be copied. This section does not apply if the copyright owner has prohibited all such copying or if the work had been published before it was deposited with the library or archive.

Regulation 7 sets out the conditions for copying to take place. The person requesting the copy must satisfy the librarian that the copy is required for the purposes of research or private study and it will not be used for any other purpose. A written declaration to this effect must be delivered to the librarian or archivist in a form similar to that set out in the Regulations. The librarian or archivist is entitled to rely on this declaration provided no contrary facts are known. Only one copy of the item may be supplied to a single person, who must pay the cost of the copying.

Lending of copies by libraries and archives

A new section 40A of the Act, introduced with effect from December 1, 1996, provides that it is not an infringement of copyright, in a work of any description, for a public library to lend a book which qualifies for library lending right under the Public Lending Right Act 1979. Nor is it an infringement of lending right for any non-profit "prescribed library" or archive to lend a work, even though library lending right does not govern such a loan.

Public administration

Sections 45 to 50 provide exceptions to infringement in the course of public administration. Section 45 provides that copyright is not infringed by anything done for the purpose of parliamentary or judicial proceedings or reporting such proceedings. The exception does not apply to published reports of such proceedings. Section 46 introduces a similar defence for proceedings of a Royal Commission or statutory inquiry and includes the issuing of the reports of that Royal Commission or statutory inquiry. The definition of "statutory inquiry" is very wide and extends to any inquiry held, or investigation conducted, in pursuance of a duty or power conferred by any enactment. When material is open for public inspection pursuant to some statutory requirement, such as at Companies House, any copying of factual information which does not involve issuing copies to the public is not an infringement of copyright, and the making of copies of the public register or other material to enable it to be inspected at more convenient times and places is similarly not an infringement.

If such statutory information is of general scientific, technical, commercial or economic interest, copies of it may be issued to the public, provided the authority of the person responsible for that register is obtained. These provisions can be extended by statutory instruments to material made open to public inspection by international organisations.

If in the course of business copyright material is communicated to the Crown by someone with the licence of the copyright owner, then for the purpose for which it was communicated or any other foreseeable purpose the Crown can copy the work and issue copies to the public. An example is submissions to an inquiry conducted by the Crown.

The material comprised in public records kept under the various Public Records Acts which are open to public inspection may be copied without infringement, as may anything which is specifically authorised by any Act of Parliament.

Anonymous or pseudonymous works

Under section 57, copyright in literary, dramatic, musical or artistic works is not infringed if it is not possible by reasonable inquiry to ascertain the identity of the author and if it is reasonable to assume that copyright has expired. This exception does not apply to Crown copyright or copyright vesting in international organisations.

Public reading and recitation

Copyright in published literary or dramatic works is not infringed by the reading or recitation in public by one person of a reasonable extract of the work if it is accompanied by sufficient acknowledgement. That reading or recitation may be recorded, broadcast or included in a cable programme service, provided that the recording, broadcast or cable programme service consists mainly of material which is not exempted from infringement under section 59. "Reasonable extract" is not defined, but presumably must be related to the length of the work as a whole. The making of a record of spoken words for reporting current events in a broadcast or for inclusion in a cable programme service is not an infringement of the copyright in those words as a literary work: (1) if the record is a direct record of the spoken words and is not taken from a previous record, broadcast or cable programme; (2) if the making of the record was not prohibited by the speaker and did not infringe any existing copyright; and (3) if the use was not prohibited by the speaker, or if the use is by or with the authority of a person who is lawfully in possession of such a record. For example, a journalist could agree to the use of his notes of a public speech for the purpose of a broadcast, provided the speaker had not prohibited the taking of notes. This provision, in section 58, is a practical solution to the problem of reporting of speeches, where it is not always clear where copyright ownership rests, because a speaker is not necessarily reading a prepared text.

Scientific abstracts

If there is no relevant licensing scheme for the publication of an abstract accompanying an article on a scientific or technical subject, then under section 60 a periodical is not infringed by the copying of the abstract and issue of copies to the public.

Recording of folk songs

Sound recordings of folk songs may be used for archival purposes without infringing copyright if the words are unpublished and of unknown authorship, if the making is not prohibited by any performer, and if it does not infringe any other copyright. In an archive maintained by a designated body, copies of such recordings may be supplied for the purposes of research and private study provided only one copy is made.

Artistic works on public display

Section 62 provides that the copyright in buildings, sculptures, models for buildings and works of artistic craftsmanship permanently situated in public places or in premises open to the public is not infringed by making a graphic work, photograph, film, broadcast or cable programme service of it, or by issuing copies of such works. Nothing done for the purposes of reconstructing a building infringes any copyright in the building or in any plans for it. This provision has interesting consequences if the building is not reconstructed but, for example, the façade only is saved and a totally new building erected behind it.

Advertisements of artistic works

It is not an infringement of copyright in artistic works to copy it or issue copies to the public in order to advertise its sale. Any other dealing with that copy infringes copyright.

Copies of artistic works by the artist

Where the author of an artistic work is not the copyright owner, he will not infringe the copyright by copying the work in the course of making another artistic work, provided that the other work is not a repetition or an imitation of the main design of his earlier work.

Public lending of copies of works

The first version of section 66, which was substituted by the present text on December 1, 1996, empowered the Secretary of State, in the absence of a certified voluntary licensing scheme, to provide for a statutory licence of the rental right in sound recordings, films and computer programs. It further provided that, in the unlikely event that a computer program was still of any use 50 years after it was first issued to the public, the copyright in it would not be infringed by the rental of it to members of the public. This provision has been replaced by a fresh section 66 which provides that, in the absence of a certified licensing scheme, the Secretary of State is empowered to treat the lending to the public of copies of literary, dramatic, musical and artistic works, films and sound recordings as being done under licence, subject only to the payment of a reasonable royalty or other payment as may be agreed *inter partes* or determined by the Copyright Tribunal.

Use of films where reasonable inquiry fails

A new section 66A, which came into force on January 1, 1996, comes to the aid of the person who wishes to show or copy an old film in circumstances where his reasonable inquiries have failed to reveal the identity of any of the humans by reference to whose death the copyright term is calculated. This defence prevails where it would be reasonable to assume that the copyright has indeed expired, or at least that it is resonable to assume that the last of the persons whose death determines the duration of copyright must have died at least 70 years prior to the taking place of the otherwise infringing act.

Use of sound recordings for charitable purposes

Section 67 provides that the copyright in sound recordings is not infringed if they are played for the benefit of a non-profit-making charitable body, provided that any charge for admission is used only for the purposes of that organisation. This somewhat incongruous exception to infringement derives from the 1956 Act. Phonographic Performance Limited, the collecting society responsible for licensing the broadcasting and public performance rights in sound recordings, was seen as being overenthusiastic in the amounts charged to charitable bodies and was thereafter constrained by legislation.

Incidental recordings from broadcasts or cable programmes

If the maker of a broadcast or cable programme service is licensed to include a copyright work in his broadcast or cable programme, he is deemed to be licensed to make sound recordings or films of that literary, dramatic or musical work, to take photographs or film any such artistic work, and to copy any such sound recording or film. This incidental licence is only for the purposes of his initial licence and any sound recordings, films or photographs made must be destroyed within 28 days of use being made of the work. This incidental right is called the broadcasters' "ephemeral" right.

Recording by the Independent Television Commission and the BBC

Both the BBC and the Independent Television Commission (which regulates Channels 3, 4 and 5) have the right to make copies of programmes broadcast by them, or, in the case of the ITC, by Channels 3, 4 and 5 which they are required to supervise. A similar right is given to the Radio Authority.

Recording for purposes of time-shifting

Section 70 permits the making, for private and domestic use, of a recording of a broadcast solely for the purpose of enabling it to be viewed or listened to at a more convenient time. The Act does not provide that a copy which is so made must be watched or listened to; nor does it provide that, after any period of time, the copy so made becomes an infringing copy.

Photographs of television broadcasts or cable programmes

Section 71 clarifies a doubt which arose in relation to the previous case law under the 1956 Act. It provides for the making for private and domestic use of a photograph of the images of a television broadcast or cable programme. The taking of such a photograph does not infringe the copyright in that broadcast or cable programme or any film included in it. This does not authorise the taking of such photographs for commercial purposes, although they may be covered by the fair dealing exception for the reporting of current events.

Exceptions in relation to showing or retransmission of broadcasts and cable programmes

As referred to above in relation to restricted acts, the showing or playing in public of a broadcast or cable programme does not infringe the copyright in a broadcast or cable programme or any sound recording or film included in it if the audience has not paid for admission. Under section 73, cable retransmission of a broadcast pursuant to the "must carry" rule in the Broadcasting Act is not an infringement of the copyright in that broadcast. The fact that there has been retransmission, though, is relevant in assessing damages if the original broadcast involved an infringement. The provision of subtitled copies of broadcasts or cable programmes for the deaf or hard of hearing or for the physically or mentally handicapped is also not an infringement of copyright. Broadcasts and cable programmes may also be recorded for archival purposes by designated bodies under section 75.

CHAPTER 13

REMEDIES FOR INFRINGEMENT OF COPYRIGHT

THE PLAINTIFF'S OPTIONS

As noted in the introduction to the previous chapter, if copyright is to possess any value to its owner, it must be capable of at least some measure of enforcement. Laws in general are enforced in one of two ways: (1) publicly, by means of the police, customs officers, trading standards officers or similar agency, or (2) privately, by legal action taken by the person who suffers from any breaches of the law. Most copyright law falls into the second category, for copyright is in essence a private legal right. It is for the owner of the copyright to go to court to prevent a wrong from taking place or to seek redress where a wrong has taken place. In legal terms, by medical analogy, it is for the copyright owner to seek a "remedy" for any infringement (actual or potential) of his legal interest. Despite this, in areas where there has been widespread infringement of copyright, such as counterfeiting of films and sound recordings, both the police and trading standards officers are becoming increasingly involved in criminal proceedings for the enforcement of copyright. This is a result of both the scope of the problem and the nature of the infringer.

ACTION AVAILABLE TO THE PLAINTIFF

Section 96 provides that, subject to the provisions of the Act, infringements of copyright are actionable by the copyright owner, and that in any action for such infringement all relief by way of damages, injunction, accounts or otherwise shall be available to the plaintiff as is available in any proceedings in respect of infringements of other property rights. In this context the "copyright owner" is the author or a person deriving title from him.

As for the remedies mentioned in section 96, that of damages is certainly the best known to the layman; it is a sum of money (which no longer need be in sterling) which compensates the plaintiff for his loss. In recent times the courts have taken a more generous view as to what sort of loss may be the subject of compensation and damages now encompass both directly-caused and some indirectly-caused but nonetheless clearly foreseeable losses. An injunction is an order by the court restraining a person from doing an act which is a breach of his legal duty. An account of profits means a direction by the court that the profits accrued from the infringement be ascertained. The plaintiff will not in general be entitled both to such an account and to damages, for the account is considered to condone the infringement.

An action in the High Court for infringement of copyright will be initiated by the serving on the defendant of a writ, which usually contains a short statement of the nature of the complaint and the relief sought. Similarly, an action in a County Court may be initiated by a summons (though in practice relatively few copyright actions are heard outside the High Court). The writ must be served on the defendant in person, unless he has authorised a solicitor to accept service on his behalf. Pending the hearing, and if a good arguable case for the alleged infringement has been made out and the balance of convenience favours the plaintiff, the court may grant a "temporary" (also known as an "interim" or "interlocutory") injunction, ordering the defendant to refrain from the alleged infringing act until the action is tried. In very urgent cases an interlocutory injunction may be ordered in the absence of the defendant. This is called an *ex parte* injunction and generally lasts only for a few days, to enable the defendant then to come before the court and object to the injunction continuing. If the plaintiff is successful in the action the injunction may be made "final" or "perpetual". In many cases, to save expense, the parties agree that the hearing at the interlocutory stage will be treated as though it were the full trial.

In addition to the injunction the plaintiff may, as provided by the statute, claim damages or an account of profits. The court may also order delivery up of infringing copies and articles specially designed or adapted to be used for making such copies (discussed below on pages 100 to 101).

The prevalence of piracy all over the world has led to recognition by the courts that the normal procedure whereby a copyright owner can seize infringing copies and equipment for making them only after proceedings have begun does not adequately protect his interests. What has been found to happen in practice is that as soon as a writ is served on an alleged infringer, the stock of infringing copies disappears, together with the equipment used for making them. Accordingly, the copyright owner may have difficulty in establishing his case and moreover, before the case comes before the court, the defendant may well have made such profits from selling the infringing copies that a judgment against him will not act as an effective deterrent.

To deal with this situation section 100 of the Act (in respect of author's works) and an equivalent section 196 (in respect of recordings of performances) provide a self-help remedy enabling a copyright owner or his agent to seize and detain intringing copies. As this is a considerable encroachment on civil liberties there are several restraints on this remedy. Before it is exercised, notice of the time and place of seizure must be given to the local police station. No force may be used, and goods may be seized only from premises to which the public has access and which are not the permanent or regular place of business of the trader offering the goods for sale or hire. Whether market stalls are a permanent or regular place of business is a question of fact in each case, but it is clear that stalls outside pop concerts or football matches are not in this category. If anything is seized, those seizing the goods must leave a notice in the form prescribed by The Copyright and Rights in Performances (Notice of Seizure) Order (S.I. 1989 No. 1006) informing the person in possession of the infringing goods of the identity of the person or company who claims to be the copyright owner and the grounds on which the seizure is made. The copyright owner may then seek an order for forfeiture or destruction of the infringing goods under section 114. This is discussed in more detail below.

Before the inclusion of section 100 in the Act, the English courts had authorised the

Anton Piller order, a new procedure named after the case in which it was first made. A copyright owner who believes his works are being substantially infringed may, even before he begins proceedings, apply *ex parte* to the High Court for an order directed to the person who will be the defendant, requiring that he allow the plaintiff to enter his premises and seize all infringing copies, and to seize or inspect all documents and other matter which may be relevant and admissible in proving that infringement had occurred. As there has been much abuse of such orders, most often in the manner in which they are exercised, they have been severely regulated by the courts. More limited orders, such as those requiring the prospective defendant to allow the plaintiff to enter and view, but not take away, property may also be authorised.

Section 97 provides that there are circumstances in which the plaintiff's remedies are limited. Where it is shown that at the time of the infringement the defendant was not aware, and had no reason to believe, that copyright subsisted in the work, the plaintiff is not to be entitled to damages, but may be entitled to any other remedy. This restriction on an award of damages is of limited importance because of the difficulty facing any commercial defendant in trying to persuade a court that he was not aware, and had no reason to believe, that copyright subsisted in the work. It is a reason, however, for putting a potential defendant formally on notice of the existence of copyright rights as soon as a copyright owner is aware of a possible infringement.

As well as the remission of damages, the court may hold that the circumstances justify their increase. Where an infringement of copyright is proved or admitted the court, having regard (among other material considerations) to the flagrancy of the infringement and any benefit shown to have accrued to the defendant by reason of the infringement, may consider that the plaintiff should be compensated by the award of such additional damages (often called "punitive" or "exemplary" damages) as it considers appropriate in the circumstances.

Legal proceedings must always commence within a specific period from the time when the cause for the action arose. As no such time is laid down in the Act, that period, for infringement actions, will be the period laid down in the relevant provisions of the Limitation Act 1980, namely six years. In some circumstances, notably where a fraud has been perpetrated on the plaintiff, the court may, however, allow him to bring his action even after the period of limitation has expired.

DELIVERY UP

Under the 1956 Act infringing copies were declared to be notionally the property of the copyright owner. For that reason a plaintiff in infringement proceedings was entitled to delivery up of the infringing items and/or to conversion damages, depending on whether the defendant had disposed of any of the infringing goods. Conversion damages were damages to compensate the copyright owner for the value of the goods of which he had been deprived. There was considerable debate about the merits of conversion damages, which were often a windfall gain to a copyright owner. For that reason the Act abolished that remedy and gave the court a discretion as to whether delivery up was an appropriate order.

Section 99 empowers the court to make an order for delivery up of infringing copies and any articles specifically designed or adapted for making them, if the copyright owner so requests. Such an order must be sought within six years of the time the infringing copy was made unless there was fraud or for some reason the copyright owner was under a disability which prevented him from bringing proceedings. Relevant disabilities are age (being under 18 years old) or insanity (see section 113).

An order for delivery up alone does not give the copyright owner the right to dispose of or destroy the infringing copies. In the absence of a further order under section 114 of the Act, the goods must be retained by the copyright owner. This often gives rise to storage problems. Orders under section 114 are available in both civil and criminal proceedings for infringement of copyright. In deciding whether to make an order forfeiting goods to the copyright owner or ordering their destruction, the court has to consider whether the other remedies available in copyright infringement actions would be adequate to compensate copyright owners. Notice may be given to all those with an interest in the infringing goods before the court. Where more than one person has an interest, the court can make such order as it considers just, including sale of the infringing copies and division of the proceedings. For the purposes of this section, an interest in an infringing copy is not confined to an interest in the copy as a copyright infringement: the interests of parties whose trade marks are infringed are equally taken into account. There has been no significant litigation yet involving section 114, but it could cause problems if for some reason a judge permitted infringing copies to be returned to a defendant. The defendant is not thus licensed to sell the infringing copies, but he is free to do so. This could lead to a multiplicity of actions.

REMEDIES AVAILABLE TO AN EXCLUSIVE LICENSEE

Introduction

Before considering the special position of an exclusive licensee, it is appropriate to examine the nature of a licence.

A licence to use a copyright, or part of a copyright, is an authority granted by the copyright owner (the "licensor" or "grantor") to another person (the "licensee" or "grantee") to do certain acts in relation to the subject-matter of the copyright. The licensee does not thereby acquire the ownership of the copyright or that part of the copyright which is the subject of the licence. The licence may be exclusive, in which case no-one else — and indeed not even the owner — can use the subject of the licence; or it may be non-exclusive, in which case others may also be licensed to use the same subject-matter.

The Act does not require that the grant of a licence, other than an exclusive licence, be made in writing. A non-exclusive licence may therefore be made orally, or even implied from conduct. This is in contrast with the evidencing of an assignment of copyright, that is, a transfer of ownership. With regard to such transaction it is laid down in section 90(3) that no assignment of copyright (whether total or partial) is to be effective unless it is in writing, signed by or on behalf of the assignor. If money has been paid for an assignment of copyright but no written assignment made, the courts may compel the execution of such an assignment.

Section 90(4) lays down that a licence granted by the copyright owner is to be binding on everyone who owns the copyright after him (his "successors in title") with the exceptions of the purchaser in good faith for valuable consideration and without notice (actual or constructive) of the licence, and of any person deriving title from such a purchaser. This means that, if A licenses his copyright to B and then transfers the ownership of it to C, B enjoys the same licence from C as he held from A. This provision, in accordance with section 91(3), is applicable in the case of a licence granted by a prospective owner of copyright as to a licence granted by the owner of a subsisting copyright. The meaning of "prospective owner of copyright" is discussed on page 65 above.

The exclusive licensee as plaintiff

Since a licence does not pass any proprietary interest in the copyright, it would not, without special provision in the Act, enable a licensee to sue for infringement of that proprietary interest. The position in this respect was not clear under the 1911 Act, which in section 5(2) provided that the copyright owner might grant any interest in the right by licence. In view of the provisions of Schedule 1, para. 25, referred to under the heading "Assignments and Licences" (pages 64 to 65 above), this uncertainty remains in respect of licences granted before the commencement of the 1956 Act.

However, the Act in section 101 makes special provision to enable an exclusive licensee to sue in his own name in respect of copyright infringement, although it may be necessary to join the copyright owner as party to the action. The Act does this by deeming the exclusive licensee, for the purpose of instituting such action, to be in the same position as an assignee of the copyright. Section 92, for the purposes of Part 1 of the Act, defines an "exclusive licence" as:

> " ... a licence in writing signed by or on behalf of the copyright owner authorising the licensee to the exclusion of all other persons, including the person granting the licence, to exercise a right which would otherwise be exercisable exclusively by the copyright owner."

"Exclusive licensee" is to be construed accordingly.

As to actions in respect of infringement of copyright under sections 101 and 102 of the Act, the effect of section 92 is that:

(a)   the exclusive licensee has (except against the copyright owner) the same rights and remedies in respect of matters occurring after the grant of the licence as if the licence had been an assignment, and such rights and remedies are concurrent with those of the copyright owner.

(b)   Where the exclusive licensee and copyright owner have concurrent rights of action neither may, without the leave of the court, proceed with the action beyond the interlocutory injunction stage unless the other is either joined as a plaintiff or added as a defendant.

(c)   A copyright owner or exclusive licensee who is added as defendant in any proceedings is not liable for any costs in the action unless he takes part in the proceedings.

The terms of the exclusive licence are taken into account in assessing damages or ordering an account of profits and in ordering delivery up or seizure whether or not both the copyright owner and exclusive licensee are parties to the action. A full explanation of the procedural points raised in section 102 lies outside the scope of this work. It may however be seen that the exclusive licensee can enjoy virtually the same rights under sections 96 and 97 as does the copyright owner. Although, for the purpose of enabling the exclusive licensee to take action in his own name, his licence is deemed to have effect as if it had been an assignment, the defendant in an action brought by an exclusive licensee is not inhibited from putting forward any defence which would have been available to him if the action had been brought by the copyright owner.

The rights of the exclusive licensee as against the copyright owner will be based on the contract (that is, the licence) between them. The exclusive licensee also has the same rights against any successor in title to the copyright owner who is bound by the licence.

Paragraph 31 of Schedule 1 provides that sections 101 and 102 are to apply to all assignments and exclusive licences entered into after the commencement of the Act. In considering the rights of exclusive licensees under licences entered into before August 1, 1989 it is necessary to consider the provisions of sections 17 and 19 of the 1956 Act for all licences entered into after July 1, 1957 and the provisions of the 1911 Act for all licences before that date.

LICENCES AS OF RIGHT

The Monopolies and Mergers Commission has power to require copyright owners to grant licences, and the Copyright Tribunal is given power under section 144 of the Act to settle the terms of such licence (as discussed at page 157 below). In infringement proceedings where such a licence is available and the defendant undertakes to take such a licence, no injunction or order for delivery up can be made and the amount available by way of damages or an account of profits cannot be more than double the amount payable by way of licence fees. This limitation does not apply to infringements committed before the licence as of right became available.

PROOF OF FACTS IN COPYRIGHT ACTIONS

Certain presumptions are authorised by the Act to facilitate proceedings in legal actions brought under it, and therefore to save the litigants' time and money. Such presumptions apply in all civil proceedings but not in criminal proceedings, other than in relation to delivery up of infringing copies. These presumptions, set out in sections 104 to 106, fall into three categories.

Presumption of authorship

Where, in the case of a literary, dramatic, musical or artistic work, a name purporting to be that of the author appeared on copies of the work as published or on the work when it was made, the person whose name appears is to be presumed, until the contrary is proved:

(1)   to be the author of the work; and

(2)   to have made it in circumstances which would not result in another person or organisation becoming the owner of the copyright.

In the case of a work alleged to be a work of joint authorship, the presumptions apply in relation to each person alleged to be one of the authors.

As far as sound recordings are concerned, where copies issued to the public bear a label stating that a named person was the owner of the copyright at the time it was first issued to the public and that it was first published in a specified year or country, then that label is admissible as evidence of the facts stated and they are presumed to be correct until the contrary is proved.

For films, copies of which have been issued to the public or shown in public or broadcast or included in a cable programme service, which bear a statement that a named person is the author or director of the film and a named person was the owner of the copyright when it was issued or made (the latter in cases where copies may not have been issued to the public), then that statement is admissible as evidence of the facts stated and presumed to be true unless the contrary is stated. On copies of films issued to the public there is a further presumption as to the place or year of first publication.

Although the same presumptions apply to computer software as apply to other literary works, there are additional presumptions if copies are issued to the public in electronic form. If the copy in electronic form bears a statement that at the date of issue a named person was the author of the copyright or it was first published in a specified country or copies were first issued electronically to the public in a specified year, such a statement shall be admissible as evidence of the facts stated and presumed correct unless the contrary is proved.

All of the presumptions in relation to sound recordings, films and computer programs apply to proceedings whether brought before or after the copies were issued or the film broadcast or shown in public.

Presumptions of subsistence and ownership where the author is not named

Where no name purporting to be that of the author appears on a work but it qualifies for copyright protection by virtue of first publication or simultaneous publication in the U.K. and a name purporting to be that of the publisher appears on copies of the work as first published, then the person whose name appears shall be presumed, until the contrary is proved, to have been the owner of the copyright at the time of publication.

Presumption of originality and first publication

If the author of the work is dead or unknown, it is presumed, in the absence of evidence to the contrary:

(1)   that the work is an original work; and
(2)   that the plaintiff's allegations as to what was the first publication of the work and as to the country of first publication are correct.

A new presumption in relation to Crown copyright has been included in the Act, in relation to the year of first commercial publication. This applies only to literary, dramatic or musical works.

These presumptions are not considered to be entirely satisfactory. It will be observed that when the author is dead, the plaintiff's allegations with regard to the originality of the work and the date and place of first publication are to be presumed true, unless the contrary is proved. If, however, the author is living, it is open to the defendant to put in issue matters which are presumed in the case of the deceased author, thus throwing onto the plaintiff the onus of proving allegations as to these matters. In order to do this it may be necessary to produce the author (perhaps at considerable inconvenience and expense) to affirm that his work was original. Judges are now becoming more robust about permitting a defendant to do so in a capricious manner. If not, proceedings in respect of minor infringements may not be thought worthwhile. However, it is generally the case that the presumptions are of importance only in interlocutory or other urgent proceedings. In most infringement cases which go to a final hearing, the matters covered by presumptions are either put in issue or admitted.

The 1956 Act also contained a general presumption as to the subsistence and ownership of copyright. It was considered by Parliament that this was not necessary as it is a presumption in all proceedings that the plaintiff has the rights asserted, unless this is put in issue by the defendant.

CRIMINAL PROCEEDINGS IN RESPECT OF CERTAIN INFRINGEMENTS

The Act provides that, in respect of certain offences against copyright, application may be made for criminal penalties to be imposed by a court. Proceedings may be brought either in magistrates' courts or in the Crown Court. Proceedings in Crown Courts may only be brought by the Crown, acting through the Director of Public Prosecutions. The DPP can, however, take over criminal proceedings commenced in a magistrates' court by a private individual.

The relevant offences are laid down in section 107. That section provides that a person commits an offence if, without the licence of the copyright owner, he:

"(a)   makes for sale or hire, or
(b)   imports into the United Kingdom otherwise than for his private and domestic use, or
(c)   possesses in the course of business with a view to committing any act infringing the copyright, or
(d)   in the course of business:
  (i)   sells or lets for hire, or
  (ii)   offers or exposes for sale or hire, or
  (iii)   exhibits in public, or
  (iv)   distributes, or
(e)   distributes otherwise than in the course of a business to such an extent as to affect prejudicially the owner of the copyright,
any article which is, and which he knows or has reason to believe is, an infringing copy of a copyright work."

There are further offences of making an article specifically designed or adapted for making infringing copies; of possessing such an article, knowing or having reason to believe that it is to be used to make infringing copies which are to be sold or hired or otherwise used in a business; and of performing a literary, musical or dramatic work or playing or showing in public a film or sound recording, knowing or having reason to believe that in so doing copyright would be infringed.

A person guilty of an offence under sub-section (1)(a), (b), (d)(iv) or (e) of section 107 is liable:

(a)   on summary conviction to imprisonment for a term not exceeding six months or a fine not exceeding the statutory maximum, or both;

(b)   on conviction on indictment to a fine or imprisonment for a term not exceeding two years, or both.

A person who, on summary judgment, is found guilty of the other offences specified under section 107 is liable to imprisonment for a term not exceeding six months or a fine not exceeding level 5 on the standard scale, or both. These penalties are a massive increase of the penalties provided under the 1956 Act.

The provisions of section 107 apply only to acts done in the U.K. and, as will have been noted, only to acts done in the knowledge that they are offences or where the person had reason to believe that they were offences.

By the Criminal Justice and Public Order Act 1994 a new section 107A was grafted on to the Act. By this provision it is the duty of every local weights and measures authority to enforce section 107 within its area. To this end, trading standards officers are empowered to make test purchases and to enter premises and seize goods. Section 107A has not yet, at the time of writing, been brought into force.

In any case brought for a copyright offence the court hearing the matter can, pursuant to section 108 of the Act, order delivery up of infringing copies and articles specifically designed or adapted for making them to the copyright owner, subject to the same test as to knowledge as for the criminal offences. Such orders can be made even if the defendant is not convicted, but not if an order would not be made under section 114 (discussed on pages 99 to 101 above), or if more than six years have passed since the articles were made (subject to the exceptions in section 113 discussed at page 101 above). Once an order for delivery up is made, infringing copies must be retained until such time as an order is made or refused under section 114. An appeal lies from an order for delivery up under section 108.

Search Warrants

Section 109 permits the issue of search warrants if there are reasonable grounds to believe that any of the offences in section 107(1)(a), (b), (d)(iv) or (e) has been or is about to be committed.

Criminal Offences by Companies

Officers of companies can be personally liable for the commission of any of the offences under section 107. For liability the person concerned needs to have consented to or connived in the commission of the offence. The officers concerned are directors, managers, secretaries or other similar officers, or anyone purporting to act as such. In the case of companies run by their shareholders rather than by directors any shareholder can be liable. This provision in the Act makes it easier to fix personal liability than the common law, which requires an officer to have acted as if he were the company.

COMPENSATION FOR COPYRIGHT OWNERS IN CRIMINAL CASES

The principal function of criminal proceedings is to punish the offender. Thus fines collected by the court are not directed to the victim of the infringement, that is, the copyright owner. This does not mean that the copyright owner must institute civil proceedings for damages before he can receive compensation; under the Powers of Criminal Courts Act 1973 it is possible for a criminal court to make an award of compensation to be paid by the accused (if convicted) to his victim.

The limit on such payments currently stands at £2,000, on summary conviction, which may make criminal proceedings an attractive alternative to civil litigation. It should be noted, however, that one cannot get "double" compensation by initiating both criminal and civil proceedings. However, it is possible to obtain other orders in civil proceedings, particularly injunctions.

Prosecutions under the Act are now common since the dramatic increase in penalties it brought about. A number of industry associations have commenced private prosecutions successfully. While these are limited to proceedings in magistrates' courts, the DPP is more easily persuaded to take a case to the Crown Court when the necessary evidence is assembled for him. Increasing numbers of prison sentences are also acting as a deterrent.

RESTRICTION OF IMPORTATION OF PRINTED COPIES

Under section 111 the owner of the copyright in a published literary, dramatic or musical work may give notice in writing to the Commissioners of Customs and Excise requesting them, during a period specified in the notice, to treat as prohibited goods printed copies of the work which are infringing copies. The period specified in such notice is not to exceed five years, and not to extend beyond the end of the period for which the copyright is to subsist. The owner of copyright in a sound recording or film may also give notice in writing to the Commissioners of Customs and Excise that infringing copies of the work are expected to arrive in the U.K. at a time and place specified in the notice, and requesting the Commissioners to treat the copies as prohibited goods. Such a notice must be specific as to the shipping details and is not of widespread utility. The section does not however apply to the importation of any article by a person for his private and domestic use.

The purpose of the section is to provide the means of forestalling the prejudice which might be caused to the copyright owner by the importation of infringing copies. Such importation is actionable under sections 22 and 23, if done knowingly (see Chapter 12 above).

Regulations prescribe the form in which the request to prohibit the importation is to be made, and provide for the supply to the Commissioners of such evidence as is specified, for the payment of fees and for the furnishing of security against any liability as they may incur. In addition to, or instead of, security the Commissioners may require indemnification from any liability or expense.

Section 111 contains some curious features: for example, it does not extend to artistic works. It is also of limited use in the single European market, as it cannot be used to prevent the importation of infringing copies, other than pirated copies, from outside the European Economic Area. In addition, the resources of Customs and Excise are such that without knowledge of specific shipments the giving of notices is of little value.

Chapter 14

THE COPYRIGHT ACTS OF 1911 AND 1956

In the above analysis of the Act, reference has been made to its predecessors, the Copyright Acts of 1911 and 1956. This chapter will touch on the significance of each of them.

The Copyright Act 1911

There are some important provisions of the 1911 Act still attaching to works in which copyright continues to subsist under the Act, and which consequently have not been related. These provisions cover:

    (1)   the statutory licence to reproduce works for sale (section 3);
    (2)   reversion of copyright (section 5(2));
    (3)   rights of the author and his assignee or licensee in respect of the extended period of copyright (section 24).

    As a preliminary it should be noted that many works governed by the 1911 Act were works in which copyright already subsisted under the pre-1911 Acts. The scope of the copyright under pre-1911 Acts was not necessarily the full copyright as under later Acts. Where a work was in existence before the commencement of the 1911 Act on July 1, 1912, and copyright subsisted in the work at that date under earlier Acts, then, on the commencement of the 1911 Act, copyright under that Act was substituted for copyright under the earlier Acts. Where a pre-1911 right had been substituted by a right under the 1911 Act, the substituted right did not include a right which had *not* subsisted in the work under the earlier Acts, except where the 1911 Act created an entirely new right: the now defunct mechanical recording right under section 19.

    Thus when the copyright subsisting in a musical or dramatic work under pre-1911 Acts constituted "copyright but not performing right", the substituted right under the 1911 Act would not include the performing right. On the other hand, the pre-1911 right might have been "performing right but not copyright", and in that case the substituted right under the 1911 Act would have the same content (section 24 of the 1911 Act). Accordingly caution is necessary with regard to the copyright content of works already in existence before the commencement of the 1911 Act. Paragraphs 34, 35 and 36 of the Seventh Schedule to the 1956 Act, effectively presented by paragraphs 3 and 4 of Schedule 1 to the 1988 Act, maintain the position under the Act as it existed under the 1911 Act in regard to these pre-1911 works, except that "performing right" is extended in this connection to include broadcasting and causing a work to be transmitted to subscribers to a diffusion service.

Statutory licence to reproduce works for sale

Under the proviso to section 3 of the 1911 Act, at any time after the expiration of 25 years (or, in the case of a work in which copyright subsisted at the commencement of that Act, 30 years) from the death of the author of a published work, copyright in the work is not infringed by the reproduction of the work for sale, subject to the prescribed notice being given and to the payment of royalties at the rate of 10 per cent of the published price of the work.

It will be noted that this proviso applies only in the case of published works, and if the reproduction is made for sale. It does not therefore apply to public performance.

This provision was not re-enacted in the 1956 Act but in accordance with the Seventh Schedule, paragraph 9(1) and (2) of the 1956 Act where, before the repeal of section 3 of the 1911 Act (on June 1, 1957), a person had, in the case of a work, given the notice required by the proviso to that section, that proviso has to have effect as if it had been re-enacted in the Act as a proviso to section 1(2), but subject to the provisions of paragraphs 4 and 5 of the Eighth Schedule, being so much of sub-sections (1) of sections 16 and 17 respectively of the 1911 Act as is applicable to the proviso.

Sections 16 and 17 of the 1911 Act, referred to in paragraph 9 of the Seventh Schedule, deal with works of joint authorship and posthumous works in relation to these provisions.

As to joint works, section 16 of the 1911 Act lays down that references to the period after the expiration of any specified number of years from the death of the author are to be construed as:

> " . . . references to the period after the expiration of the like number of years from the death of the author who dies first or after the death of the author who dies last, whichever period may be shorter."

Since this provision can hardly mean "the like number of years from the death of the author who dies last, whichever period may be the shorter", it presumably means "the like number of years from the death of the author who dies first or immediately on the death of the author who dies last, whichever period may be the shorter". This interpretation would seem harsh where the second author dies soon after the first, for the copyright would die with him. Presumably Parliament intended that copyright would expire at the end of the specified number of years from the death of the first author, unless the second author was still alive, in which case copyright would continue to subsist until his death and *not* until the specified number of years after it.

Reversion of copyright

The principle of reversion is that an assignment of copyright, or a grant of any interest in the copyright, may not run beyond a specified term which is shorter than the full term of protection and that, at the end of this specified period, the rights assigned or interest granted revert to the author or his legal personal representative. The principle — which still has its advocates, although it was abandoned in the 1956 Act — is motivated by the possibility that the author may have parted with his right for what, in the light of events, proved to be an insufficient consideration, and that the obligatory reversion to him or his heirs will enable him or them to make a bargain more commensurate with the revealed value of the right for the remaining term of protection.

There is no doubt that in the past many authors in need have sold their copyrights outright for an unduly small consideration. Once the assignment has been effected, the author cannot under the law of contract claim any further benefit, in the absence of contractual terms which expressly or implicitly promise it to him. This is why copyright reversion, with its chance of a "second bite at the cherry", is an attractive proposition to the author.

The reversionary principle was abandoned in the 1956 Act on the recommendation of the Copyright Committee of 1951. The Committee's principal reason was that the retention of the principle was inconsistent with the U.K.'s continued adherence to the Berne Copyright Convention.

Underlying the objections to the principle is the view that contracting parties should be at liberty to agree on terms which they consider equitable for such period as may be without having to consider the effect of statutory intervention in the conditions of the contract. The effect of such intervention may indeed be to diminish the consideration in return for which the assignment or grant is made.

Inherent in this view is the supposition that authors will be well aware of, or will take advice on, the reasonableness or otherwise of any contract into which they may enter with those to whom they may assign the copyright or grant an interest in it. Such advice is always available from the professional associations to which most authors belong. On the other hand, most publishing contracts are concluded on terms decided by the publisher, so the author often has to accept whatever terms he is offered, regardless of any advice he may have been given.

The 1911 Act, in the proviso to section 5(2), provided that:

" ... where the author of a work is the first owner of the copyright therein, no assignment of the copyright, and no grant of any interest therein, made by him (otherwise than by will) after the passing of this Act, shall be operative to vest in the assignee or grantee any rights with respect to the copyright in the work beyond the expiration of twenty-five years from the death of the author, and the reversionary interest in the copyright expectant on the termination of that period shall, on the death of the author, notwithstanding any agreement to the contrary, devolve on his legal personal representative as part of his estate, and any agreement entered into by him as to the disposition of such reversionary interest shall be null and void, but nothing in this proviso shall be construed as applying to the assignment of the copyright in a collective work or a licence to publish a work or part of a work as part of a collective work."

A "collective work" is an encyclopaedia, yearbook or similar work, or a newspaper, magazine or similar periodical, or any work written in distinct parts by several authors. A song is not, however, a "collective work" because its words and music constitute two separate works.

The effect of this proviso is that if, after the passing of the 1911 Act on December 16, 1911, the author assigned the copyright in his work, or granted an interest in the copyright, for the full term of the copyright, or for a term extending beyond the end of 25 years after his death, then 25 years after his death the assignment or grant terminated, and the copyright or interest reverted to the author's legal personal representative, that representative would have power to exercise the copyright afresh for whatever new consideration might be agreed, but subject also to the specified exceptions in the cases of testamentary disposition and collective works, and subject also to the author having been the first owner of the copyright in the work.

In accordance with the Seventh Schedule to the 1956 Act, para. 28(3), this proviso is to apply to assignments made and licences granted before the commencement of that Act as if it had been re-enacted. Accordingly, where a copyright was assigned or licensed before June 1, 1957, the assignment or licence would cease to have effect 25 years after the author's death. For example, the copyright in a work assigned by the author in 1954 (when the 1911 Act was in force) would, if the author died in 1970, have reverted to the author's legal personal representative in 1995, unless the work fell within the scope of the specified exceptions and unless of course a new assignment of copyright was made after the Act commenced. There are obviously many works to which these reversionary provisions are still applicable; but this principle is not applicable to assignments or licences made or granted after the commencement of the 1956 Act. Paragraphs 27(1) and 27(2) of Schedule 1 to the 1988 Act have preserved this position, the effects of which can be expected to be felt until well into the next century.

The proviso to section 5(2) of the 1911 Act applies where the assignment or grant was made after the passing of the 1911 Act but the work was created before that date, but not where the assignment or grant was made before the passing of the 1911 Act.

Some claims to reversionary rights which could have been asserted have never been made, since, inevitably, many personal representatives know little about copyright. Authors of works in respect of which assignments were made or interest granted before June 1, 1957 should, if they have any expectation that their copyrights could be of value after their death, draw this expectation to the attention of their heirs.

Reversion is automatic and does not have to be claimed in order to become effective. The utilisation by another of a work in respect of which the author's heirs are entitled to the reversion is an infringement of copyright, actionable in the same way as any other infringement.

Extended copyright under the 1911 Act

Under the 1911 Act the term of copyright, subject to certain exceptions, was during the author's lifetime and for 50 years precisely thereafter. This was longer than the terms provided in earlier Acts. The protection period under the Literary Copyright Act of 1842 was the lifetime of the author plus seven years, or during 42 years from date of publication, whichever was the longer. The protection period for performing rights in dramatic or musical works was during the lifetime of the author plus seven years, or during 42 years from the date of the first performance of the work.

The 1911 Act consolidated the several earlier Acts under which works have been protected, substituting copyright under that Act for the copyright subsisting under the earlier Acts. In section 24(1) it was provided that this substituted right was to subsist for the term for which it would have subsisted if that Act had been in force when the work was made.

Who, therefore, is the beneficiary of the extended term when the author had, before July 1, 1912 when the 1911 Act came into force, assigned copyright in his work, or granted an interest in the work? The answer to this question is found in the proviso (a) to section (1) of the 1911 Act, which is as follows:

> "If the author of any work in which . . . [copyright] subsists at the commencement of this Act has, before that date, assigned the right or granted any interest therein for the whole term of the right, then at the date when, but for the passing of this Act, the [existing] right would have expired the . . . [substituted right] shall, in the absence of express agreement, pass to the author of the work, and any interest therein created before the commencement of this Act and then subsisting shall determine."

The expression "author" includes for this purpose the legal personal representative of a deceased author. It should be noted that this proviso applies only when the assignment made or interest granted was for the full period of copyright, and by the author of the work. It would not apply, therefore, if the assignment had been made or interest granted by someone other than the author because the copyright had vested originally in that other person. In that case it would be the assignee or grantee, subject to contrary agreement, who would be the beneficiary of the extended term.

If the right had been assigned or licensed for a period less than the full term, then the substituted right would pass to the author or his legal personal representative, as from the commencement of the 1911 Act, for the term of protection as provided in that Act, but without annulling the assignment or grant for a limited period.

These provisions may be illustrated as follows:

— work published 1910;
— substituted right replaces existing right 1912;
— copyright assigned by the author for full period of protection in 1925;
— author dies 1944;
— but for the passing of the 1911 Act the copyright would have expired in 1952;
— assignment determines and substituted right passes to author's legal personal representative in 1952;
— copyright under 1911 Act subsists at the commencement of the Act and, but for the extension of copyright term under the 1995 Regulations, would have expired on December 31, 1994;
— copyright expires on December 31, 2114.

The 1911 Act recognised, however, that these provisions could cause hardship to the original assignee or licensee, who would, unless some relief were allowed to him, have no interest for the extended period of protection in a work on the exploitation of which he might have expended money, and whose success might be substantially due to his efforts. Accordingly, the proviso goes on to specify that the person who immediately before the date at which the right would have expired (under the earlier Acts) was the owner of the right or interest in the work is to be entitled at his option either under (i) of the proviso:

"... on giving such notice as hereinafter mentioned, to an assignment of the right or grant of a similar interest therein for the remainder of the term of the right for such consideration as, failing agreement, may be determined by arbitration;"

or (ii)

"... without any such assignment or grant, to continue to reproduce or perform the work in like manner as theretofore, subject to the payment, if demanded by the author within three years after the date at which the right would have so expired, of such royalties to the author as, failing agreement, may be determined by arbitration, or, where the work is incorporated in a collective work and the owner of the right or interest is the proprietor of that collective work, without any such payment."

The notice referred to in section 24(1)(a)(i) must have been given not more than one year nor less than six months before the date at which the right would have expired, and have been sent by registered post to the author or his personal representative, or, if he could not with reasonable diligence be found, be advertised in *The London Gazette* and in two London newspapers. It will be noted that where, under (ii) of the proviso, the work is incorporated in a collective work, and the owner of the right or interest is the proprietor of that collective work, he is entitled to continue to reproduce the work "in like manner as theretofore". An individual contribution to a collective work could not be separately reproduced by virtue of this provision because such reproduction would not be "in like manner as theretofore". The Seventh Schedule to the 1956 Act, in paragraph 38, was concerned with the effect on these provisions of the Act. It will be appreciated that while the period of 42 years after publication must now have elapsed in the case of works published before July 1, 1912, the period of seven years after the death of the author may not have elapsed on the commencement of the Act; in that case the copyright will not at that time have reverted under the proviso to section 24(1) of the 1911 Act.

In accordance with paragraph 38 of the Seventh Schedule, where at the commencement of the 1956 Act copyright continued to subsist in a work to which paragraph (i) of the proviso was applicable, then paragraph (a) was to have the corresponding operation under the Act in relation to that work. Accordingly, when the copyright had, before the commencement of the 1956 Act reverted pursuant to that proviso, then the copyright under that Act also vested in accordance with the reversion. Similarly, if the effect of the proviso would have been that the copyright would have reverted at some time after the date of commencement of the 1956 Act, if that Act had not been passed, then the copyright would nevertheless revert at that time; any interest of any other person in that copyright then subsisting by virtue of the proviso would then determine.

[Sub-paragraph (2) of paragraph 38 preserves, in relation to copyright under the 1956 Act, the effect of any event which occurred or notice which was given before the commencement of that Act which, by reason of the operation of paragraph (a) of the proviso in question, affected the ownership or otherwise of the copyright conferred by the 1911 Act. It is therefore clear that the right referred to in option (ii) is still exercisable under the 1956 Act.

On the other hand, sub-paragraph (3) of paragraph 38 provided that any right which, at a time after the commencement of the 1956 Act, would by virtue of paragraph (a) of the proviso in question have been exercisable in relation to the work, or to the right conferred by the 1911 Act, if that Act had not been passed, would be exercisable in relation to the work or to the copyright under the 1956 Act. These terms are so wide that they seem to remove any doubt that may exist under sub-paragraph (2) as to the preservation under the Act of option (ii) when that right was exercisable before the commencement of the Act, while they also preserved both options when they would become exercisable at a time before the commencement of the 1956 Act.

The operation of these provisions with regard to works of joint authorship, where the expiry of the pre-1911 copyright was ascertainable with reference to the period of seven years following the author's death, was nowhere precisely indicated. It would be reasonable to suppose that the *post mortem* period should be reckoned from the death of the author who dies last, as otherwise the rights of a joint author who had survived for more than seven years after the death of a joint author who died first could have been extinguished during the former's lifetime. This position has not been altered by the Act, paragraph 2(2)(a) of Schedule 1 of which adds that references in the Schedule to copyright:

" ... include the right conferred by section 24 of [the 1911] Act in substitution for a right subsisting immediately before the commencement of that Act."

Summary of the 1911 Act's significance

It may assist in the understanding of these somewhat complex provisions of the 1911 Act to summarise their general purport.

First, the section 3 proviso concerns a statutory licence to reproduce published works for sale 25 years (in some cases 30 years) after the author's death where copyright subsisted under the 1911 Act, whether the work was created before the commencement of that Act on July 1, 1912 or not. This faculty is preserved under the Act in respect of works for which the prescribed notice had been given before the commencement of the Act.

Secondly, the section 5 proviso concerns reversion to the author's legal personal representative 25 years after the author's death of copyright assigned or granted by him (otherwise than by will) after July 1, 1912 and not later than June 1, 1957, although reversion in the case of such works may take place after the latter date.

Thirdly, the section 24 proviso concerns the rights of the author and his assignee or licensee in respect of the extended period of copyright granted by the 1911 Act where an assignment was made or licence granted before that Act commenced on July 1, 1912.

THE COPYRIGHT ACT 1956

This Act, which came into force on June 1, 1957, is divided into six parts; there are also nine schedules, which supplement the provisions of these parts.

Part I: Copyright in original works

In the 1956 Act legal protection attached not only to works of authors — that is, to literary, dramatic, musical and artistic creations — but also to subject-matter which was not an author's work. The word "work" is therefore used in that Act only with reference to authors' creations (sometimes referred to as "primary" works) and not to such other subject-matter.

It follows that copyright, as provided for in Part I of the 1956 Act, is copyright in authors' works, such copyright being independent of the copyright in subject-matter other than authors' works, which is provided for in Part II.

Part II: Copyright in derivative works

Once a "primary" work has come into existence, it may be rendered into the form of a "secondary" work by its translation from one medium to another. Thus a piece of music may be recorded, a manuscript may be typeset, a play may be made into a film, and so on.

The rendering of a literary, musical, artistic or dramatic work into one of the media dealt with in Part II of the Act — sound recordings, cinematograph films, broadcasts and published editions of works — attracts copyright protection. This copyright is independent of the copyright, if any, subsisting in authors' works which may be incorporated in the recording, film, broadcast or edition.

That the copyrights as provided in Parts I and II of the Act are additional to and independent of each other is laid down in section 16, sub-section (6) of the 1956 Act.

Part III: Remedies for infringement of copyright

These remedies are, for the greater part, available to copyright owners generally. Their provision in a separate Part of the 1956 Act meant that they did not have to be provided both in Part I and Part II. Remedies under this Act were in most respects less extensive than those under the 1988 Act, except for the now abolished "conversion damages", which effectively enabled many successful plaintiffs to secure double damages.

This Part of the 1956 Act also dealt with the rights of an exclusive licensee and with certain presumptions which might be admitted in legal proceedings respecting copyright.

Part IV: Performing Right Tribunal

The Tribunal's terms of reference were narrower than the Copyright Tribunal (discussed in Chapter 18 below). It was not constituted to decide generally on copyright disputes, or even generally on disputes concerning the public performance right. Its jurisdiction was limited to disputes between "licensing bodies" as limitatively defined, and persons requiring licences for what may be broadly termed the public performance and broadcasting rights in works, sound recordings and television broadcasts. It will be noted that, despite the Tribunal's name, its functions covered, within the prescribed limitations, the broadcasting right.

Part V: Extension of restriction of operation of the Act

The territory of jurisdiction of this Act was in the first place the United Kingdom of Great Britain and Northern Ireland, but under this Part of the Act its provisions were extended (with or without modification) to the Isle of Man, the Channel Islands, and the colonies and dependencies of the U.K.; they were also made to apply, in return for reciprocal protection, to works of foreign origin, an expression which was taken as including the independent countries of the British Commonwealth.

Part VI: Miscellaneous and supplementary provisions

This Part of the Act included, in particular: provisions relating to assignments of copyright (that is, the transfer of the ownership of the copyright); licences, which do not entail transfer of the ownership but authorise the licensee to exercise the copyright in specified conditions; prospective ownership of copyright (ownership of the copyright in works not yet created); false attribution of authorship; also a number of provisions affecting earlier provisions of the Act including a single "definition" section in which words used else-where in the Act were given a specific meaning for the purposes of the Act.

The Schedules

The Schedules dealt with what might be termed special situations including, in the Seventh Schedule, the transitional provisions, that is, those which decide the application of the Act to works in which copyright subsisted, when the Act came into force, under the provisions of the Copyright Act 1911 where these latter differed from the provisions of the Act.

CHAPTER 15

COPYRIGHT AND INTERNATIONAL LAW

THE BERNE COPYRIGHT UNION

Introduction

Copyright is essentially international in character. This was recognised even before the advent of modern techniques such as cinematography, mechanical recording and broadcasting had given an immense impulse to the international exploitation of works, since the reasons which dictated the national protection of authors' works were equally applicable at the international level. Accordingly, the Berne Copyright Union was founded in 1886, although before then international copyright protection had existed through bilateral arrangements entered into by like-minded countries.

It should be noted that the Convention of the Berne Union uses the expression "literary and artistic works" in relation to the subject-matter with which it is concerned, and that, subject to one qualification, this expression is equivalent to the term "literary, dramatic, musical and artistic works" as used in the U.K. copyright legislation. The qualification concerns cinematograph works, for which protection is provided in the Convention as original works. However, the Convention does not define the author of the cinematograph work, and while, under the U.K. Act, that author is the producer of the film for many purposes, in many other countries of the Union that author can only be a person who, as author, composer, director or otherwise, has made a creative contribution to the film. With this qualification, therefore, the Convention of the Union is not concerned with subject-matter other than the traditional copyright works.

Legal nature of the Union

The countries belonging to the Berne Union have undertaken to grant reciprocal protection to each others' works, in effect assimilating to the national repertoire, and protecting according to the same principles, works of which another country of the Union is the country of origin. The Convention does not require that the countries belonging to the Union adopt similar legislation, but does lay down a body of rules to which that legislation must conform. Thus the Union can accommodate countries such as the U.K. which protect authors' rights under what in this book is called the copyright system, and countries whose concept of the author's right is somewhat different.

It can even happen, in some extreme cases, that the copyright owner in one country of the Union is not the same person (apart from any question of assignment of rights) as the copyright owner recognised by the copyright law of another country of the Union, as, for example, in the case of the employee author.

It is one of the fundamental principles of the Convention that protection is granted automatically and without the fulfilment of any formality such as registration, deposit of a copy of the work or the display of a copyright notice.

Until the Stockholm revision of the Convention, adopted in 1967, "country of origin" of the work under the Convention meant, in the case of unpublished works, the country of which the author was a national and, in the case of published works, the country of first publication. Thus the unpublished work of a British national, as soon as it was protected under British law, was also protected under the law of all other countries of the Union, independently of the fulfilment of any formality.

The position under the Stockholm revision (which the U.K. has not yet ratified) is that the principle of nationality of works is extended to include the country of which the author is a national irrespective of whether (if the work is published) first publication takes place in a Union country. This important change of principle does not however mean that, for countries which accede to the Stockholm text, works which have previously lost protection through first publication in a non-Union country will suddenly regain protection.

Since a work first published in a country of the Union is taken to have its origin in that country, and the Union requires the protection of works having their origin in a Union country, even the works of a non-Union country obtain protection in all countries of the Union.

As regards simultaneous publication in Union and non-Union countries, until 1948 the Convention of the Union provided that when a work was published simultaneously in a country outside the Union and a country of the Union, the latter was to be regarded as the country of origin. It was, therefore, left to Union countries to consider what they would regard as simultaneous publication. Since 1948, however, the Convention has provided that a work is to be considered as published simultaneously in several countries if it is published in two or more countries within 30 days of its first publication.

Revisions of the text

The Convention has been revised periodically to amend the text in the light of technical and other developments in the reproduction and diffusion of authors' works. Amendments currently being considered relate to matters such as electronic storage of works, photocopying and the introduction of a rental right. National laws will usually need some modification to conform to the new text of the Convention and such revision, if it takes place, will sometimes be very dilatory. Accordingly, membership of the Union on the part of a given country does not necessarily mean that it has adhered to the latest text of the Convention. By way of example, on January 1, 1997 there were 121 Member States of the Union. Only 105 adhere to any part of the most recent (1971) text. Some of the more important revisions are described in the following paragraphs.

The Berlin revision of 1908 introduced the principle of protection for 50 years post mortem, but not as an obligation. To meet differences in the period of protection after the author's death as between one country of the Union and another it provided for the so-called comparison of terms. In other words, when there was divergence between two terms, the protection period was determined by the law of the country where protection was claimed, but was not to exceed the term fixed in the country of origin of the work.

The Brussels Convention of 1948 made obligatory a minimum term of protection for the author's lifetime and for not less than 50 years thereafter, the comparison of terms system being maintained only where the term exceeds this minimum in one of the terms to be compared. Some exceptions are admitted to the general rule in respect of cinematograph works, photographic works, works of applied art, anonymous, pseudonymous and post-humous works.

The Brussels text recognised for the first time (but not as an obligatory rule) the right generally known by its French name of *droit de suite*. There does not appear to be a generally accepted equivalent term in English for this right, which is not known in English law. The term has been translated as "right of subsequent disposal", but it is now more widely known as the "resale royalty right" discussed on page 56. The right, in this Convention specification, provides that the author, or after his death the persons or institutions authorised by national legislation, shall, in respect of original works of art and original manuscripts of writers and composers, enjoy the inalienable right to an interest in any sale of work subsequent to the first disposal of the work by the author.

Neither the Brussels text nor any other Union Convention provides for the Public Lending Right, which is found in the copyright legislation of a small number of countries, and which U.K. authors now enjoy after some years of vigorous campaigning. That right provides a small payment in respect of a notional number of borrowings of books in public libraries, thus compensating authors for loss of income resulting from the privilege enjoyed by the public of borrowing rather than buying the book. Public Lending Right is discussed under that heading in Chapter 20 below.

The principal significance of the Stockholm revision of 1967 has already been discussed above. Attached to the text, and forming an integral part of it, was a Protocol in favour of developing countries. However, as related below under the heading "Relaxations in favour of the developing countries", this Protocol has now been superseded by the Appendix to the Paris Act 1971 of the Berne Union.

At the 1967 Stockholm Conference there was also adopted a new Convention establishing the World Intellectual Property Organisation (WIPO, also known under its French acronym OMPI). Membership of WIPO is open to any state which is a member of the Berne Union, the Paris Union (for the protection of patent rights) and certain other international organisations, and whose purpose is "to modernise and render more efficient the administration of the Unions established in the fields of the protection of industrial property and literary and artistic work". Under this Convention the responsibility for the administration of the Berne Union was shifted from the Swiss Government to the member states acting together in an Assembly. WIPO is housed in a striking modern building in Geneva, and has been criticised on account of the great expense of its maintenance. That organisation has, on the other hand, made a great impact on the introduction and drafting of laws in all areas of "intellectual property", especially among the countries of the Third World.

It is important to note that countries may ratify or accede to the administrative provisions of the Stockholm Convention without either ratifying or acceding to the substantive clauses of that Act or the Protocol attached to them. The U.K. has ratified these administrative clauses, but is not otherwise bound by the Stockholm Act.

The U.K. ratified the Paris Act of 1971 on September 29, 1989 and made adjustments to the necessary U.K. copyright law in the Act.

As at January 1, 1997 the countries named below were members of the Berne Union:

Albania	Guinea	Peru
Argentina	Guinea Bissau	Philippines
Australia	Guyana	Poland
Austria	Haiti	Portugal
Bahamas	Holy See	Republic of Korea
Bahrain	Honduras	Republic of Moldova
Barbados	Hungary	Romania
Belgium	Iceland	Russian Federation
Benin	India	Rwanda
Bolivia	Ireland	St Kitts and Nevis
Bosnia/Herzegovina	Italy	St Lucia
Brazil	Jamaica	St Vincent and the
Bulgaria	Israel	Grenadines
Burkina Faso	Japan	Senegal
Cameroon	Kenya	Slovakia
Canada	Latvia	Slovenia
Central African Republic	Lebanon	South Africa
Chad	Lesotho	Spain
Chile	Liberia	Sri Lanka
China	Libya	Surinam
Colombia	Liechtenstein	Sweden
Congo	Lithuania	Switzerland
Costa Rica	Luxembourg	Thailand
Côte d'Ivoire	Madagascar	Togo
Croatia	Malawi	Trinidad and Tobago
Cuba	Malaysia	Tunisia
Cyprus	Mali	Turkey
Czech Republic	Malta	Ukraine
Denmark	Mauritania	United Kingdom
Ecuador	Mauritius	United Republic of
Egypt	Mexico	Tanzania
El Salvador	Monaco	United States of America
Estonia	Morocco	Uruguay
Fiji	Namibia	Venezuela
Finland	Netherlands	Yugoslavia
France	New Zealand	Yugoslav Republic of
Gabon	Niger	Macedonia (former)
Georgia	Nigeria	Zaire
Germany	Norway	Zambia
Ghana	Pakistan	Zimbabwe
Greece	Paraguay	

Unfortunately it must be said that in some of these countries protection is rather more nominal than effective and that their copyright legislation is not by any means always compatible with the Berne Convention and with the Universal Copyright Convention (see below). It will also be noted that some countries do not even nominally protect authors' works. They include a number of Middle Eastern states.

THE UNIVERSAL COPYRIGHT CONVENTION

It will have been noted that a sizable, but decreasing, number of countries are not members of the Berne Union. The legislation of some did not conform to the Berne standards. Others, because of fundamental differences between their system of protection and that of the Union, did not accede to the Berne Convention. This was the case with the countries comprising the former Soviet Union, some of the countries with which it held close political connections, and, before 1989, the U.S.

The U.S. and some other countries outside the Union were able, by means of bilateral arrangements and such procedures as the simultaneous publication mentioned above, to have copyright relations with the Union countries. However, the need to establish more direct and practical bases for such relations, and in particular to establish a bridge between countries which required formalities, and countries such as those of the Union, which do not demand such formalities was increasingly felt. This need led to the adoption in 1952 of the Universal Copyright Convention (UCC), sponsored by UNESCO.

The purposes of the UCC could be achieved only if minimum obligatory requirements were stipulated and in fact, beyond requiring a minimum period of protection, the UCC demands little more of its adherents than that they undertake to provide "adequate and effective protection", a requirement which will carry as much or as little significance as the legislatures of the contracting countries decide to give to it.

The Convention was made much more specific in the 1971 Paris revision, in particular by providing for the first time that protection was to include:

> "the basic rights ensuring the author's economic interests, including the exclusive right to authorise reproduction by any means, public performance and broad-casting."

However, the UCC[1] goes on to provide that "any contracting state may, by its domestic legislation, make exceptions" to these rights "that do not conflict with the spirit and provisions of this Convention" and that:

> "any state whose legislation so provides shall nevertheless accord a reasonable degree of effective protection to each of the rights to which exception has been made".[1]

Again, what is meant by "reasonable degree of effective protection" is left to the discretion of the contracting states. This is apart from the relaxations in favour of developing countries which are discussed under the following heading.

The minimum period referred to is the lifetime of the author and for 25 years thereafter, but any country which limits this term for certain classes of works to a period computed form first publication of the work is entitled to maintain these exceptions; and when a state does not compute the term of protection on the basis of the author's lifetime, it is entitled

---

[1] Article IV *bis* (2).

to compute that term from the date of first publication of the work, or from its registration before publication, as the case may be, but the term of protection is to be not less than 25 years from such date (subject to some exceptions).

The UCC has performed one very important and useful service. It provides that any contracting state which under its domestic law requires as a condition of copyright the compliance with formalities (such as deposit, registration, payment of fees, manufacture or publication in that state) is to regard these requirements as satisfied with respect to all works protected in accordance with the Convention, even if they are written by non-nationals and are first published outside its territory if, from the time of first publication all copies of the work published with the authority of the copyright proprietor bear the symbol © accompanied by the name of the copyright proprietor and the year of first publication placed in such manner and location as to give reasonable notice of copyright.

Since the U.S. is a party to the UCC, this provision offered a relatively simple means of securing U.S. copyright for works of non-U.S. origin without compliance with the onerous formalities required before the U.S. joined the Berne Union.

Article XVII of the UCC in its original text of 1952 provided that the Convention is not to affect in any way the provisions of the Berne Convention, and in application of that provision a Declaration was annexed to the Article to which the states belonging to the Berne Union, which were also signatories to the UCC, had to subscribe. The Declaration provided, in effect, that works of countries which withdrew from the Berne Union after January 1 1951 would not be protected by the UCC in countries of the Berne Union, and further that the UCC was not in general to apply to relations between Berne Union countries with respect to works originating in those countries.

As at January 1, 1997 the countries named below were parties to the UCC:

Algeria	Cyprus	Israel
Andorra	Czechoslovakia	Italy
Argentina	Denmark	Japan
Australia	Dominican Republic	Kenya
Austria	Ecuador	Lagos
Bahamas	El Salvador	Lebanon
Bangladesh	Fiji	Liberia
Barbados	Finland	Liechtenstein
Belgium	France	Luxembourg
Belize	Germany	Malawi
Brazil	Ghana	Malta
Bolivia	Greece	Mauritius
Bulgaria	Guatemala	Mexico
Cambodia	Guinea	Monaco
Camaroon	Haiti	Morocco
Canada	Holy See	Netherlands
Chile	Hungary	New Zealand
Colombia	Iceland	Nicaragua
Costa Rica	India	Niger
Cuba	Ireland	Nigeria

Norway	Republic of Korea	Sweden
Pakistan	Russia	Switzerland
Panama	Rwanda	Trinidad and Tobago
Paraguay	Saint Vincent and the	Tunisia
Peru	Grenadines	United Kingdom
Philippines	Senegal	United States
Poland	Spain	Venezuela
Portugal	Sri Lanka	Zambia

RELAXATIONS IN FAVOUR OF THE DEVELOPING COUNTRIES INCORPORATED IN THE PARIS 1971 REVISIONS OF THE BERNE AND UNIVERSAL COPYRIGHT CONVENTIONS

Historical background

The UCC has attracted a large number of countries, including many of the so-called developing countries, of which, according to a definition of the United Nations Organisation, there are some 80. Among these countries many are former colonies in the British, French and Dutch empires, and as such their copyright laws were those of the colonial power. When these countries became independent the question arose of whether they were, like that power, members of the Berne Union. Speaking generally, the former French colonies considered that they were and the former British colonies held that they were not.

It has also been apparent that many developing countries objected to the price payable by them as copyright importers. That the developing countries are entitled to cultural as well as material aid is not generally disputed; but it would not be right to envisage the furnishing of the former solely at the expense of authors and publishers, any more than it would be right that material aid such as medicines or tractors should be supplied solely at the cost of the producers of those materials.

However, great pressures were exerted by the developing countries at the Stockholm Revision Conference of the Berne Union Convention in 1967 for the right to remain in, or join, the Berne Union with the privilege, for the period of their development, of enjoying important relaxations of the Convention rules. It was as a result of these pressures that the Protocol in favour of the developing countries emerged as an integral part of the substantive (copyright) provisions of the Stockholm Convention of the Union.

Copyright owners opposed the Protocol on the ground that it was an unnecessary encroachment on the integrity of the standards hitherto upheld by the Union because there was already in existence a "low-level" Convention, that is the UCC, and because they considered that the sacrifice of their rights which they were called on to bear was unreasonably heavy. In the event, although the Protocol was adopted, the hopes which the developing countries placed in it have not been realised, partly because of the opposition to it of the U.S., and partly because the exponential rate of advance in science and technology rendered much copyright material relating to those disciplines obsolete before it could effectively be exploited under the terms of the Protocol. The developed countries which already belonged to the Union, moved by the desire to see the U.S. also accede to that organisation, and perhaps relieved to find a reason for not acceding to the Act about which they had grave misgivings, in general indicated that they did not, for the present, intend to ratify the Stockholm text. Except that, as already mentioned, the U.K. has ratified the administrative provisions only of that text, this was also the attitude of the British Government.

The Paris amendments of 1971

In the light of the U.S. Declaration and their own hesitations, the governments of the principal countries belonging to the two great Conventions decided to institute together a far-reaching inquiry into the whole field of international copyright relations. Out of this inquiry there emerged a set of proposals supported generally by developed and developing countries alike as a fair compromise between their respective views. Copyright owners were again called on to make sacrifices, but of a far less drastic character than those that would have been entailed by the Protocol.

At the conferences in Paris during July 1971 at which the two Conventions were simultaneously revised, the draft texts incorporating this compromise were generally adopted, although numerous amendments, some of importance, were made to them. In essence, what this compromise amounted to was:

(1)   relaxation of the exclusive nature of the Berne rights in favour of the developing countries only;

(2)   strengthening of the very imprecise prescriptions of the UCC, coupled with the right in certain cases for developing countries to make exceptions to them;

(3)   alignment of the Berne relaxations with the UCC exceptions, so that a developing country member of the Berne Union would not, in respect to these special provisions, be at a disadvantage with a country party to the UCC only;

(4)   modification of Article XVII of the UCC and its appended Declaration so as to permit developing countries to withdraw from the Berne Union without thereby forfeiting protection under the UCC.

The Berne relaxations and the UCC exceptions allow developing countries to institute regimes of non-exclusive, non-transferable licences for translation and reproduction for educational purposes, including broadcasting for that purpose. Strict conditions are attached to the granting of such compulsory licences by the governments of the developing countries, including the obligation on their part to ensure payment of royalties at standards normally applicable in the two countries concerned, and the effective transfer of such royalties. In particular these licences will not be grantable for purely cultural purposes, as they could have been under the Protocol — that is, to an almost unlimited extent — while developing countries of the Berne Union may not reduce the post mortem period of protection as laid down in that Convention, that is, not less than 50 years. Under the UCC the minimum post mortem protection period will continue to be 25 years. Export of copies made under the compulsory licence provisions will be subject to strict limitations.

Accordingly, while the Berne relaxations and the UCC exceptions correspond, the level of protection otherwise prescribed under each Convention (precise under Berne, very general under the UCC) differs. A country can adhere to both Conventions, applying

Berne in relation to other Berne countries and the UCC to countries party only to that Convention, with the right in each case, if it is a developing country, to apply the relaxations or exceptions as the case may be.

Application of "material reciprocity" by a developed country, in order to gain access to the use of works originating in a developing country of the Berne Union which uses the relaxation faculty, is not permissible.

The Berne relaxations are incorporated in Articles V*bis* to V*ter* of the UCC and in an Appendix to the Paris Act, completely replacing the Stockholm Protocol. The Paris text of the Berne Convention corresponds in other respects to the Stockholm text.

The U.K. ratified the Paris Act of the UCC on September 29, 1989, together with that Act of the Berne Convention.

THE AGREEMENT ON TRADE RELATED ASPECTS OF INTELLECTUAL PROPERTY RIGHTS (TRIPs)

Although the TRIPs Agreement is not strictly a copyright convention, its impact upon copyright at the national level is of almost immeasurable importance. The TRIPs Agreement was one plank in a whole raft of international agreements upon which floated the Third (Uruguay) Round of GATT, the General Agreement on Trade and Tariffs, an international agreement on the reduction of international trade barriers which was concluded in 1994.

The TRIPs Agreement, which was formally concluded in Marrakech in 1995 and came into effect from January 1, 1996, makes provision for four areas of concern to copyright owners: the scope of copyright protection, the enforceability of copyright, the range of remedies available against infringers and the gap which is sometimes perceived between a country's international obligations and the manner in which they are reflected in its national law.

As to the scope of copyright protection, TRIPs provides that the main obligations under the Berne Convention are to be adopted by TRIPs members, whether they are members of the Berne Union or not. TRIPs does not require compliance with Berne's moral rights provisions since they are not seen as being "trade-related". Although the number of countries which belong to TRIPs is almost exactly the same as the number of Berne Union members, the two membership lists are not coextensive. TRIPs, additionally, is open even to countries which, because of their uncertain international status, are not eligible for Berne Union membership (of which the most significant is Taiwan).

In addition to adherence to the main substantive provisions of the Berne Convention, a TRIPs member must also ensure that a full range of remedies is available: damages, injunctive remedies and delivery up of infringing articles. Apart from judicial remedies, each country must provide effective administrative relief against foreign infringers, through adequate customs controls. Each country's enforcement system, whether judicial or administrative, must be transparent in the sense that the law must be seen to be accurately and consistently applied; a right of appeal or judicial review should be permitted. Finally, any country which believes that another TRIPs member has failed to comply with its TRIPs obligations may lodge a complaint with the World Trade Organisation (WTO), the Geneva-based policeman of not only TRIPs but also of the other trading agreemental which make up the Uruguay Round of GATT. Early experience of the WTO indicates that it is likely to be efficient in enforcing complaints made against Member States, not least because there is always the threatened sanction that the benefits of the Uruguay Round will be witheld from states which are in dereliction of their international obligations.

It is too early to see how effective TRIPS will be with regard to developing countries. Unlike the leading industrial nations, which had until January 1, 1996 to put their domestic copyright law in order, developing nations were given a five-year period of grace (10 years in respect of the least developed states and those countries which were adjusting from socialist to market economies). This means that it will be 2006 before copyright owners can lay claim to the full benefit of TRIPs' obligations.

WIPO COPYRIGHT TREATY

On December 20, 1996 two new copyright treaties were signed: the WIPO Copyright Treaty and the Performances and Phonograms Treaty. Consensus as to a third treaty, covering the protection of databases, could not be reached but it is probable that further diplomatic initiatives will have resulted in its resuscitation by the time the next edition of this book is published.

The WIPO Copyright Treaty is designed as a bolt-on extra for Berne Convention adherents. It requires, for the first time in an international copyright convention, the protectability of computer programs as literary works as well as the protection of databases "as such". The author's rights of distribution and communication are spelled out: the latter appears to embrace the right to put a copyright-protected work on to an internet website, although it does not use those words. Article 10 provides that defences to copyright infringement, both in respect of works mentioned in the Treaty and in respect of works covered by the Berne Convention, shall be confined to "special cases" rather than blanket defences. Signatories must also protect copyright works against tampering with any technological means which may be used for their protection, for example, by means of encryption at the point of transmission or by use of a "dongle", a piece of hardware which restricts or regulates the use of copyright-protected software. Signatories must also protect copyright owners against the "decoding" of products by the obliteration or destruction of any rights management information which is embodies in or on them.

This treaty comes into force three months after WIPO has received 30 instruments of accession or ratification. At the time of writing, none has yet been received.

INTERNATIONAL CONVENTION FOR THE PROTECTION OF PERFORMERS, PRODUCERS OF PHONOGRAMS AND BROADCASTING ORGANISATIONS

Introduction

The rights of record manufacturers (called in the above-named Convention "producers of phonograms") in their sound recordings, of film producers in their films, and of broadcasters in their broadcasts are sometimes referred to collectively as "neighbouring rights" or "ancillary rights", because they are considered as deriving from, or serving as a medium of communication of, authors' works. This is perhaps an over-simplified conception because, while it is possible to consider sound recordings and broadcasts as purely technical productions (although this is sometimes disputed), it is claimed with some plausibility that there is a creative element in film production, at least on the part of the director of the production. A similar claim has also been made on behalf of performing artists.

What is certain is that the activities of record makers, film producers, broadcasting organisations and performing artists are generally based on authors' works. It is submitted accordingly that in the protection of the legitimate and important interests of these persons a prime consideration should be not to impair the rights of authors.

In many countries the problem of reconciling the protection of neighbouring rights with those of authors is considered delicate enough to require an extremely cautious approach; indeed it is still only a minority of countries which has adopted a fully considered regime in this field.

Consequently, the above-named Convention, which was signed at Rome in 1961, has so far attracted only a relatively small number of countries, each of whom must, under the terms of the Convention, be a member of the Berne Union or the UCC. Members so far include the U.K., for which the Convention came into force from May 18, 1964. At the time of writing, some 52 countries have adhered to the Convention. The European Commission has proposed that all Member States become parties to the Convention. Perhaps not surprisingly, in order to attract further membership, the Convention allows very large possibilities of reservation and exception, even in respect of some of its principal provisions, in order to accommodate as far as possible the various solutions adopted, or which may be adopted in the future, to the problems raised by neighbouring rights.

It will be observed in particular that the Convention does not cover the rights of film producers. Both the Berne Union Convention and the UCC do so, but without defining the author of such works, so that it is open to national legislation to consider the producer of a film as its author (which, in effect, is what is done in the Act). It is also open, as in the legislation of some countries, to consider that only a true author (including possibly such contributors to the work as the film director) can be regarded as the author of a film.

Legal provisions

The basic principle of the Convention is that each contracting state undertakes to grant national treatment to performers, producers of phonograms and broadcasters of contracting states, subject to conditions identifying the subject-matter of the Convention as originating in a contracting state. National treatment in the U.K. is provided for the subject-matter in question by Parts I and II of the Act.

The term of protection under the Convention is to last at least until the end of a period of 20 years computed from the end of the year in which:

(1)   the fixation (recording) was made — for phonograms and for performances incorporated therein;
(2)   the performance took place — for performances not incorporated in phonograms;
(3)   the broadcast took place — for broadcasts.

The Convention provides that if as a condition of protecting the rights of producers of phonograms, or of performers, or both, in relation to phonograms, a contracting state, under its domestic law, requires compliance with formalities, these are to be considered as fulfilled if all the copies in commerce of the published phonogram or their containers bear a notice consisting of the symbol ℗, accompanied by the year or date of the first publication, placed in such a manner as to give reasonable notice of claim of protection; and if the copies or their containers do not identify the producer or licensee of the producer (by carrying his name, trade mark or other appropriate designation), the notice is also to include the name of the owner of the rights of the producer; and if the copies or their containers do not identify the principal performers, the notice shall include the name of the person who, in the country in which the fixation was effected, owns the rights of such performers.

The current membership of the Rome Convention is:

Argentina	Finland	Niger
Australia	France	Nigeria
Austria	Germany	Norway
Barbados	Greece	Panama
Bolivia	Guatemala	Paraguay
Brazil	Honduras	Peru
Bulgaria	Hungary	Philippines
Burkina Faso	Iceland	Republic of Moldova
Chile	Ireland	St Lucia
Colombia	Italy	Slovakia
Congo	Jamaica	Slovenia
Costa Rica	Japan	Spain
Czech Republic	Lesotho	Sweden
Denmark	Luxembourg	Switzerland
Dominican Republic	Mexico	United Kindom
Ecuador	Monaco	Uruguay
El Salvador	Netherlands	Venezuela
Fiji		

WIPO PERFORMANCES AND PHONOGRAMS TREATY

Like the WIPO Copyright Treaty, this treaty was concluded on December 20, 1996. In many respect it mirrors the provisions of the Copyright Treaty, but applying them *mutatis mutandis* to performances and phonograms. One startling innovation, in Article 5, is the requirement that the author's moral rights to be identified as author and to object to distortions and mutilations of a work be conferred also upon performers. Since rights under this treaty may not be subject to any formalities, the performer's right to be identified as such — assuming that the U.K. chooses to ratify the treaty — will be enjoyed automatically and will not be subject to the onerous requirements of assertion which currently govern the availablity of that right in respect of authors.

This treaty comes into force three months after WIPO has received 30 instruments of accession or ratification. At the time of writing, none has yet been received.

EUROPEAN AGREEMENT CONCERNING PROGRAMME EXCHANGES BY MEANS OF
TELEVISION FILMS

This Agreement, signed at Paris in 1958, was promoted by the Council of Europe to meet difficulties in the international exchange of filmed programmes arising from differences in national legislation with regard to the authorship of cinematograph and television films. As has been indicated earlier in this Chapter, the owner of the copyright in films can vary from country to country. The U.K., for example, can treat a film as being created by a corporation, while its European neighbours regard it as being created by all who make artistic contributions to it (which, as the Whitford Report points out, may include cameramen and those responsible for the design of the film's sets).

The Agreement is specifically drafted to exclude from its effects the copyright in literary, dramatic, musical and artistic works from which the film is derived, or by which it is accompanied; it also excludes the copyright in films other than television films, and the copyright in the exhibition of television films otherwise than on television.

The operative clause of the Agreement lays down that in the absence of any contrary or special stipulation (meaning any restrictive condition agreed between the maker of the film and persons who contribute to the making of it), a broadcasting organisation under the jurisdiction of a country which is party to the Agreement has the right to authorise in the other countries which are parties to the Agreement the exploitation for television of television films of which it is the maker.

A broadcasting organisation, under the Agreement, is the maker of the television film if it has taken the initiative in, and responsibility for, the making of the film, and "television film", as defined in the Agreement, includes all visual or sound and visual recordings intended for television.

It will be noted that a film producer who is not also a broadcaster and who hires or sells his film directly to a broadcasting organisation in a foreign country is not within the scope of the Agreement, although he can hire or sell his film to a broadcaster in his own country to whom the Agreement will apply.

At the time of writing the following countries are parties to the Agreement: Belgium, Cyprus, Denmark, France, Greece, Ireland, Israel, Luxembourg, the Netherlands, Norway, Spain, Sweden, Tunisia, Turkey and the U.K. The Agreement was effective in the U.K. from July 1, 1961.

EUROPEAN AGREEMENT ON THE PROTECTION OF TELEVISION BROADCASTS

This Agreement, like the one referred to above, was sponsored by the Council of Europe but, while its general purpose is the same as that of the earlier Agreement, its scope is wider. This later Agreement was signed in 1960 and both Agreements accordingly antedated the Rome Convention of 1961 for the Protection of Performers, Producers of Phonograms and Broadcasting Organisations. It is stated in the Preamble to the 1960 Agreement that:

"pending the conclusion of a potentially universal convention on 'neighbouring rights' at present in contemplation it is fitting to conclude a regional Agreement restricted in scope to television broadcasts and of limited duration."

It was further provided in the Agreement as originally signed that it was to cease to be effective at such time as a convention on neighbouring rights, including the protection of television broadcasts, had entered into force for at least a majority of the states which, being members of the Council of Europe, were parties to the Agreement.

In 1965 a Protocol was added to the Agreement, motivated by the fact that the Rome Convention had attracted only a small number of countries, removing the temporary character of the Agreement and making it of unlimited duration. The Protocol also provided that after January 1, 1975 no state might remain or become party to the Agreement which was not also a party to the Rome Convention. A further Protocol has extended this date to January 1, 1990. In the light of European Commission's proposals for all Member States to become parties to the Rome Convention, the Agreement is likely to cease to be of importance.

European Agreement for the Prevention of Broadcasts Transmitted from Stations Outside National Territories

This Agreement, sponsored by the Council of Europe, has for its purpose the prevention of "pirate" broadcasting. In accordance with its Article 1 the Agreement is concerned with broadcasting stations which are installed or maintained on board ships, aircraft or any other floating or airborne objects and which, outside national territories, transmit broadcasts:

(1)   intended for reception; or
(2)   which are capable of being received, wholly or in part, within the territory of any contracting party; or
(3)   which cause harmful interference to any radio communication service operating in accordance with the Radio Regulations.

Each contracting party undertakes to take appropriate steps to make punishable as offences, in accordance with its domestic law, the establishment or operation of broadcasting stations as defined above, as well as acts of collaboration knowingly performed. The following are to be regarded as acts of collaboration:

(1)   the provision, maintenance or repairing of equipment;
(2)   the provision of supplies;
(3)   the provision of transport for, or the transporting of, persons, equipment or supplies;
(4)   the ordering or production of material of any kind, including advertisements, to be broadcast;
(5)   the provision of services concerning advertising for the benefit of the stations.

Stations broadcasting from outside territorial waters, or otherwise outside national territories, are of course beyond the national jurisdiction, whether pursuant to the copyright law or any other enactment. They can, therefore, use copyright material without the authorisation of, or payment to, the copyright owners.

At the time of writing the countries which are parties to the Agreement are: Belgium, Cyprus, Denmark, France, Germany, Greece, Ireland, Italy, Liechtenstein, the Netherlands, Norway, Portugal, Spain, Sweden, Switzerland, Turkey and the U.K. The Agreement became effective in the U.K. on December 3, 1967 following the enactment of the Marine, etc., Broadcasting (Offences) Act 1967.

CONVENTION FOR THE PROTECTION OF PRODUCERS OF PHONOGRAMS AGAINST UNAUTHORISED DUPLICATION OF THEIR PHONOGRAMS.

This Convention, signed at Geneva on October 29, 1971, provides that:

> " ... each contracting state shall protect producers of phonograms who are nationals of the other contracting states against the making of duplicates manufactured without the consent of the producers and against the importation and distribution of such duplicates, provided that any such making or importation is for the purpose of distribution to the public ... "

"Phonogram" is defined as it "any exclusively aural fixation of sounds" and "producer" as "the person who, or the legal entity that, first fixes the sounds embodied in the phonogram".

The term of protection under the Convention is to be not less than 20 years from the end of the year in which the sounds embodied in the phonogram were first fixed or of the year in which the phonogram was just published.

If, as a condition of protecting the producers of phonograms, a contracting state requires compliance with formalities, these are to be considered as fulfilled if all authorised duplicates of the phonogram distributed to the public or their containers bear a notice consisting of the symbol (P), accompanied by the year or date of the first publication, placed in such a manner as to give reasonable notice of claim of protection, and if the duplicates or their containers do not identify the producer or his successor in title, or the licensee (by carrying his name, trade mark or other appropriate designation), the notice is to include the name of the producer, his successor in title or the licensee.

Producers of phonograms are also protected under the Rome Convention of 1961 (described above). Until, however, more countries join these Conventions (52 have joined the Rome Convention, 54 the Geneva one), or the WIPO Performances and Phonograms Treaty, the need for protection will remain a pressing one. Piracy of commercial recordings is now being perpetrated on such a scale that it has been calculated that more pirated recordings are in circulation throughout the world than legitimate ones. It will in any case be seen that the scope of the protection accorded by the new Convention is much narrower than that of the Rome Convention and the WIPO Performances and Phonograms Treaty.

Of course, the unauthorised reproduction of a record which incorporates a copyright work will infringe the copyright in that work, and it will accordingly be possible for the owner of that copyright (the author or his legal successor, generally a publisher) to prosecute the infringer in any country where there is an adequate copyright law. In practice, however, there are many countries of the world where the copyright law is not adequate, or does not exist at all, and in others the very scale of the infringement has defeated the efforts of the copyright owners. It is to be hoped that this Convention will attract a sufficiently large number of countries (particularly those in which infringement is rampant) to enable the record manufacturers, armed with their (for the greater part of these countries) new legal right, to cope better with this problem, not only in their own interest but also in that of the authors, their legal successors and the performers.

The current membership of this Convention is as follows:

Argentina	France	Norway
Australia	Germany	Panama
Austria	Greece	Paraguay
Barbados	Guatemala	Peru
Brazil	Holy See	Republic of Korea
Bukina Faso	Honduras	Russian Federation
Chile	Hungary	Slovakia
China	India	Slovenia
Colombia	Israel	Spain
Costa Rica	Italy	Sweden
Cyprus	Jamaica	Switzerland
Czech Republic	Japan	Trinidad and Tobago
Denmark	Kenya	United Kingdom
Ecuador	Luxembourg	United States
Egypt	Mexico	Uruguay
El Salvador	Monaco	Venezuela
Fiji	Netherlands	Zaire
Finland	New Zealand	

BRUSSELS CONVENTION ON THE PROTECTION OF SATELLITE TRANSMISSIONS

This Convention, promoted by the European Broadcasting Union in 1974, has not yet been signed by the U.K. Its intended function is to protect signals transmitted by "point-to-point" satellites against distribution by "pirate" ground stations, for whom such signals were not intended, and who would distribute those signals, by wire or by wireless means, to domestic receivers. To some extent its provisions have now been overtaken by technological development.

The U.K. is unlikely to become a party in the light of the European Community Directive on Copyright in Satellite Transmissions and Re-Transmission. This Convention came into force on August 25, 1979 and now has 21 members (Armenia, Australia, Austria, Bosnia/Herzegovina, Croatia, Germany, Greece, Italy, Kenya, Mexico, Morocco, Nicaragua, Panama, Peru, Portugal, Russian Federation, Slovenia, Switzerland, Trinidad and Tobago, U.K. and Yugoslavia).

VIENNA AGREEMENT FOR THE PROTECTION OF TYPEFACES AND THEIR INTERNATIONAL DEPOSIT

This Agreement, made in 1973, provides for the protection of distinctive sets of letters used as typefaces. It does not cover the protection of published editions of works (discussed on pages 37 to 38) which is often referred to as "typeface" copyright. To fulfil the terms of the Agreement, a member state can protect typefaces by one of these means;

ordinary copyright law, industrial design law, or establishing a "special notional deposit."

Typefaces are now apparently protected in the U.K. as works of artistic copyright (see pages 33 to 34).

The Vienna Agreement is not yet in force and only two of the eleven signatory states have so far ratified it. The signatories are France, Germany, Hungary, Italy, Liechtenstein, Luxembourg, the Netherlands, San Marino, Switzerland, the U.K. and Yugoslavia.

CONVENTION FOR AVOIDANCE OF DOUBLE TAXATION ON COPYRIGHT ROYALTIES

Representatives of 44 countries met in Madrid in the winter of 1979, at a conference jointly convened by WIPO and UNESCO, to discuss the taxation problems which inevitably arise when royalties payable for the use of the copyright work in one country are due to an author who is resident in another. The substance of the Convention which resulted from this conference is that its members undertake to make every possible effort to avoid double taxation of copyright royalties, whether through the adoption of domestic legal provisions or (as frequently happens already) through the entering of bilateral tax treaties with other Member States.

This Convention will enter into force three months after the deposit of the tenth instrument of ratification. By January 1, 1982 five states had signed the Convention, and only two had ratified it. The signatories are Cameroon, Czechoslovakia, Egypt, Holy See and Israel.

TREATY OF ROME

While the Treaty of Rome is not specifically a treaty governing copyright law, the accession of the U.K. to the European Economic Community in 1972 has consequences for copyright owners. The Treaty of Rome and the aspirations of its adherents affect copyright both with regard to its exploitation and with respect to the feasibility of harmonising the domestic copyright laws of the various Member States.

Exploitation of copyright

The Common Market is, in essence, an institution for the enhancement of trade between its members. The provisions of the Treaty of Rome accordingly seek to prohibit the erection of artificial barriers within it. To this end, Article 30 states that:

> "Quantitative restrictions on imports and all measures having equivalent effect shall, without prejudice to the following provisions, be prohibited between Member States."

The owner of copyright, if he seeks to enforce the territoriality of his copyright by excluding others from importing goods into a particular territory, is putting a "quantitative restriction" on the importation of those goods.

It was at one time considered that Article 30 did not apply to copyright. This is because Article 36 stated that Article 30 (among others) did not preclude prohibitions or restrictions on imports where the protection of industrial and commercial property (that is, copyright) was the justification for the restrictive activity. Article 36 would appear, however, to justify the existence of intellectual property rights but not always their exercise. What is now plain is that any use of copyright so as to divide the countries of the European Union into separate markets will not be encouraged. Thus, for example, a British record manufacturer who publishes a record in both the U.K. and France may not use his copyright to prevent the importation into the U.K. of the records lawfully marketed by him in France.

The principle of the free flow of legally marketed goods within the Community is so strong that it can even permit market distortions. Thus the European Court has ruled that records manufactured in the U.K. (where the musical recording royalty is lower than in Germany) cannot be excluded from Germany, even though this gives an unfair competitive advantage to U.K. manufacturers. Such distortions should eventually be resolved through harmonisation of national copyright laws (see below).

Two other provisions of the Treaty of Rome which attract the exercise of copyright in the European Union are Articles 85 and 86. Article 85 prohibits all agreements and concerted practices which may affect trade between Member States and which have as their object or effect the prevention, restriction or distortion of competition within the Common Market. Article 86 prohibits any abuse of a dominant trade position which affects trade between Member States. Neither of these provisions is, of course, exclusively applicable to copyright; but whether one seeks to exploit one's copyright within the E.C. alone or through licences, one should be wary of them. Article 86 has been held by the European Court to permit the Commission to order copyright owners to license their copyright if failure to do so would amount to an abuse of a dominant position. Contravention of these provisions, apart from being (in likelihood) a civil wrong in the courts of the U.K., can result in a substantial fine being imposed by the Commission of the European Communities.

Harmonisation

The stated aims of the European Union include the progressive harmonisation of domestic laws, on the assumption that every divergence of national laws is inherently capable of distorting the model of perfect competition to which the Community aspires. Following its 1988 Green Paper, "Copyright Issues Requiring Immediate Action", the Commission has had its Directive on the Legal Protection of Computer Programs[2] adopted by the Council of Ministers. This Directive provided for protection of computer software as a literary work (as was accepted previously in the United Kingdom). Its provisions required minor amendments to U.K. law as set out in the Act, which are set out in the Copyright (Computer Programs) Regulations 1992.[3] Further Directives on the Rental and Lending Right, Satellite and Cable Retransmission, Duration of Term and Database Protection have since been issued. All but the latter (which must be implemented in the U.K. and the other Member States by January 1, 1998) have now been incorporated into British law.

[2] 91/250/EEC.
[3] S.I. 1992 No. 3233.

CHAPTER 16

COPYRIGHT AND INFORMATION TECHNOLOGY

Like most other intellectual property rights copyright is in principle a general right and not one which is industry-specific in its applicability. Thus just as the law of patents applies across the range of industries in which innovations occur, including pharmaceuticals, engineering, photography and electronics, and design law protects equally those designs which are applied to domestic appliances, clothing, furniture or motor vehicles, so too copyright applies across a wide range of industries and functions including book publishing, newspapers, the recording industry, cartography, education and now the computer industry. It has been cynically suggested that, while book publishing provided the cradle for copyright, computers have dug its grave. However, as may be seen from the Act itself, copyright has proved highly adaptable and provides a secure bedrock of legal protection upon which investors in new works and products can place their confidence. This confidence has been established and maintained with only minimal industry-specific amendments to the norms of copyright law.

This chapter addresses three areas of concern to modern copyright owners. The first is the impact upon copyright law of the increasing and now nearly universal use of computers. The second is the widespread use of electronic means of sending and receiving mail. The third is the protection of information databases, which are normally stored and accessed by computers. Inevitably, each of these headings contains reference to materials which are addressed specifically or alluded to elsewhere in this book. However, for ease of reference they are also addressed here.

COMPUTERS AND COPYRIGHT

Computer programs

Since computers may be used for the composition, storage, editing, distribution, transmission and copying of all manner of copyright subject-matter, it is to be expected that copyright is the principal legal means by which the use of such subject-matter can be restrained, licensed or controlled. In the U.K. all works created on computers enjoy copyright protection in like measure as if they had been created on other media. Additionally, literary, dramatic, musical and artistic works created by a computer also attract copyright protection if the circumstances of their creation are such that no human contribution to their authorship can be identified (section 9(3) of the Act). Such works do not attract moral rights and enjoy a copyright term of only 50 years following the end of the calendar year of their creation (section 12(7)).

Computer programs are protected as literary works. For the purpose of copyright law, protection is granted both to computer programs and to preparatory design materials for computer programs (sections 3(1)(b) and (c)), regardless of the form or language in which they are expressed and of the medium upon which they are stored. Back-up copies of computer programs may be made (section 50A), but only where it is necessary to make them. It may be doubted whether it is normally necessary to make a back-up copy of any software which is supplied in the form of a manufacturer's diskette which, having been uploaded on to a computer's hard disk, effectively serves as its own back-up. However, the backing-up of software which is downloaded from an online service or a distant website will be more easily justified. The Act contains two other defences to infringement which are unique to computer programs and which owe their existence to the enactment of the European Software Directive (the "Software Directive").[1] The first, in section 50B, permits the decompilation of software when certain specified conditions are fulfilled. This enables software writers to study the interface between computer programs and thus enable one program to operate upon, or in relation to, another program. The second, in section 50C, permits a lawful user of the program to make copies or correct errors if such use is necessary for his lawful use and is not contractually prohibited. A further defence, relating to all "works in electronic form", permits the purchaser of such a work from its previous owner to use or copy it in the same manner as its former owner, if there are no contract terms to the contrary (section 56).

Electrocopying and electronic publication

The two terms mentioned above are not legal terms, but are found in common parlance within the information technology and publishing industries respectively. "Electrocopying" is a general term for copying by any electronic means and it will be seen that, even in 1988, the concept of copying by electronic means had been adequately provided for by statute. By section 17(2) of the Act copying is defined as "reproducing the work in any material form" and a coda to this definition adds: "This includes storing the work in any medium by electronic means". Since section 17(6) then adds that copying "includes the making of copies which are transient or are incidental to some other use of the work" it is plain that the unauthorised screen display of all or a substantial part of a work stored in a computer is a copying of it, just as is the result of the transfer of a file from one disk or other storage medium to another, even if the file is not itself opened and read.

A work may be copied electronically in one of two ways. The copying may be done by an analog(ue) process or by a digital one (analog, the American spelling, is generally preferred in computer industry circles). Analog copying is carried out through the use of some variable physical quantity (normally electricity) to represent equally variable subject-matter such as sounds, letters or numbers. Since this form of copying is effectively performed by the making of a close mechanical analogy, the continual recopying of copied items will result in the degradation and eventual disintegration of the image or subject-matter copied as the approximate quality of the analogised copy becomes more approximate. This effect can be verified by making photocopies of photocopies or by taping copied audio or video cassettes. In contrast, digital copying involves the use of

---

[1] Council Directive 91/250/EEC of May 14, 1991, implemented in the U.K. by the Copyright (Computer Programs) Regulations 1992 (S.I. 1992 No. 3233).

discrete rather than variable quantities; copying is always perfect because it involves a one-to-one correspondence between each unit of the work copied and the resulting copy. The copy, being perfect, can be the first in a chain of copies which will not end, since the one-to-one correspondence of original work to copy remains constant. It has been suggested from time to time that copyright law requires amendment so as to take into account the apparent threat of endless perfect copies. This view is misguided. Copyright treats an unauthorised copy of a work as being an infringement because it is unauthorised, whether it is a good copy, a moderate one or a bad one. Additionally, even under the law as it currently stands it is open to a copyright owner to exploit the fact that both analog and digital copying exists by licensing separately the right to make, or to exploit, both analog and digital copies (or recordings or broadcasts) of his work. It is worthy of note, in this context, that the European Commission has not called for special legislation to address the position of copyright owners with regard to digital recording and broadcasting technologies, despite having invited European copyright-based industries to demand it by issuing a Green Paper, *Copyright and Neighbouring Rights in the Information Society* in the late summer of 1995.

"Electronic publication", like "electrocopying", is a non-legal term which has some grounding in the words of the Act. "Electronic publication" is a term used loosely to indicate the making available of the texts of newspapers and journals in any new technological form, whether on a conventional floppy disk, in CD-ROM format, through an online "host" or via the internet. The Act actually defines "publication" (and related expressions, such as "publish") in terms which, by section 175(2)(b), include "making the work available to the public by means of an electronic retrieval system". Note that this definition does not require the publication to be exclusively, or initially, by means of an electronic retrieval system. Nor does it require any member of the public to have availed himself of the opportunity of retrieving the work. The implications of this definition are substantial and may be of fundamental importance to international copyright: if any work which is stored at a website on the internet is available to a U.K. internet user, that work is presumably taken to be published in the U.K. (and thus in a Berne Union country) and could arguably be said to be entitled to a measure of copyright protection in other Berne Convention countries even if the server which stores its "physical" essence lies outside the Berne Union. This matter, and many other issues relating to electronic publication, require careful thought. As yet, there is very little judicial guidance upon which to rely. It is submitted that traditional concepts of copyright law should be able to cope with new questions, such as the automatic routing of the users from one website to another when the other has a different copyright owner than the first. Despite their technical novelty, they should, from a legal point of view, be soluble.

ELECTRONIC MAIL

Since electronic mail (usually abbreviated to "E-mail", "e-mail" or, increasingly, "email") looks set to challenge both the conventional postal system and the delivery of documents by fax as the prime means of communicating personal written messages between individuals and organisations, or even within organisations, it is appropriate to consider its impact on copyright. As previously stated, copyright is a "one right fits all" sort of right, so the reader need not feel surprised to learn that copyright protects email in the same manner as it protects conventional mail. Emails, like ordinary letters, normally constitute original literary works, though they may occasionally carry art and musical work too. Any unauthorised use of them constitutes a potential infringement, although many unauthorised uses which are made of emails (for example, copying them on to interested third parties or reproducing them in full in the course of an electronically generated reply) will almost certainly be regarded in legal terms as being covered by an implied licence. It may however be questioned whether any use of an email which contravenes the general norms of conduct (the "netiquette") which pertain within a particular service or on a particular noticeboard upon which emails are posted can be said to be permitted by the implication of a licence.

DATABASE PROTECTION UNDER U.K. LAW

In the U.K. copyright can subsist in a literary work consisting of a "table or compilation" separately from the copyright which may subsist in any works comprised in the table or compilation under section 3(1). Thus collection of information – databases (including electronic databases), enjoy the same level of copyright protection as any other literary work.

It has been argued that some online databases are also protected as "cable programmes" as defined in the complex and lengthy definition of such works under section 7. However, this may only be said of non-interactive databases, since interactive databases are excluded from the definition of "cable programme service" (s. 7(2)(a)).

Computer programs are not necessarily databases, though they are also a "literary work" which is protected by copyright, and though many online databases are customarily accessed by means of the use of a computer program which may be supplied or licensed together with it.

INTRODUCTION TO THE NEW E.U. DATABASE DIRECTIVE

It has been estimated that the volume of the increase annually in information generated today equals the total information in circulation in the world 50 years ago. If (as seems possible) this is so, we should not be surprised that information has become a resource of great value today and has become a tradable commodity. Many specialised companies produce or operate databases, many of which are woven together in a complex inter-relationship of international data hosts, providers and consumers. This, plus divergences in the laws of E.U. Member States regarding the legal protection of databases (see below) means that harmonisation is needed so that database creators and operators can compete fairly against their international rivals.

The Directive for the Legal Protection of Databases ("the Directive") has a long history. The Commission's Green Paper on Copyright and the Challenge of Technology[2] addressed for the first time the harmonisation of database protection in the various E.U. Member States. A proposal for a draft directive on the legal protection of databases was submitted by the Commission in April 1992. This proposal was met with confusion and bewilderment within many sections of the database-producing industries, who had not considered that there was any inadequacy in the degree of protection already available

[2] COM (88) 172 Final, June 7, 1988.

under national law, particularly in the U.K. (which hosted an estimated 50 per cent of the European database industry at that time).

An amended proposal was adopted in October 1993 and a Common Position was reached by the Council of Ministers on July 10, 1995. This led to the Final Directive[3] on the Legal Protection of Databases, which was adopted on March 11, 1996.

The deadline for implementation of this Directive in all E.U. Member States is January 1, 1998. So far no Member State has implemented the Directive. In August the U.K. published a consultative document on the implementation of the Directive, which is disscussed below.

THE DIRECTIVE IN BRIEF

What is a database?

The definition of "database" is

> "a collection of independent works, data or other materials arranged in a systematic or methodical way and individually accessible by electronic or other means" (Article 1(2)).

"Accessible by electronic ... means" suggests that the definition is not limited to traditional databases but includes all forms of online databases, thus taking into account the rapidly increasing importance of modern communication networks. Recital 13 tells us that this phrase is to be interpreted widely so as to encompass electronic, electromagnetic, electro-optical and analogous means. It, therefore, matters not what kind of carrier the product is stored on, be it hard disk, floppy disk, CD-ROM, CD-I or anything else.

Recital 20 makes clear that protection under the Directive

> "may also apply to the materials necessary for the operation or consultation of certain databases, such as thesaurus and indexation systems".

Computer programs used in the making or operation of electronic databases are, however, by virtue of Article 1(3), expressly excluded from the scope of the Directive. They are protected under the E.U. Software Directive.

Phonograms were also expressly excluded in previous drafts, but this exclusion was dropped. However, Recital 19 provides useful guidance when it states that

> " ... as a rule, the compilation of several recordings of musical performances on a C.D. does not come within the scope of this Directive, both because, as a compilation, it does not meet the conditions for copyright protection and because it does not represent a substantial enough investment to be eligible under the *sui generis* right."

Although computer programs are the only subject-matter to be expressly excluded, others are implicit in the qualification that a database must be "independent". We have little guidance in the Directive as to the meaning which is to be vested in this word, but we may hypothesise as follows: Recital 17 says that the Directive especially excludes single works

---

[3] 96/9/E.C.

such as films, musical compositions or books comprising distinct elements or materials (*e.g.* frames or chapters) which, though perhaps separately accessible, are interrelated and dependent on one another. This could give rise to problems with regard to some multimedia products, for example complex games, which are viewed by the user as a single work but which are made up of layer upon layer of separately identifiable features.

The definition of database also requires that it be "arranged in a systematic or methodical way". What does this mean? Recital 21 says it does not mean that the materials have to be physically stored in an organised manner, which is of crucial significance for electronic databases. More than this cannot be confidently predicted.

The requirement that the contents of a database be "individually accessible" should also be noted. The contents of multimedia products are, by definition, interactively (*i.e.* individually) accessible. The same can be said of online databases which are driven by search software.

What databases are protected?

The Directive extends to "any form" of database, whether electronic or not (unlike the initial proposals, which only dealt with electronic databases). What policy underlies the extension of protection so as to cover not only electronic databases but also manual ones? Three reasons have been offered for this, as follows:

- the distinction between electronic and non-electronic databases is easier to identify than it is to define;
- it eliminates the problem that two different databases with the same content, one electronic, the other not, might receive different levels of protection, even though the investment in compiling the data may have been the same in each case;
- an inclusivist approach towards the protection of all forms of database is in line with the TRIPs Agreement and the WIPO Copyright Treaty (see below).

THE DIRECTIVE AND COPYRIGHT PROTECTION

Article 3(1) provides that databases which, "by reason of the selection or arrangement of their contents, constitute the author's own intellectual creation shall be protected as such by copyright". Article 3(2) makes clear that "the protection of databases provided for by this Directive shall not extend to their contents and shall be without prejudice to any rights subsisting in those contents themselves". Thus it is the structure of the database (or its "expression", according to Recital 15) which is protected. The Directive's originality test (that a copyright-protected database must be the author's "own intellectual creation") means that countries such as the U.K. and Ireland which still allow copyright protection for compilations meeting the lower "sweat of the brow" or "skill and labour" originality standard may have to reduce the scope of copyright protection for databases. Interestingly, neither in fact did for software – the problem was effectively ignored when the Software Directive was implemented. This may happen again, since the test of originality in the Database Directive corresponds to that of the Software Directive.

No other criteria shall be applied to determine a database's eligibility for copyright protection. In particular, no aesthetic or qualitative merits may be considered (Recital 16).

Once is it deemed protected by copyright, a database will be protected by copyright for the normal duration of 70 years from the end of the year in which the author dies.

Another limitation on copyright protection arises from the requirement that a copyright-protected database be the result of a process of "selection or arrangement" (this phraseology is also found in the Berne Convention, the TRIPs Agreement and the WIPO Convention on Copyright). Electronic databases are by their nature rarely "selective", as their commercial value mostly lies in their comprehensive nature. The selection function which copyright requires is a function which, in the normal course of things, would appear to lie with the user.

The "arrangement" of the contents of a multimedia product can be understood in two ways. If understood to mean the way its contents are physically stored on the data medium, it can be argued that this is determined by the use of computer programs. Even if it is understood to mean the manner in which the contents are presented to the user, the freedom of the user to choose the contents he or she wants to look at still depends on software. In either case, there seems no reason why the producer should benefit.

Until we see how the courts or U.K. implementing legislation interpret these terms, it is difficult to tell how they will work in practice.

Copyright restricted acts are similar to those provided in most national copyright laws and include:

(a)   temporary or permanent reproduction
(b)   translation
(c)   adaptation or any form of alteration
(d)   any form of distribution to the public
(e)   communication, display or performance to the public
(f)   making a database available by means other than the distribution of tangible copies (*e.g.* by means of online transmission).

There are four optional exceptions to the restricted acts which provide E.U. Member States with the facility to enact certain statutory defences: reproduction for private purposes, teaching or scientific purposes, reasons of public security or reasons of administrative or judicial procedure. However, a "catch-all" clause enables Member States to apply exceptions which are "traditionally authorised under national law". Despite this, the U.K. appears to intend to limit the "fair dealing" exception in respect of research to non-commercial research only.

Who owns the copyright in a database? In keeping with the norms of copyright in literary works, the right holder is the author, defined as the natural person or group of natural persons who create the database or, where the legislation of the Member State so permits, the legal person designated by that legislation.

It is notable that the Directive does not harmonise the rules concerning first ownership. This is in contrast to earlier proposals, which contained a presumption that the employee who creates a database in the course of his employment is the first owner of the copyright. It is also in contrast with the Software Directive, which contains a presumption that the employer is the first owner.

In at least one respect, the copyright for which the Directive requires provision to be made under national law differs from more traditional forms of copyright. Moral rights are outside the scope of the Directive, so that Member States are free to apply their own provisions if they choose to do so (Recital 28). Of the four so-called moral rights which exist under U.K. copyright law, it is difficult to see how in practice any of them is likely to be of more than occasional and tangential relevance to the database industries.

THE DIRECTIVE AND "SUI GENERIS" PROTECTION

Article 7(1) creates a new right, in addition to but inferior to copyright, where

> "...there has been, qualitatively or quantitatively, a substantial investment in either the obtaining, verification or presentation of the contents"

of a database. This right is the right to prevent unfair extraction.

The new *sui generis* right applies irrespective of the eligibility of the contents of the database for copyright protection (unlike the 1992 proposal, which withheld *sui generis* protection from all databases which included copyright protected material). The right applies irrespective of the eligibility of the database for copyright protection under Article 3(1).

For the purposes of this new right, "substantial investment" may consist of the input of financial resources and/or the expending of time, effort and energy (Recital 40). This is effectively a "sweat of the brow" approach. Restricted acts in respect of *sui generis* right are the unauthorised extraction and/or re-utilisation of the whole or a substantial part. This is subject to the commercial interest of the maker and is capable of being ascertained in relation to criteria which are both qualitative and quantitative.

"Extraction" covers all different forms of temporary or permanent transfer of at least a substantial part of the contents of a database to another medium, however this transfer is achieved.

"Re-utilisation" means any form of making available to the public all or a substantial part of the contents of a database by the distribution of copies, by renting or by on-line or other forms of transmission. Public lending is not mentioned in this context. The repeated and systematic extraction and/or re-utilisation of insubstantial parts of the contents of a database which conflicts with the normal exploitation of the database, or unreasonably prejudices its maker, is also prohibited. Nor may a lawful user prejudice the rights of owners of copyright in the contents of a database.

The exceptions to infringement largely relate to "extraction" and are similar to those under the copyright provisions: they enable extraction to be made lawful for private purposes, teaching or scientific research and public security or judicial proceedings. However, unlike the copyright provisions, there is no "catch-all" clause.

The right holder is the maker of the database, *i.e.* the person taking the initiative and the risk of investing. This may or may not also be the author.

The *sui generis* right may be voluntarily assigned and licensed. The statutory licensing of works subject to the *sui generis* right, subject to a reasonable royalty, had been suggested in order to prevent monopolies. This proposal was much criticised and was consequently dropped after the second draft. Control of abuses of the *sui generis* right within the E.U. will, therefore, have to be left to Article 86 of the Treaty of Rome, as was done in respect of copyright in collections of data in the *Magill* case. However, when the Commission reviews the operation of the Directive after three years, it must pay particular regard to the question of whether the *sui generis* right has led to any abuse of a dominant position or any other interference with competition.

Protection lasts for 15 years from the start of the year following completion of the database, but this is a misleading statement of the practical effect of the Directive in most instances involving commercial databases. Substantial changes in the contents which result in the database being considered to be a substantial new investment will result in the database being regarded as new, with a further term of protection. Thus dynamic databases such as telephone lists will be protected in effect indefinitely (it is debatable whether this is consistent with the underlying principle that copyright in compilations is intended to protect skill and effort put into preparing the compilation as a whole). It is only static databases of materials that are not themselves protected by copyright which will in practice lose protection after 15 years. In the U.K. existing databases upto 15 years old, and which do not attract copyright protection, will qualify for *sui generis* protection. Databases currently protected by copyright will remain protected by copyright for the remainder of their copyright terms.

INTERNATIONAL CONSIDERATIONS

The position of non-E.U. countries

By contrast to copyright, in which the major international conventions require countries to grant reciprocity of protection to authors of other Member States, the *sui generis* right only applies to databases whose makers are nationals of E.U. Member States or who have their habitual residence in the E.U. (Article 11(1)). Companies are treated in the same way (Article 11(2)). Beyond this, protection may only be extended to databases by means of reciprocal agreements. This is a particular problem for the U.S., in which the extent to which copyright protection prevents the copying of databases has become increasingly uncertain in recent years.

The Directive's discrimination against non-E.U. States has to be viewed against the backdrop of the U.S. Semiconductor Chip Protection Act which discriminated against, among others, European citizens and companies. Such discrimination is permitted under TRIPs Article 3 (National Treatment) and Article 4 (Most Favoured Nation Treatment) if it is expressed in terms of "protection of intellectual property". Unlike copyright, the new *sui generis* right is not one of the defined categories of intellectual property within the TRIPs treaty.

International treaties

The Berne Convention protects "collections of literary works such as encyclopaedias and anthologies which by reason of their content, constitute intellectual creations" (Article 2(5)). This obviously has some impact upon the protection of databases.

In this context, two points should be made:

- The Berne Convention does not cover electronic databases. However, the WIPO Copyright Treaty adopted on December 20, 1996 includes and protects electronic databases (Article 5: "Compilations of data or other material, in any form, which by reason of the selection or arrangement of their contents constitute intellectual creations, are protected as such. This protection does not extend to the data or the material itself and is without prejudice to any copyright subsisting in the data or material contained in the compilation"). Similarly, the TRIPs Agreement adopted on December 22, 1995 protects "compilations of data or other material, whether in machine readable or other form" (Article 10). This adds little to existing U.K. law.

● The term "intellectual creations" causes the same problems as the *droit d'auteur* countries have with respect to electronic databases. In the light of this, the European Commission proposed in February 1996 the international harmonisation of the *sui generis* right protection of databases along the lines of the Database Directive. However, the WIPO Treaty on Intellectual Property in respect of Databases, which would have followed the E.U. Database Directive, was not agreed as part of last December's negotiations. There will be an extraordinary session of WIPO Governing Bodies during September of this year to decide on a schedule of further preparatory work on that draft. An intergovernmental meeting is thought likely in 2000.

The Proposed Regulation

In August 1997 the Department of Trade and Industry published a consultative paper to which it appended a draft of the Copyright and Rights in Databases Regulations 1997. Since the draft is relatively uncontroversial and its provisions appear to fall squarely within the requirements of the Directive, it is likely to be adopted with little risk of major amendment. Part I of the draft provides for the date of commencement to be January 1, 1998 and for its application throughout the U.K. Part II amends the Act to enable it to make adequate provision for the protection of databases which achieve the necessary level of creativity. Part III establishes the *sui generis* database right, while Part IV contains savings and transitional provisions. There are two additional Schedules to the draft: the first addresses the "public interest" dimension of database right by limiting the effect of its exercise in respect of parliamentary or judicial proceedings, materials open to public inspection, public records and acts performed under statutory authority; the second deals with the reference of licensing schemes for database rights to the Copyright Tribunal.

In short, with regard to copyright, the draft provides that a database is an original literary work only if "by reason of the selection or arrangement of the contents of the database, the database constitutes the author's own intellectual creation", in accordance with Article 3(1) of the Directive; it removes the fair dealing exception from the doing of restricted acts for the purpose of commercial research; it also affirms the right of a person who is entitled to use a databse to perform such acts as are necessary for the exercise of the right to use it and renders void any contract term which seeks to prevent such use.

As to database right, the draft vests ownership in the database's "maker", that is "the person who takes the initiative in making a database and assumes the risk of investing in its making". A provision analogous to Crown copyright governs databases made on behalf of the Crown; infringement involves the extraction or re-utilisation of all or a substantial part of it (this includes repeated and systematic insubstantial extractions). The term of protection will be 15 years. Only where the maker is a national or resident of an EEA state, or a company incorporated in such a state, will a database attract protection.

CHAPTER 17

COLLECTIVE LICENSING

INTRODUCTION

Collective licensing is now a very prominent feature of the copyright scene, and indeed it may not be long before all the acts restricted by copyright in literary and musical works, excepting only publishing and adaptation, will be collectively administered. This is so much a necessity in present conditions that the official attitude to it in the U.K. seems to be one of endorsement, subject only to the proviso that the collecting societies' charges are, unless fixed by statute, referable to an independent and government-appointed tribunal, which has power to vary them.

The monopolistic nature of collective licensing has been recognised in the U.K., most recently by the Monopolies and Mergers Commission (MMC) Reports into Phonographic Performance Limited and the Performing Right Society and by the European Commission in its decisions on French discotheques. The lack of an alternative is recognised as requiring controls to ensure that collecting societies do not abuse their market power.

Collective licensing is of two kinds: "blanket" licensing and centralised licensing per item. Blanket licensing means the grant of a licence that effectively conveys the rights in the entirety of a vast or even virtually all-embracing repertoire. Centralised licensing means licensing through a central organisation of the rights in individual works, though possibly on standardised lines. Examples of both kinds exist in the U.K.

It is clear that blanket licensing is not altogether congruous with the traditional "exclusive right" granted to authors under copyright law. Indeed it was accepted by them, and in particular by their publishers, but only with reluctance. However, in adopting it as a necessity they have argued that, since some of their rights could in practice only be exercised in this way under modern conditions, they should not be thought to have renounced their claim to an exclusive privilege of control over their creations which is based on the creative act itself. Nevertheless, there is no doubt that they thereby give a hostage to their economic fortunes insofar as they are subject, directly or indirectly, to influences beyond their control, including that of the government. In countries such as the U.K., which is greatly productive in all the creative spheres and where authors are assured of support for their interests up to the highest levels, this may not be of great moment, although the reaction of the government to the regulation of collecting societies, as indicated in their acceptance of the MMC Report into Phonographic Performance Limited (HMSO 1988, Cm. 530), is clearly coloured by considerations of import/export consequences. In copyright importing countries, including some of the advanced countries as well as developing countries, this is a highly significant consideration.

PRACTICAL CONSIDERATIONS

The operation of a single licensing society for each area of copyright, or of a single body for all collective licensing areas, would seem to possess obvious advantages over competition between competing societies. Administrative costs, which have to be covered by royalties, would be increased if there existed a plurality of licensors, since individual works are not in price competition with one another and, if each society had a large repertoire, users might be compelled to hold more than one licence. It is, moreover, a great convenience to the users to be able to deal with a single body.

The problem that has activated the blanket licensing system is that of controlling and ensuring payment for the use of works, and it is best appreciated in relation to the public performance and broadcasting of non-dramatic (non-stage) music, which is now so pervasive as absolutely to defy regulation by contract between individual copyright owners and music users. The necessity for blanket licensing in this field is so compelling that societies for this purpose now exist in all countries where copyright is effective. In the U.K. the society of this kind is the Performing Right Society Limited (PRS), 29–33 Berners Street, London W1P 4AA.

HOW DOES A TYPICAL COLLECTING SOCIETY FUNCTION?

The system operated by public performance societies such as the PRS is that in each country the composers, authors (lyric writers) and music publishers combine to assign or exclusively license their non-dramatic (non-stage) public performance and broadcasting rights to a national association, which is thus in effective possession of the national repertoire of copyright music for non-dramatic public performance and broadcasting. Each national society may also, under contracts of reciprocal representation with the similar associations in other countries, include in its licence cover the rights in the repertoire of all these other associations; in short, it may grant a coverage of worldwide extent. At intervals, as agreed by the reciprocal contracts, a clearing is effected between the national societies of their respective credits.

Each national society establishes tariffs for its blanket licence on a scale proportionate to the prospective use or as endorsed by the users or the Copyright Tribunal. The multiple users, such as breweries, retail shop chains, discotheques and others, clear performances through a single contract negotiated by their head offices. Under this system even a user on the scale of the BBC or the independent television and radio broadcasters, using some hundreds of thousands of works every year on a constantly changing repertoire, can by a single annual licence clear the broadcasting rights in that repertoire so that they no longer have problems about their authority to broadcast "non-dramatically" virtually any work they or their performing artists wish to use. Because large-scale licences are negotiated centrally, it is indeed probable that few performers (and even in some cases the responsible managers of entertainment premises licensed at source) are ever aware of their legal liability in respect of the public performance and broadcasting of copyright works.

The societies endeavour so far as possible to keep strict records of works used in order to be able to distribute royalties collected both to their own members and to their affiliated foreign societies in proportion to the recorded use of copyright works. The U.K. broadcasters co-operate fully with the PRS in this regard, but there are obviously many circumstances in which programme returns cannot reasonably be expected (juke boxes in public houses and background music in shops, for example). The society will generally distribute royalties from such establishments on the basis of programmes effectively received on the ground that these will be generally representative, or it may allocate such royalties for other functions authorised by the members, including welfare services.

These licensing bodies are highly conscious of their responsibilities, at least in the more advanced countries. However, they are never likely wholly to escape from external interests. This criticism does not, however, usually attach to the system as such but to operational procedures, which are necessarily highly complex. Perhaps the least satisfactory aspect of the system is that in the developing countries, in some of which copyright may be more nominal than effective, and in others where the balance of royalties is always and inevitably a debit one, the societies may have difficulties of various kinds that impair their effectiveness. But the system works, and the big users at least would not want to change it.

What happens if There is no "Monopolistic" Collecting Society?

In the case of dramatic works, whether straight plays or musical plays or operas, there is an entirely different situation. In the U.K. and generally in the copyright countries it is still the practice to control the stage and broadcasting rights in such works individually, although this is usually done for authors by their publishers or professional agents. Thus there is in the U.K. no organisation centralising the licensing of such works. However, the continued expansion in the technologies of communication, in particular cable television and broadcasting via satellites, will make control of use and infringement increasingly difficult in this area of copyright, so that collective licensing may become necessary in it also. In fact, in Continental Europe and generally in the countries of the author's right system, as contrasted with the copyright system, this is already done. The E.U. Directive on satellite broadcasting and cable retransmission are likely to encourage the development of such societies in the U.K. The Directive requires copyright licensing for cable retransmission to be accomplished collectively, rather than by individual copyright owners.

Rights in Sound Recordings

Blanket licensing is currently operated in the U.K. by Phonographic Performance Limited (PPL), Ganton House, 14–22 Ganton Street, London W1V 1LB, which licenses the performing and broadcasting rights in sound recordings (as distinct from the reproduction right, if any, in the works recorded). However, these are rights that are at present granted in few other countries. E.U. proposals in relation to the ratification of the Rome Convention or the WIPO Performances and Phonograms Treaty should ensure that such rights at least exist within Europe. They do not yet, however, exist in the U.S. PPL does collect royalties for use of sound recordings produced outside the U.K., but such royalties are distributed directly to beneficiaries in the U.K.

Mechanical Recording Rights in Musical Works

Centralised licensing is operated in the U.K. and abroad by the Mechanical-Copyright Protection Society Limited (MCPS) of Elgar House, 41 Streatham High Road, London

SW16 1ER, the agency for the licensing of the mechanical recording rights in musical works. MCPs has now merged operationally with the PRS. With the repeal of the statutory mechanical recording right in section 8 of the 1956 Act, the MCPS has, after proceedings before the Copyright Tribunal, agreed blanket licences for most commercially produced sound recordings with the U.K. record industry's trade association, the British Phonographic Industry Limited (BPI). It has also negotiated special arrangements of a blanket nature with the BBC and the commercial television companies in respect of "off air" recordings of educational material, but otherwise in this field licences are normally granted on a per item basis.

The PRS, because of a special situation in the U.S., licenses on a per item basis its members' synchronisation rights, that is the right to incorporate specially written film music on the film soundtrack. These synchronisation rights are licensed to film producers under arrangements designed to ensure that performance royalties are paid for the performance of the music in cinemas in the U.S.

Following the recommended actions of the Whitford Committee the Copyright Tribunal now has jurisdiction over this synchronisation right, together with, in the case of musical works at least, licences in respect of the reproduction right generally.

FURTHER DEVELOPMENT

It is generally accepted that there will have to be an extension of centralised and blanket licensing to cope with the modern problems of multiple copying and pervasive communication of authors' works. The Act now contemplates schemes of this kind for two vital areas — that is, reprography and audio-visual recording — in which, unlike the fields of public performance, the recording of musical works and broadcasting, this solution is not yet operative.

There is, however, yet another area in which collective administration is necessary, although it was outside the Whitford Committee's remit; that is the Public Lending Right (see Chapter 20), which is not a copyright and which is supported by a government subsidy.

Already there exist associations formed to administer the rights in these areas. At the time of writing they are:

The Authors Lending and Copyright Society Limited (ALCS)
33 Alfred Place
London WC1E 7DP
Tel: 0171 255 2034
Fax: 0171 323 0486

The Publishers' Licensing Society (PLS)
90 Tottenham Court Road
London W1P 9HE
Tel: 0171 436 5931
Fax: 0171 436 3986

The Education Recording Agency (ERA)
33 Alfred Place
London WC1E 7DP
Tel: 0171 436 4883
Fax: 0171 636 2402

The objectives of these new groups are to press for and make practical the establishment of collective (or blanket) licensing of the use of works and the collection and distribution to the rights owners of the royalties, levy proceeds or government subsidy attaching to the exercise of these rights. In the case of VARS these royalties would include those resulting from the exercise of the *droit de suite* if that right is granted in the U.K. (see page 56).

Most national collective licensing societies belong to the International Confederation of Authors' and Composers' Societies (CISAC), whose headquarters are in Paris. CISAC does not purport to direct the constitution, rules or methods of operation of its affiliated societies, but it does lay down certain principles of good administration to which its member societies are expected to conform. CISAC also collaborates with UNESCO and WIPO in aiding the developing countries to stimulate the production of creative works by their national authors, among other ways through effective copyright protection.

CISAC's work is strictly independent of all political or religious affiliations.

CHAPTER 18

COPYRIGHT TRIBUNAL

INTRODUCTION

The Copyright Tribunal is the successor to the Performing Right Tribunal established under the 1956 Act. The new name, the Copyright Tribunal, is a recognition that the Tribunal is now concerned with copyright licensing as a whole, rather than just performing rights.

The need for such a Tribunal has been recognised since 1929 when a Select Committee of the House of Commons recognised that collecting societies were the only practicable way for performing rights to be dealt with. For societies to function effectively they need to have a monopoly and as monopolists can abuse their position. The Select Committee said:

> "Your Committee consider that a supermonopoly can abuse its powers by refusing to grant licences upon reasonable terms so as to prejudice the trade or industry of persons carrying on business in this country and to be contrary to the public interest, and that it should be open to those persons to obtain relief in respect of such abuse by appeal to arbitration or some other tribunal. This should apply only in those cases where the ownership or control of copyright has been transferred to an Association."

In the light of this recommendation the U.K. delegation to the Brussels Conference in 1948 for the revision of the Berne Copyright Union Convention made a declaration that the U.K. was free to enact legislation necessary in the public interest to prevent or deal with any abuse of monopoly powers. A similar reservation has been made to subsequent revisions to the Berne Convention.

Recognition of collecting societies as monopolies has extended to the European Commission, many of whose copyright cases have dealt with collecting societies. Even if copyright is not itself a monopoly, because it prevents someone only from copying or making use of a work and does not restrict anyone who freshly invents or creates a work, collecting societies cannot often operate effectively unless they are monopolies.

The copyright committee set up in 1951 (The Gregory Committee) to advise on the revision of the Copyright Act 1911 also considered the matter of collective licensing. For the reasons adduced by the 1929 Committee, it recommended that a new Act should include provisions for a tribunal having jurisdiction not only over authors' performing and broadcasting rights, but also over record makers' performance rights in their recordings. Under the 1956 Act the Performing Right Tribunal had jurisdiction over both the broadcasting and public performance rights of authors and those of owners of copyright in sound recordings and broadcasts. The Performing Right Tribunal's jurisdiction was not limited to the restraint of abuse. Section 25(5) of that Act required it to consider the matters in dispute and, after giving the parties a right to be heard, to make such order as was determined to be reasonable in the circumstances.

The Whitford Committee recommended that the Performing Right Tribunal should be renamed the Copyright Tribunal and that it be given a rather wider jurisdiction to settle disputes arising from any blanket licensing scheme operated by any collecting society. This was on the basis that reprographic copying and the reproduction of musical works and film soundtracks would eventually be the subject of blanket licensing schemes. The Whitford Committee also recommended that the Tribunal should have the power to review the statutory royalty for the reproduction of musical works in the form of sound recordings. There is no longer such a statutory licence (it was abolished by the Act), but the resultant licensing scheme is within the jurisdiction of the Tribunal.

Performing Rights in International Law

Under the Paris text of the Berne Convention of 1971 authors have the exclusive right of public performance and broadcasting of their works and also that of any communication to the public by wire or to rebroadcast the work. However, the Convention provides that member countries may determine the conditions under which those rights are exercised. The Rome Convention, the International Convention for the Protection of Performers, Producers of Phonograms and Broadcasting Organisations 1971, provides under Article 15(2) that any contracting state may provide the same kind of limitations with regard to the producers of phonograms and broadcasting organisations as it provides in connection with the protection of copyright in literary and artistic works.

Membership of the Copyright Tribunal

The Copyright Tribunal is established pursuant to section 145 of the Act. Its membership was widened with the introduction of the Act because of complaints about the slowness of cases before the Performing Right Tribunal. Such slowness was no surprise, given that all members were part-time and that parties invariably underestimated the length of cases. The Copyright Tribunal, however, retains the same administrative difficulties as the Performing Right Tribunal, still being located in the Patent Office and having only one full-time member of staff, administering a Tribunal whose decisions can have multi-million pound effects.

With the widening of its jurisdiction to encompass all forms of collective licensing under Chapter VII of the Act, together with specific heads of jurisdiction such as powers consequent on Monopolies and Mergers Commission reports and television programme listings, the Tribunal has a greatly increased workload.

The Act provides that the Tribunal shall consist of a chairman and two deputy chairmen appointed by the Lord Chancellor and between two and eight ordinary members appointed by the Secretary of State for Trade and Industry. Currently the Chairman is a retired solicitor and the Deputy Chairmen, a practising barrister and a Scottish solicitor. One of the three is required to sit on any reference together with two or more other members. There are currently only six other members.

Procedure

Section 150 gives the Lord Chancellor power to make procedural rules for the Copyright Tribunal including the incorporation of the procedural powers set out in the Arbitration Act 1996. The current rules are the Copyright Tribunal Rules.[1] They were amended following the introduction of the Broadcasting Act 1990 by the Copyright Tribunal (Amendments) Rules 1991[2] and are based on the rules of the former Performing Right Tribunal. Their purpose is to ensure the expeditious disposal of proceedings. Forms are prescribed for the commencement of proceedings before the Tribunal. The rules specify who should be parties to proceedings and require the Tribunal to apply the rules of natural justice, giving parties a right to state their cases in writing or orally. The overriding provision of the Rules gives the Tribunal power to regulate its own procedure.

Applications or references to the Tribunal may be advertised and the resultant advertisement must provide information about objections to applications and applications to be made a party to the proceedings. The Chairman of the Tribunal has yet to exercise his discretion not to advertise proceedings before the Tribunal. If a party applies to intervene in Tribunal proceedings, the existing parties have a right of objection.

Proceedings are commenced by the filing of a notice accompanied by a statement of case. Thereafter, the other party and any intervenor is required to serve a reply or answer to the applicant's statement of case, rather like a defence in court proceedings. The Chairman of the Tribunal has the power to give directions as to the further conduct of proceedings, including deciding when and if there are to be oral hearings, procedure relating to evidence, the exchange of written arguments and the form of evidence on applications. The Tribunal has issued a Practice Direction, dealing in great detail with directions in proceedings before it. These directions are similar to those in High Court litigation, although they are less formal. Evidence is usually by way of signed statement rather than by affidavit. The rules do provide for procedural steps such as discovery, which are dealt with in a more limited manner than in court proceedings, as the issues to be determined by the Tribunal are generally wider and not as clearly defined. The Tribunal is given power to administer oaths or to take affirmations and to issue subpoenas.

In the absence of an order to the contrary, proceedings are in public and evidence may be given orally. While this is the case few have been interested in the past in Tribunal proceedings and, as the Tribunal usually sits in the Patent Office, security arrangements and considerations of space severely curtail the public gallery.

Parties have a right to be represented before the Copyright Tribunal. Unlike the courts, any person may act as an agent for a party before the Copyright Tribunal. An agent must be appointed in writing and notice of appointment needs to be served on the Tribunal. There are wide rights of audience for barristers, solicitors or legally unqualified persons. The hours of opening of the Tribunal are specified, with a somewhat late start at 10.00 a.m., and an early finish, 4.00 p.m. Aside from what is set down specifically in the

[1] S.I. 1989 No. 1129.
[2] S.I. 1991 No. 201.

rules, the Tribunal has the power to regulate its own procedure and has been forced to depart from the strict letter of its procedural rules in so doing.

The rules appear to be comprehensive and consistent with the expeditious disposal of cases. The major drawback is the nature of the Tribunal itself. Although the number of members has been increased since the Tribunal was renamed under the Act, its members are either retired or have another job. This means an inevitable delay in proceedings, co-ordinating the diaries of busy people.

The Tribunal is required to give its decisions in writing. The Secretary is directed to make copies of the Tribunal's decisions available for public inspection and, if need be, to advertise short particulars of a decision.

APPEALS

Under section 152 of the Act appeals are available to the High Court, or in the case of proceedings in Scotland, to the Court of Sessions, on a point of law arising from a decision to the Tribunal. There is no appeal on the facts found by the Tribunal. Appeals must be brought within 28 days of the decision, or in such other period as the court allows. The lodgement of such an appeal effectively stays the Tribunal's proceedings. Parties may also apply to have orders of the Tribunal suspended pending decisions on such points of law.

COSTS

The Tribunal has the right under section 151 to order payment of costs by either party, which costs may be taxed. It has exercised this power in the same manner as it is exercised by the courts. It is also empowered to collect fees. A new section 151A, introduced on November 1, 1996 following the passage of the Broadcasting Act 1996, provides for a direction or order which relates to the broadcasting of a work or its inclusion within a cable programme service to include an award of simple interest.

JURISDICTION OF THE TRIBUNAL

The Tribunal's functions, as defined in section 149 of the Act, are to hear and determine those matters allotted to it under the Act. The current list of these is as follows: reference of licensing schemes; applications with respect to entitlement to licences under licensing schemes; references or applications with respect to licensing by licensing bodies, or appeals against the coverage of licensing schemes or licences; applications to settle royalties or other sums payable for the rental of sound recordings of films or computer programs (this jurisdiction has not yet been vested in the Tribunal); applications to settle terms of copyright licences as of right; application to consent on behalf of performers under Part II of the Act dealing with performers' protection; determination of the royalty or other remuneration paid to the trustees for the Hospital for Sick Children on the performance of *Peter Pan*; applications to settle payment for use as of right of sound recordings in broadcasting and cable programme services; and applications under Schedule 17 of the Broadcasting Act 1990 to determine applications for payment for the use of information about television programmes as of right.

The major part of the Tribunal's jurisdiction, as it has been historically, is in relation to collective licensing, which is dealt with in relation to licensing schemes and licensing bodies. A "licensing body" defined in section 116 of the Act as a society or other organisation whose main object is the negotiation or granting of copyright licences and whose objects include the granting of licences covering the works of more than one author. The licensing body may be either the owner of copyright or an agent for the copyright owner. It can only be a collective licensing body. Single and collective works are excluded from this head of jurisdiction, as are works commissioned by a single entity. This presumably excludes the licensing of works such as Time-Life cookery books. A "licensing scheme" is also defined in section 116 as a scheme setting out the classes of case in which the operator of the scheme is willing to grant copyright licences and the terms on which those licences will be granted. Summary provisions relating to licensing schemes together with the other parts of the Tribunal's jurisdiction are set out below.

LICENSING SCHEMES

The types of licensing schemes over which the Tribunal has jurisdiction are licensing schemes relating to literary, dramatic, musical or artistic works or films and their reproduction, performance, broadcasting or inclusion in a cable programme service. There is no jurisdiction over licensing schemes relating to adaptation or the right to issue copies of the work to the public. There is jurisdiction over all licensing schemes in relation to sound recordings, broadcasts, cable programme services and typographical arrangements of published editions. A special jurisdiction may be brought into force, relating to the exercise of the rental right in sound recordings, films and computer programs, if a statutory instrument to that effect is made by the Secretary of State.

Performing and broadcasting rights in musical works have long been regulated by the Performing Right Society Limited and similar rights in sound recordings by Phonographic Performance Limited. Those two companies are the most frequent parties to Copyright Tribunal proceedings.

Section 118 gives licensing bodies the right to refer proposed schemes to the Tribunal. The Tribunal may then determine whether or not the scheme is reasonable in all the circumstances. Existing licensing schemes can be referred either by potential licensees or their representatives under section 119. Either the licensing body or potential licensees may refer existing schemes while an order relating to them is in force, although not within a year of the making of the order.

If potential licensees have been denied a licence they may apply for a licence, or apply for amendment of the terms of that licence, under section 121, in which case the Tribunal may determine the terms of the licence. Such orders are reviewable. In all cases where there is an order of the Tribunal in force in relation to a licensing scheme, and where those within a class to whom the order applies either pay the charges set out in that scheme, or give an undertaking to pay those amounts when they are ascertained, and otherwise comply with the terms of the licences, they are given immunity from copyright infringement.

LICENSING BY LICENSING BODIES

The Tribunal also has jurisdiction in relation to licences by licensing bodies other than pursuant to a licensing scheme covering the same copyright rights as existing schemes.

Prospective licensees may refer such licences to the Tribunal under section 125 either for the grant of a licence or for its continuance. Such orders are reviewable under sections 127 and 128. Compliance with the licence constitutes a defence to copyright infringement.

MATTERS TO BE TAKEN INTO ACCOUNT BY THE COPYRIGHT TRIBUNAL

When dealing either with licensing schemes or with licences by licensing bodies the Tribunal is directed by section 129 to have regard to the availability of other schemes, the granting of other licences in similar circumstances and the terms of those licences. It must also exercise its powers so as to ensure that there is no unreasonable discrimination between licensees and the scheme or licence and other schemes or licences granted by the same person. In practice the Tribunal relies heavily on voluntary agreements relating to the same or related uses of copyright and looks to see whether there is increased value in, or use of, the copyright licensed under the scheme to the licensees before it. It also compares similar schemes operated by the PRS and PPL. Sections 130 to 134 contain guidance as to matters to be taken into account by the Tribunal in relation to other parts of its jurisdiction.

PHOTOCOPYING LICENCES

There is no statutory licence for reprographic copying, or photocopying, in the United Kingdom other than a limited licence given by section 36 for use by educational establishments of small regular amounts of published musical, literary or dramatic works. 'Educational establishments' are schools and other institutions identified by statutory instrument. The question of whether there should be a statutory licence is one which has been considered in other countries which have introduced such licences for educational institutions. The Copyright Licensing Agency Limited in the U.K. does grant voluntary licences for photocopying and has reciprocal links with other similar licensing and collecting bodies. It acts as agent for its members who are publishers and authors. To date it has concentrated on licensing photocopying by educational institutions and has granted blanket licences for schools and universities. It is now turning its attention to commercial photocopying in industry and the law. The Newspaper Licensing Agency also operates a scheme which permits the photocopying of newspaper items which appear in its members' publications.

The provisions of the Act dealing with reprography deal with photocopying and all other means of making facsimile copies, including copying from works stored electronically. To give similar protection as would have been given had there been a statutory licence, section 136 of the Act implies into every licence granted by a licensing body, which does not detail the particular works covered by the licence, an undertaking by the licensing body to indemnify the licensee against liability incurred by having infringed copyright by photocopying works of an author not party to the scheme.

Schemes for photocopying in educational institutions can be extended under section 137 to cover works of the same description as those covered, if those works have been unreasonably excluded and if the interests of the owner of copyright are not unduly prejudiced. Owners of copyright may apply for variation or discharge of the order and may appeal to the Copyright Tribunal. Any such appeal under section 139 must be brought within six weeks of the making of the order, or if brought later, will not affect the legality of anything done in reliance on the order before the decision takes effect. The Secretary of State also has the general power under section 140 to appoint an inquiry to consider whether existing licence schemes for photocopying in educational establishments should be extended. To some extent these provisions are seeking to regulate by threat of legislative intervention, rather than in an orderly manner. Given that the underlying policy relating to collective licensing is to control any potential abuse of a monopoly position, the rationale for this sort of sanction is hard to see. Surely there is less chance of there being an abuse if a statutory licence is introduced at the outset. If the social good of permitting educational establishments to photocopy freely is recognised by the government, this too would accord with such policy.

Rental

As is mentioned above, the Secretary of State may give the Copyright Tribunal power to set the sum payable for the rental of sound recordings, films and computer programs. If such an order is made, the rental to the public of copies of literary, dramatic, musical and artistic works, films and sound recordings is to be treated as licensed by the copyright owner, subject to the payment of such reasonable royalty as is agreed or determined by the Copyright Tribunal. The power given to the Secretary of State in section 66 is obviously intended to be held in reserve to be used by the government if it appears that owners of copyright in these works are abusing their powers and not permitting rental of these works. Such an order is unlikely ever to be made, particularly as the European Commission has established that it has power to order licensing of copyright if a copyright owner abuses his monopoly position under Article 86 of the Treaty of Rome. An order cannot be made if there is in existence a licensing scheme as defined above.

Certification of Licensing Schemes for Educational Establishments

Under section 143, proposed or existing licensing schemes in relation to copying by educational establishments of broadcasts or cable programmes, sub-titling of broadcast and cable programmes for those with impaired hearing, and photocopying for educational institutions may be certified by the Secretary of State. This is not a Copyright Tribunal power, but should be mentioned for completeness. Such certification may be made if works can be identified with sufficient certainty. Once a scheme is certified it is available for use by educational institutions and other such beneficiaries and cannot be amended without a further order, including an order after a Copyright Tribunal hearing.

Powers Exercisable in Consequence of Competition Reports

Section 144 provides that where the Monopolies and Mergers Commission finds either that a refusal to grant licences, or the conditions imposed in existing licences are against the public interest, it may modify those conditions or provide that licences shall be available as of right. Such power may be exercised only by the Secretary of State following an MMC report and only if it does not contravene an international convention to which the U.K. is a party. Failing agreement between the parties, the Copyright Tribunal has jurisdiction to settle the terms of such licences.

INCLUSION OF SOUND RECORDINGS IN BROADCASTS

The Broadcasting Act 1990 includes a statutory licence of the copyright in sound recordings used in broadcasts and cable programme services. The statutory licence is to ensure that the relevant collecting society, PPL, cannot impose needle time restrictions, that is to say restrictions on the amount of time the playing of records can take up during a broadcast, and cannot impose unacceptable terms of payment on broadcasters. This section was inserted in the Act following the inquiry by the Monopolies and Mergers Commission into the activities of Phonographic Performance Limited in 1989.

The Copyright Tribunal has jurisdiction under section 135D to settle the terms of payment under the statutory licence, which will be what it determines to be reasonable in the circumstances. It also has jurisdiction under section 135E to settle the conditions of any such licence.

TELEVISION AND RADIO PROGRAMMES

Section 176 of the Broadcasting Act 1990 requires certain broadcasting organisations to make available at least 14 days before the relevant programmes go to air advance information about those programmes. The broadcasters concerned are basically the BBC (for both television and radio), the ITV television programme contractors and Channels 4 and 5. Satellite broadcasters licensed under the Broadcasting Act are also covered. The only condition which they can impose once such information is made available is as to copyright. The licensing of the copyright in the programme schedules is dealt with in Schedule 17 of the Broadcasting Act. That Schedule provides a statutory licence of the copyright in date, time and title information about the programmes, with the fee payable being set by the Copyright Tribunal, in the absence of agreement between the copyright owner and the publisher. In such an application the Tribunal's only statutory guidance is to decide what is reasonable in all the circumstances. The statutory licence came into force on March 1, 1991. The Tribunal has made a decision on the amount payable, which was amended by agreement following the lodgement of an appeal.

CHAPTER 19

RIGHTS IN PERFORMANCES

While this book is concerned mainly with the rights of authors in copyright works, the 1988 Act established new rights in performances which have become of increasing importance both nationally and in international treaties and which have recently been the subject of substantial reform. These rights were brought into existence to remedy yet another unsatisfactory situation which had arisen as a result of Parliament taking a piecemeal approach to problems raised between the 1911 and 1988 Acts. As with many areas covered by the Act, the problem to be solved is much easier to set than it is to answer. In short it is this: should performers and the companies for whom they exclusively record be given rights which go beyond the traditional law of copyright?

Performing artists historically had no copyright or property right in their performances. In the early days of copyright there were no recording techniques capable of capturing the subtleties of performance, so that if one wished to see Sarah Bernhardt act, one had to attend her place of performance. The copying of a performance originally meant no more than the emulation by one artist of the performance of another. However, the advent of film inevitably changed this. One fine performance could be seen by all and in perpetuity. For the first time, it became possible for a performing artist to compete against himself in order to attract an audience. It seemed clear that performers deserved protection, and this was originally granted by the Dramatic and Musical Performers' Protection Act 1925. This was modified by a 1958 Act and supplemented by the Performers' Protection Acts of 1963 and 1972. These created a range of criminal offences, but did not provide any means whereby the performer could secure compensation in a civil action. The Whitford Committee considered the problem and recommended that, while a performer should not be given copyright in a performance, he should be able to obtain a civil remedy such as damages or an injunction against the offender.

RIGHTS AND PERFORMANCE UNDER THE 1988 ACT

Part II of the 1988 Act creates two sets of rights: those given to performers and those given to persons having recording rights. The first protects the man on stage, the second his backer, promoter or, more importantly today, his recording company.

Section 180 defines "performance" to mean a live performance in one of the following classes:

(a)   a dramatic performance (which includes dance and mime),
(b)   a musical performance,
(c)   a reading or recitation of a literary work, or

(d)   a performance of a variety act or any similar presentation.

There is no requirement for the performance to be of any particular standard nor for it to be written or capable of repetition. Rather than specifying what the rights are, the Act describes how they will be infringed.

Since December 1, 1996 a performer has been able to exercise not only the right to give his consent to the making of a recording or the broadcasting of his performance (section 182) but also the following three rights, known as "performers' property rights" rather than copyright: the reproduction right (section 182A), the distribution right (section 182B) and the rental and lending right (section 182C). The reproduction right is the right to permit a person to make a copy of a recording of the whole or part of a performance; this right does not affect the making of a copy for private and domestic use, for which the performer's permission is not required. The distribution right is the right to permit the issue to the public of recordings of all or part of a performance. This includes the issue of copies within the EEA which were not previously circulated there, as well as the issue of copies outside the EEA, whether those copies were previously issued within the EEA or not. The rental and lending right, ie the right to permit the rental and lending of copies of performances, operates in much the same way as the author's rental and lending right.

The performers' property rights are governed by new sections 191A to 191M, which make provision for such matters as their assignment, licensing and testamentary disposition.

The definition of "recording" means a film or sound recording not only made directly from the live performance but also made from another recording or broadcast of a performance. Accordingly, a performer's rights are also infringed by a person who, without the performer's consent shows or plays in public the whole or a substantial part of a performance, or broadcasts it or includes it in a cable service.

As with copyright, the acts of importation or dealing with a recording of a performance in the course of business are also infringements of the performer's rights.

The second set of performer's rights is given to any person having an "exclusive recording contract" with a performer under which that person is entitled to make recordings of the performer with a view to their commercial exploitation. The right must be exclusive, which means that even the performer is not allowed to make recordings of his own performance. This situation commonly applies in the recording industry. The rationale for giving recording companies such rights is that they may well be more interested in taking action than the artist himself. A recording company is be almost certain to be more upset about a "bootleg" recording of a live pop concert than the performer, who knows that his reputation may be enhanced by copies of such a recording becoming available to the public. The recording company will, however, lose money, as this recording will compete with its authorised recording. The rights of the exclusive contractor are infringed by the carrying out of acts similar to those which infringe the performer's rights. However, the exclusive contractor's rights are not infringed if the performer consents to the making of the recording.

There are a number of exceptions to the rights conferred which allow the Copyright Tribunal (see Chapter 18) to give consent where a performer cannot be identified or tracked down or where he unreasonably withholds his consent. This prevents "extras" from holding productions to ransom by demanding further payments for recordings. The

Copyright Tribunal is also empowered under section 182D to determine, in the absence of agreement, how much equitable remuneration a performer is entitled to received in respect of the public performance, broadcasting or cable transmission of a recording of all or part of his performance.

The performer's rights created by the Act are independent of copyright or any moral right relating to any work which is included in the performance. They also have a different duration, lasting 50 years from the end of the calendar year in which the performance first took place or, if a recording of the performance is released during that period, 50 years from the end of the year in which it it is released. In contrast to copyright, the action for breach of these rights must be framed as an action for breach of statutory duty.

The remedies for breach of a recording right include the usual remedies available for copyright infringement, among them an order for delivery up.

Sections 198 to 204 of the Act create criminal offences, covering a number of business activities relating to "illicit recordings". These are recordings made without the performer's consent and otherwise than for private purposes. The offences cover not only the making and dealing in such recording but also the broadcast or showing of them. The offences are punishable by a maximum six-month sentence.

Performers will be able to protect their rights only if the conditions for qualification in the Act are met. In particular, the idea of "qualifying country" is important. Under section 206 this includes the U.K., the European Union and any other country granting reciprocal protection. The last class includes those countries which have acceded to the 1961 Rome Convention protecting performer's rights. Fewer countries therefore qualify, as this Convention is far less popular than the Berne Convention (see Chapter 15, above).

Chapter 20

PROTECTION OUTSIDE THE COPYRIGHT SYSTEM

Introduction

As is apparent from the title, most of this book deals with the law of copyright. Inevitably this overlaps with the law governing designs, as discussed in Chapter 10. However, there are also a number of other areas of the law which may be of interest to the reader, because they may provide remedies for infringement of the reader's rights in addition to rights of copyright, or where such rights of copyright are hard to prove or do not exist. It will not be practicable to do any more than give a brief introduction to these topics here, but is worth doing so because it would be a mistake to give the impression that copyright exists in a legal vacuum. In the commercial world there may well be more than one way for an author to protect his interests.

Public Lending Right

After many years' vigorous campaigning by authors and (some claim) publishers, the Public Lending Right Act 1979 introduced the principle that an author is entitled to compensation for any loss of book sales consequent on the borrowing of his books by users of public lending libraries. The Public Lending Right (usually known as PLR) is not incurred automatically, but depends on a complex scheme of registration under which the author and each book in respect of which he seeks to claim PLR must conform to various criteria.

The Public Lending Right Act 1979 is very short and contains little substantive law concerning PLR. It provides for the operation of a Scheme (the Public Lending Right Scheme 1982) in which all the details of PLR are contained. The Scheme is appended to the Public Lending Right Scheme 1982 (Commencement) Order 1982. The Scheme came into full operation on July 1, 1983.

Under the 1979 Act PLR is to be conferred initially on the author or authors of a book, whether the copyright is owned initially by the author or by anyone else (see "Ownership of Copyright", Chapter 7, above). PLR is transmissible, which means that the author can be parted from it by the term of any contract; and the right applies only to books, excluding from its ambit any other type of item (notably gramophone records and, more recently, compact discs, CD ROMs and videotapes) which may be borrowed from libraries. The duration of PLR is that which, until recently, applied also in respect of copyright in works, expiring 50 years from the author's death. There is no special provision of the duration of anonymous or pseudonymous works, presumably because the author of a work must be known and proved to the Registrar of Public Lending Right before registration can be effected. It is not yet known whether it is intended to extend the post mortem duration of PLR by a further 20 years, but this may be expected as a matter of course. If it does not, some interesting legal problems may arise from the lending of books by libraries during the final copyright period of 20 years within which a book's eligibility for PLR has ceased but the author's right to control lending has not expired.

Under the Scheme an author (which may include an author not entitled to be credited on the title page) is eligible to register his claim to PLR if his only or principal home is in the U.K., although applications are also received from authors living in Germany. A book is registrable for PLR if it contains at least 32 pages, although poetry and drama books need only be 24 pages long. Previously there was a distinction between text and illustration for counting pages but this has now been removed.

Once a book is registered, the author can look forward to receiving annual payments in respect of its borrowings. Since it is currently impracticable to monitor and record every loan of every book in every public library across the country, a system of loan sampling has been devised. The sampling is done by careful recording of loans in a number of libraries distributed across the U.K. and selected in accordance with criteria of size, location and demography. The libraries whose loans are sampled are replaced every four years in order to limit the impact of local oddities of borrowing habits.

On the basis of the loan sampling procedure, each registered book is taken to have been borrowed on a conjectural number of occasions. The person registered as being entitled to receive the annual PLR payment will receive in 1993 the sum of 1.86 pence, multiplied by the number of notional loans made in respect of any given book. If this sum is less than £1 per author, it will not be payable, presumably because it is administratively not worth handling; if, on the other hand, the sum exceeds £6,000, the figure actually received may be reduced in accordance with the complex formula where the author of that book is also the registered author of other books in respect of which PLR is payable.

The U.K. Government currently sets aside £5 million per annum for the operation of PLR. A proportion of this is spent on administration of the Scheme, the rest being divided between those entitled to receive it.

PLR is administered by the Registrar of Public Lending Right, from whom application forms and further guidance are available. The Registrar's address is Bayheath House, Prince Regent Street, Stockton-on-Tees, Cleveland TS18 1DF. Advice concerning the entitlement of U.K. authors to claim PLR abroad may be obtained from the Authors' Lending and Copyright Society Limited, 430 Edgware Road, London W2 1EH.

CONFIDENTIAL INFORMATION

The law governing confidential information applies both to oral and written disclosures. The English courts have sought to enforce the idea that people should keep secret matters that are disclosed to them in confidence. All the authorities come from case law; there is no general statute covering the area, although some types of confidential information may be governed by the Official Secrets Acts. The English courts do not recognise any right of "privacy" as such.

The laws of copyright and confidential information often both provide protection in commercial situations. For example, the recipient of a confidential document may copy it and then publish it. The first act will be an infringement of copyright, the second a breach of confidence. If, however, the document is not copied, but there is a disclosure of the ideas it contains, then there can be no copyright infringement and the copyright owner will have to rely on the law of confidential information for relief. The termination of a business relationship between business partners or between employers and employees are particularly likely to give rise to an action for a breach of confidence.

The classic statement of the law of confidence is found in the case of *Coco v. Clark* in which the court set out a three-limbed test which would be required if the plaintiff was to show breach of confidence. First the information must have the necessary quality of confidence about it. Secondly, that information must have been disclosed to the recipient in circumstances giving rise to an obligation of confidence. Thirdly, there must be an unauthorised use of that information, possibly to the detriment of the party communicating it.

Turning to the first requirement, it is clear that information made freely available to members of the public cannot later be subject to an obligation of confidence. However, it is possible that information may be collected from publicly available sources and compiled into a document which may itself be confidential. Information which is confidential cannot be disclosed simply because there is public interest in it being made widely available. However, the courts have in the past held that where the information is likely to be suppressed if disclosed to the proper authorities, then there may be justification for it being published in a national newspaper. This is clearly an area where there is a conflict between the obligation of confidence and the right of the public to know of misdeeds. As such, the outcome of any case cannot be predicted with any certainty, and everything depends on the circumstances. The courts will not restrain a breach of confidence unless it is in the public interest to do so.

The obligation of confidence may be express, or may be implied by the behaviour of parties. If it is express, then it may also be governed by the law of contract (see below). It will always be easier for the court to rule on an express obligation of confidence than to have to imply one, and authors should bear this in mind before they disclose anything they wish to be kept secret. Where there is a written contract which is silent on the question of confidence, the court may still imply an obligation. Where there is no written contract, the court will look at the circumstances surrounding the disclosure and assess confidentiality on objective grounds, asking the question whether it would have appeared to a person to whom the disclosure was made that the information was being given to him in confidence.

Where the court is considering a relationship of employer and employee (or, as is often the case, ex-employee), there is again a need to strike a balance between allowing people to transfer freely from one job to another and protecting an employer's rights in the information specific to his business. Employees have to observe a duty of fidelity to their employers. This means that they must neither disclose trade secrets nor damage the employer's goodwill in his business. The more senior and more highly rewarded an employee is, the stronger this duty will be. The ex-employee will be allowed to take with him the mental tools of his trade, but not his employer's trade secrets. Information which is not a genuine trade secret but which is not publicly known may be protected by a reasonable term in the employee's service contract.

There are other relationships in which the law will impose a duty on parties to act for the benefit of another party. These include relationships between a director and his company and between partners and their partnership. The duty imposed on such persons by reason of their position (known as a "fiduciary" duty) may give rise to an obligation of confidence but is not necessarily of the same scope.

Because there are no statutorily defined "restricted acts" relating to confidential information there is, in theory, no limit to the number of ways in which confidential information may be misused. There will be a breach not only where confidential information is disclosed when there is an absolute bar against disclosure, but also where limited disclosure has been allowed and further dissemination takes place and where confidential information is used in secret without authority.

As with other areas of this law, the extent to which the unauthorised disclosure must be to the plaintiff's detriment is not clearly defined and everything will depend on the circumstances of the case.

The remedies available for breach of confidence depend on the stage at which it is caught. The plaintiff will usually hope to stop any disclosure taking place and will try to obtain an injunction. The plaintiff may also be entitled to damages or an account of profits.

TRADE MARKS

People in trade have for hundreds of years marked their goods in a distinctive way so that customers will recognise their goods and rely on their sign as indicating that the goods will be of a certain quality. In recent years the use of particular packaging and trade marks has become widespread, especially in the field of retail goods. Since the creation of the Trade Marks Registry, traders have been able to rely either on the statutory framework or on the common law to protect their trade marks. The overlap with copyright protection may occur where the trade mark or brand is a logo, picture or even a wrapper for a chocolate bar, which is also a copyright work or where an item carries both a copyright work and a trade mark. The trade mark concerned may be registered or unregistered.

Unregistered marks

The tort of passing-off as it is recognised today was developed by the courts at the end of the nineteenth century and protects rights in "goodwill". The principle of the tort is that one trader is not entitled to represent his goods as if they are those of someone else. The courts have sought to protect the goodwill in a business. Although it seems a simple word, "goodwill" has proved extremely difficult to define. One judge noted that it was the sort of thing that would be recognised if seen. In brief, it may be thought of as the force which makes customers come back for more. The power to encourage further trade is valuable and therefore worth protecting. Where a competitor makes a misrepresentation liable to damage a trader's goodwill, relief may be sought. The type of damage which the plaintiff may show is most commonly lost sales, or at least the likelihood of such loss. Where the plaintiff is in the business of granting licences to third parties to exploit his goodwill, there may also be a misrepresentation of the connection between the defendant and the plaintiff which will not only damage the plaintiff's reputation but also lead to a loss of licensing opportunity in the relevant area.

The successful plaintiff will usually ask the court for an injunction to restrain any further action by the defendant. He may also be awarded damages or an account of profits. The majority of passing-off cases which come before the courts do so as interlocutory applications (*i.e.* applications for urgent relief). The outcome usually brings an end to the whole action, as the losing party most often gives up at this stage.

Registered marks

It is also possible for certain trade marks to be registered under the Trade Marks Act 1994 or under the terms of the European Trade Mark Regulation. It is not possible to consider here the question of which marks may be registrable. Registration is in theory limited to the goods or services in which the proprietor trades or to similar goods (or services). A trade mark may be registered in one or more classes, which cover most types of goods and services.

Once the mark has been registered, it is possible to enforce it to prevent the use of an identical or similar mark which is used in the course of trade in relation to the goods for which it is registered.

As with the law of passing-off, a registered trade mark may also be a copyright work, the copying of which by a competitor may lead to an action for both copyright and registered trade mark infringement. Under section 10 of the Trade Marks Act 1994, a wide range of acts may infringe a registered trade mark. Unfortunately, the section is an extremely complex one and the true scope of the registered proprietor's rights is uncertain particularly where the allegedly infringing use is not an exact copy of the trade mark as registered.

If the defendant has used the mark for goods other than those for which he is registered, then the proprietor may not be able to rely on the fact that he has secured a registered mark. However, he may have an action in passing-off or copyright infringement. Unlike passing-off, the registered proprietor does not have to show any likelihood of damage, as this is inferred from the fact of the mark's registration. The range of remedies for infringement of registered trade marks includes injunctions, damages and accounts of profits. Once again, the majority of actions reaching the courts are applications for interlocutory injunctions.

Just as there is no copyright in a person's name, it is usually accepted that there is no copyright in the name of a book, play, poem or art work. Since, however, the author of a work may feel that another author is interfering with his commercial expectations by adopting an identical or similar title, it is generally prudent to avoid the risk of passing-off by choosing a title which is unlikely to be confused with anyone else's. In America, where the tort of passing-off is buttressed by a wider tort of unfair competition, some firms of lawyers specialise in conducting title searches in order to advise their clients as to the risks inherent in their choice of title.

There is no copyright in a fictitious character as such, although copyright may rest in the work of fiction itself. Thus early this century, a writer of Sherlock Holmes stories, who used the "character" of the great detective but did not copy the original Conan Doyle texts, was held not to have perpetrated a copyright infringement (although such utilisation of a character may constitute passing-off). The Whitford Committee was urged to recommend the introduction of a copyright in characters, but the technical difficulties in defining such a law and the lack of a cogent case for such a reform led to the rejection of the idea.

BREACH OF CONTRACT

Finally, a word about the law of contract. Many copyright works will be the subject of oral or written contracts between the creator and another party, which may set out their understanding on a number of matters of importance including, for example, how the work created is to be used, by whom and for how much. A breach of a binding contract may entitle the innocent party to apply to the court for relief, including damages or specific performance. The latter remedy is one under which the court compels the party to perform his side of the bargain. It is, therefore, of great importance for parties to a contract to ensure that they understand the obligations they are entering into so as to avoid a dispute once it is too late. It should be noted that breach of a copyright licence may well be both a copyright infringement and a breach of contract and the plaintiff may have to base his action on one ground rather than the other.

CHAPTER 21

COPYRIGHT CLEARANCE AND PRACTICAL ADVICE

Copyright comes into existence automatically, that is without fulfilment of formalities, subject only to its meeting certain conditions laid down in national legislation, such as, for example, that the work must exist in writing or in some other material form. International copyright is also granted automatically in all Berne Convention countries, and insofar as some countries do demand formalities, these can be met in the way (described in Chapter 15) set out in the Universal Copyright Convention.

This is obviously an enormous convenience for creative workers, but on the other hand, since there is no central copyright registry to which application for copyright clearance can be made, problems may arise for copyright users in clearing rights or in ascertaining whether a particular work is in copyright or not.

In the case of published works, application will normally be made in the first instance to the publisher. Some authors entrust the management of their professional interests to agents, and some literary and artists' agents are listed in the London Yellow Pages directory. There are also the collective licensing societies (see Chapter 17, above), which, it is thought, will deal helpfully with inquiries falling within the scope of their respective operations. It will plainly facilitate answers from any quarter if postal inquiries are accompanied by a stamped addressed envelope.

Internationally, UNESCO's International Copyright Information Centre (7 Place de Fontenoy, Paris 75700, France) exists primarily to assist users in the developing countries to secure copyright clearance on favourable terms, especially in the case of educational works. The Centre has, however, also published model statutes to aid the setting-up of public or private national copyright information centres.

The professional associations that exist in every branch of arts and letters do not have among their purposes that of informing the public generally on copyright problems; indeed, they seldom have the resources to do so, but they will often assist inquirers wherever it would be reasonable to expect them to reply. The same may be said of the British Copyright Council, of 29 Berners Street, London W1P 4AA, which is not an administrative body but a forum of consultation and study among associations of copyright owners. The Council does, however, issue a booklet explaining in general terms the obligations of copyright users.

The problem of copyright clearance was considered at some length by the Whitford Committee in paragraphs 845 to 851 of its Report. Representations on this matter were made to the Committee principally by newspaper and magazine publishers, who often need quick clearance, and who suggested that when copyright owners cannot be traced after reasonable inquiry and/or advertisement, it ought to be possible for a work to be reproduced without infringing copyright provided it is accompanied by an offer to pay reasonable reproduction fees to the copyright owner if he later comes forward. The copyright owners felt that most of the systems proposed were too easily open to abuse.

The Committee finally recommended that the statutory tribunal which it proposed should be set up should be empowered to give such clearances. However the government did not endorse this suggestion, and it is not included within the Copyright Tribunal's powers. Such licensing was felt to be an unwarranted encroachment on authors' rights and incompatible with the U.K.'s international obligations.

In the context of copyright clearance, it should be noted that ownership of the material on which a work is recorded or in which it is incorporated does not in itself confer ownership of the copyright in the work. Thus a letter will normally belong to the recipient, but copyright in the letter – as a literary work – will belong to the writer. In letters to the press the right to edit for publication is generally taken as implied (as is the right to print them). The same principle is true of a painting or work of sculpture, the purchase of which does not in itself convey the copyright to the purchaser.

Accordingly, when in doubt as to whether a work that it is desired to use is in copyright or as to whom to apply for permission to use it, and on the understanding that the proposed use falls outside the scope of fair dealing (see pages 87 to 89), applications should be made to the quarter from which the required information or authority can most probably be obtained. In the case of published literary and musical works that quarter will generally be the publisher but, if the proposed use is the public performance of musical works, it will be the Performing Right Society (PRS) and, if it is the mechanical reproduction of musical works, it may be the Mechanical-Copyright Protection Society (MCPS). Further information about the PRS and the MCPS, including their addresses, is provided in Chapter 17.

It is thought that in this way the required information or authority can generally be elicited without difficulty. The area in which difficulty is most likely to be encountered is that of photographs, because a particular photograph may be found in a number of different outlets, and because the copyright in photographs quite often belongs to individuals, with whom it may be difficult to make contact.

The collective licensing societies, being intermediaries between the copyright owners and the copyright users, are designated to answer inquiries from the general public concerning their specific branch of copyright. The professional associations referred to above, whose function is to promote and advise on the interests of their own members, although highly qualified in their respective spheres, are not such intermediaries. However, readers of this book may have reason for wishing to contact a professional or commercial association in the field of arts and letters, and such a list is accordingly appended, thank to the good offices of the British Copyright Council. The collective licensing societies, dealt with in Chapter 17, have been omitted and it should be emphasised that this list does not purport to be comprehensive.

APPENDIX

LIST OF ASSOCIATIONS

Association		*Address*
The Artists' Union	Exists to advance the interests of artists and improve the status of artists generally. Membership is open to all visual artists.	128 Gordon Road, South Woodford, London E18 1RD
The Association of Authors' Agents	Represents the majority of British agents, who in turn act in business matters for many British authors and their heirs and also many foreign authors.	79 St Martin's Lane, London WC2N 4AA
The Association of Illustrators	Exists to promote and protect the interests of illustrators. It provides advice to members on professional, legal, union and contractual matters.	1st Fl., 32–38 Saffron Hill, London EC1N 8FH Tel: 0171 831 7377 Fax: 0171 831 6277
The Association of Learned and Professional Society Publishers	An association of the publishing activities of over 100 British learned and professional organisations and individuals in publishing. It exists to promote the development of publishing and the flow of publications to its members.	48 Kelsey Lane, Beckenham, Kent BR3 3NR Tel: 0181 658 0459 Fax: 0181 663 3583
The Association of Professional Composers	An unincorporated non-profit-making society founded in 1980 to further the collective interests of its members and to inform them on professional and artistic matters.	4 Brook Street, London W1Y 1AA Tel: 0171 629 4828 Fax: 0171 629 4515
The Benesh Institute of Choreography	Exists to protect the interests of dance notators.	12 Lisson Grove, London NW1 6TS Tel: 0171 258 3041 Fax: 0171 724 6434

Association		*Address*
The British Academy of Songwriters, Composers and Authors (BASCA)	Represents British writers of songs and light music. It exists to assist both established and aspiring British songwriters with advice, information and encouragement.	The Penthouse, 4 Brook Street, London W1Y 1AA Tel: 0171 629 0992 Fax: 0171 629 0993
The British Videogram Association Ltd (BVA)	A body which exists to help combat piracy.	10 Maddox Street, London W1
The Chartered Institute of Journalists	Represents the professional and trade union interests of its members and is certified as an independent trade union under the Employment Protection Act 1975. It gives equal rights of membership to all journalists including freelances.	2 Dock Offices, Surrey Quays, Lower Road, London SE16 2XL Tel: 0171 252 1187
The Christian Copyright Licensing Association	Represents a number of composers and publishers of religious music and the licensing of lyrics of religious music, other than by photocopying.	P.O. Box 1339, Eastbourne BN21 4YF Tel: 01323 417 711 Fax: 01323 417 722
The Composers' Guild of Great Britain	An unincorporated society whose object is to further the professional and artistic interests of its members.	4 Brook Street, London W1Y 1AA Tel: 0171 629 5229 Fax: 0171 629 6599
The English PEN	One of the 78 centres which together constitute International PEN — a worldwide, non-political association for writers working for freedom of expression and against repressive regimes of whatever ideology. PEN is open to any writer, editor or translator actively engaged in any branch of literature.	7 Dilke Street, London SW3 Tel: 0171 352 6303
The Federation of British Artists	A grouping of 25 organisations in the visual arts field. It provides central support and information services together with exhibition and meeting facilities for its member associations, representing painters, sculptors, engravers, illustrators and graphic artists.	17 Carlton House Terrace, London SW1Y 5BD Tel: 0171 930 6844

Association		*Address*
The Incorporated Institute of Photographers	Represents about 4,000 practising photographers in the U.K., and is the principal qualifying organisation for professional photographers. It looks after the interests of professional photographers generally at all levels.	Amwell End, Ware, Herts.
The Music Publishers' Association Limited	Promotes and protects the interests of British publishers of serious and popular music as the trade association of music publishers. It seeks to originate and promote improvements in the law on musical copyright and endeavours to keep its members up to date on all matters affecting or of interest to them.	3rd Floor, Strandgate, 18–20 York Buildings, London WC2N 6JU Tel: 0171 839 7779 Fax: 0171 837 7776
The National Union of Journalists	Represents over 32,000 members employed in newspapers, magazine and book publishing, public relations and broadcasting, including copyright and contracts.	Acorn House, 314 Gray's Inn Road, London WC1X 8DP Tel: 0171 278 7916 Fax: 0171 837 8143
The Periodical Publishers' Association	Has the overriding aim of safeguarding through its members the freedom and well being of the periodical press. Members represent 75 per cent of periodicals by circulation.	Imperial House, 15–19 Kingsway, London WC2B 6UN Tel: 0171 404 4166 Fax: 0171 404 4167
The Poetry Society	The national society for the encouragement of the poetic art. It is open to poets and poetry lovers, runs a library and information service, administers competitions, and conducts verse-speaking examinations.	22 Betterton Street, London EC2 9BU Tel: 0171 240 4810 Fax: 0171 240 4818
The Publishers' Association	Represents over 90 per cent of Britain's book publishing industry by turnover in all areas of book production. Its main objective is to maintain a climate in which this vigorous and highly competitive industry can thrive.	19 Bedford Square, London WC1B 3HJ Tel: 0171 580 6321 Fax: 0171 636 5375

Association		*Address*
The Royal Academy of Arts	Founded in 1768 to promote the "Arts of Design" through an annual (summer) exhibition of fine art works of the highest merit, the running of the oldest art schools (of paintings and sculpture) in the country and, from 1870, loan exhibitions of international reputation showing works of art and artefacts of all countries and periods.	Burlington House, Piccadilly, London W1V 0DS Tel: 0171 439 7438 Fax: 0171 434 0837
The Royal Institute of British Architects	The chartered qualifying association for architects in England and Wales. It represents over 21,000 salaried and freelance practitioners and provides legal and professional advice to members.	66 Portland Place, London W1N 4AD Tel: 0171 580 5533
The Royal Photographic Society	The leading body in photography, embracing both amateurs and professionals and ranking as a learned society. The RPS operates the National Centre of Photography in Bath, which includes a library and information service.	The Octagon, Milsom Street, Bath BA1 1DN Tel: 01225 462841 Fax: 01225 448688
The Society of Authors	An independent trade union (not affiliated to the TUC) which exists to promote the interests of authors of literary and dramatic works in all media. It gives its members detailed legal and business advice, including the vetting of contracts. It has specialist groups for translators, broadcasting, educational, children's and medical writers.	84 Drayton Gardens, London SW10 9SB Tel: 0171 373 6642 Fax: 0171 373 5768
The Society of Industrial Artists and Designers	The chartered qualifying and representative association for over 6,000 designers working for industry and commerce in the United Kingdom and overseas. It gives practical and professional advice to members in many fields, including copyright and contracts.	12 Carlton House Terrace, London SW1Y 5AH

Association		*Address*
The Video Copyright Protection Society Ltd	Active in opposing video piracy and promoting legal and other measures for the protection of the video recording industry.	Visnews House, Cumberland Avenue, London N10 7EH
The Writers' Guild of Great Britain	The writers' trade union affiliated to the TUC, representing writers' interests collectively and individually in film, radio, television, the theatre and publishing. The Guild comprises practising professional writers in all media united in common concern to improve the conditions in which they work.	430 Edgware Road, London W2 1EH Tel: 0171 723 8074/6 Fax: 0171 706 2413
Association of Photographers	The Association was founded in 1968 as the Association of Fashion, Advertising and Editorial Photographers. It represents the interests of and aims to improve the rights of all professional photographers in the United Kingdom, as well as promoting the highest standards of work and practice across the industry.	9–10 Domingo Street, London EC1Y 0TA Tel: 0171 608 1441 Fax: 0171 253 3007
The British Actors' Equity Association (Equity)	Membership includes actors, variety performers, stage management, designers, directors, dancers, opera singers and many others. It negotiates standard agreements, is affiliated to the TUC and, internationally, to the International Federation of Actors (IFA).	Guild House, Upper St Martins Lane, London WC2 2AB Tel: 0171 379 6000 Fax: 0171 379 7001
The British Computer Society	The major representative body of the computer profession in Britain. It is open to all associated with computer operations. It aims to promote understanding of data processing, to improve the status of the profession and to give guidance on matters of interest to its members, the industry and the public.	1 Sanford Street, Swindon SN1 1HJ Tel: 01793 417 417 Fax: 01793 480 270
British Film and Television Producers Association	The Association represents the interests of U.K. producers of film and television programmes.	Paramount House, 162–170 Wardour St, London W1V 4LA

Association		*Address*
The Copyright Licensing Agency	It is the U.K.'s reproduction rights organisation with responsibility for looking after the interests of rights owners in copying from books, journals and periodicals. A non-profit-making company limited by guarantee, it is "owned" by its members, the Authors' Licensing and Collecting Society (ALCS) and the Publishers' Licensing Society (PLS).	88 Tottenham Court Road, London W1P 9HE Tel: 0171 436 5931 Fax: 0171 436 3986
Design and Artists' Copyright Society	DACS was created in 1983 for the protection of British artists' copyright and collection of copyright dues in the U.K. and throughout the world. It licenses, on behalf of artists, artistic works in any medium.	Parchment House, 13 Northborough Street, London EC1V 0AH Tel: 0171 336 8811 Fax: 0171 336 8822
Education Recording Agency Limited	ERA issues blanket licences to educational establishments covering recording off-air from broadcast and cable programmes for the purpose of educational instruction.	74 New Oxford Street, London WC1A 1ES Tel: 0171 436 4883 Fax: 0171 636 2402
Federation Against Software Theft	FAST enforces rights in computer programs by seeking and collecting evidence of piracy and bringing legal (usually criminal) proceedings against infringers.	1 Kingfisher Court, Farnham Road, Slough, SL2 1JF Tel: 01753 527 999 Fax: 01753 532 100
International Federation of Phonographic Industries	IFPI licenses public performance, broadcasting and cable distribution rights in certain sound recordings, mainly foreign recordings not commercially available in the U.K. market.	54–62 Regent Street, London W1R 5PJ Tel: 0171 878 7900 Fax: 0171 878 7950
The Musicians' Union	Has 42,000 members covering the whole spectrum of musical activities, including performance, teaching, arranging and composition. It negotiates with employers and is active in the field of performers' rights.	60/62 Clapham Road, London SW9 0JJ Tel: 0171 582 5566 Fax: 0171 582 9805

INDEX

ADAPTATION
  burlesque or parody as, 50
  definition, 50
  restricted act, as, 50
  restricted acts applying to, 51
ANONYMOUS WORKS
  copyright in, 44
  infringement, exceptions to, 94
ANTON PILLER ORDERS, 100
APPEALS
  Copyright Tribunal, from, 154
  precedent, doctrine of, 21
ARCHIVISTS
  copying by,
    replacement of works, for, 92, 93
    statutory provisions, 91
    unpublished works, of, 93
ARTISTIC WORKS
  artist, copying by, 95
  artistic, whether required to be, 31, 32
  categories of work being, 31
  definition, 31, 32
  designs applied industrially, 76
  fixation, requirement of, 39, 40
  graphic work as, 32
  infringement, exceptions, 33
  models, 32
  originality, requirement of, 38, 39
  photograph as, 33
  public display, on, 95
  sculpture as, 32
  unknown authorship, of, 70
ASSIGNMENT
  design right, of, 77
  future copyright, of, 65
  reversionary principle, 110–112

ASSIGNMENT—*cont.*
  rights, of, 45
  transmission of copyright by, 64–65
AUTHOR
  ascertaining identity of, 53
  definition, 53
  encouragement of, 17
  fair play, copyright as, 17
  joint, 41
  other countries, attitude towards role
    of in, 13
  ownership. *See* OWNERSHIP OF
    COPYRIGHT PROTECTION,
    QUALIFICATION FOR
  recording, consent to, 14
  rights. *See* AUTHORS' RIGHTS
  status of, 26
  transmissibility of copyright, 14
  unknown, 104
AUTHORS' RIGHTS
  Berne Convention, under, 152
  common law, at, 18
  France, in, 16, 17
  Germany, in, 16–17
  international protection, 9
  law, protection of, 12
  limitation on, acceptance of, 18
  paternity, of, 52, 56, 59–60
  protection of, 1
    moral basis for, 2
  public interest, balanced against, 18
AUTHORSHIP
  presumption of, 103–104

BERNE COPYRIGHT CONVENTION
  authors' rights under, 152

BERNE COPYRIGHT CONVENTION—*cont.*
  Berlin revision, 119
  Brussels Convention, 119, 120
  developing countries, relaxations in
    favour of, 124–126
  legal nature of, 118, 119
  moral rights in, 57
  revisions of, 119–120
  Stockholm revision, 120
  use of terms, 118
BERNE UNION
  members of, 121
BREACH OF CONFIDENCE
  remedies for, 165
BRITISH LIBRARY
  deposit of books in, 70
BROADCASTING
  protection of, 10
BROADCASTS
  archival purposes, recording for, 50
  definition, 35
  encrypted, 35
  European Agreement for the
    Prevention of Broadcasts
    Transmitted from Stations Outside
    National Territories, 131–132
  European Agreement on the
    Protection of Television Broadcasts,
    130–131
  fraudulent reception of, 72
  free public showing, 49
  ITC and BBC, recording by, 96–97
  photographs of, 97
  protection of, 10, 32
  right to, 48
  showing or retransmission of, 97
  sound recordings included in, 158
  time shifting, 49, 97
BRUSSELS CONVENTION ON THE
  PROTECTION OF SATELLITE
  TRANSMISSIONS, 133

CABLE PROGRAMMES
  archival purposes, recording for, 50
  definition, 10, 36
  exclusions from protection, 37

CABLE PROGRAMMES—*cont.*
  fraudulent reception of, 72
  free public showing, 49
  ITC and BBC, recording by, 96–97
  licence to transmit, 48
  photographs of, 97
  protection of, 36
  reception, places of, 37
  showing or retransmission of, 97
  sound recordings, inclusion of, 158
  telecommunications system,
    programmes sent by, 36
  time shifting, 49
CHANNEL ISLANDS
  Copyright, Designs and Patents Act
    1988 extended to, 80
COLLECTIVE LICENSING
  advantages of, 146, 147
  blanket, 146, 147
  centralised, 146
  Copyright Tribunal, jurisdiction of,
    154
  European Commission cases on, 151
  further development of, 149
  mechanical recording rights in musical
    works, of, 149
  monopolistic nature of, 146
  societies,
    advice from, 169
    International Confederation, 150
    none, position where, 148
    single, operation of, 146
    system of, 147
  sound recordings, of, 148
COLLECTIVE WORKS
  ownership of copyright in, 53–54
COLONIES
  Copyright, Designs and Patents Act
    1988 extended to, 80
COMMUNICATIONS
  revolution in, 10
COMPANIES
  criminal offences by, 106–107
COMPENSATION
  criminal cases, in, 107
COMPILATIONS, 29

COMPUTER PROGRAMS
  adaptation, 50
  back-up copies, 172, 187
  literary works, 137
  presumption of authorship, 103–104
  protection of, 10, 137–138
  rental,
    setting sums for, 157
COMPUTER-GENERATED WORKS
  duration of copyright in, 43
CONFIDENTIAL INFORMATION
  application of law, 163–165
  breach of confidence, remedies for,
    165
  confidence, obligation of, 164
CONTRACT
  breach of, 167
  parts of copyright limited by, 46
CONVENTION FOR THE AVOIDANCE OF
  DOUBLE TAXATION ON COPYRIGHT
  ROYALTIES, 134
CONVENTION FOR THE PROTECTION OF
  PRODUCERS OF PHONOGRAMS AGAINST
  UNAUTHORISED DUPLICATION OF THEIR
  PHONOGRAMS, 132–133
COPY-PROTECTION
  devices designed to circumvent, 71
COPYING
  definition, 45
  substantial part of work, of, 45
COPYRIGHT
  advice on, 169
  assignment of, 64–65
  automatic grant of, 168
  buying, selling and hiring, 13
  clearance, 168–169
  codification of law, 9
  common law, at, 3
    abolition, 7
    after 1709, 6, 7
    Statute of Anne, test cases after, 7
    unpublished works, in, 7
  criminal cases, compensation in, 107
  crisis of, 10
  definition, 3
  designs, in, 76–77

COPYRIGHT—cont.
  duration of. See DURATION OF
    COPYRIGHT
  expansion of, 8–10
  future, 65–66
  infringement. See INFRINGEMENT
  letters patent, 2
  literary property, as, 13
  moral right, as, 15–16
  offences, 105
  other languages, in, 13
  ownership. See OWNERSHIP OF
    COPYRIGHT
  property right, as, 14–15
  public interest, balance of, 18
  publisher's right, as, 12
  purpose of, 8
  reversionary principle, 110–112
  right to copy, not merely, 1
  Stationers' Company, of, 3, 4
  statutory,
    duration of, 6
    publication, secured by, 6
    sources of, 2
  subsistence, presumption of, 94
  system, foundation of, 17–19
  transmission of, 13, 14
  use of term, 12, 13
COPYRIGHT ACT 1911
  codification of law by, 9
  extended copyright under, 112–115
  provisions still applying,
    generally, 109
    reversion of copyright, 110–112
    works for sale, statutory licence to
      reproduce, 109–110
  significance, summary of, 114
COPYRIGHT ACT 1956
  generally, 9–10
  Parts of, 115–117
  Schedules, 117
  transitional provisions, 44
COPYRIGHT LAW
  civil law countries, in, 20
  extension provisions, 80–81
  motive of, 17–19

COPYRIGHT LAW—*cont.*
scope, enlargement of, 9, 10
sources of,
common law, 20–21
European law, 22–23
international treaties, 22
legal decisions, 20–21
statute-based case law, 21–22
statutes, 20. *See also* COPYRIGHT ACT
1911, etc.
Statute of Anne, 4–7, 12
COPYRIGHT LICENSING AGENCY
photocopying licences, grant of, 89
COPYRIGHT TRIBUNAL
appeals, 154
applications or references to, 153
competition reports, powers exercised
in consequence of, 157
costs, 154
decisions of, 153, 154
jurisdiction,
collective licensing, in relation to,
155
educational establishments,
certification of licensing schemes,
for, 157
generally, 154
licensing bodies, over, 155
licensing schemes, over, 155
photocopying licences, over, 156
programme information, settling fee
for, 158
sound recordings included in
broadcasts, over, 158
licences of rights, settling terms of, 103
matters taken into account by, 155
membership, 152–153
Performing Right Tribunal, successor
to, 151
photocopying licences, dealing with, 156
procedural rules, 153–154
proceedings, commencement of, 153
rental, setting sums for, 157
representation before, 153
Whitford Committee
recommendations, 152

COPYRIGHT, DESIGNS AND PATENTS ACT
1988
application in countries to which not
extended, 82–84
Chapters, 24–25
copyright law, as principal course of, 20
countries to which extended,
amendment in, 82
extension provisions, 80–82
miscellaneous and general provisions,
71–73
other countries, extension to, 41
Parts, 24
Schedules, 25
transitional provisions, 79
work within meaning of, 26
COURTS
hierarchy of, 21
CROWN COPYRIGHT
consents, addresses for, 69
duration of, 66–67
first publication, presumption of, 105
practice, in, 68–69
subsistence of, 66
works having, 66–67

DATABASES
background to Directive, 139–140
copyright protection and Directive,
141–143
definition, 140–141
meaning, 140–141
protection, 141, 143–144
sui generis protection, 143–144
DECODERS
unauthorised, importation and sale of,
73
DEPENDENCIES
Copyright, Designs and Patents Act
1988 extended to, 80
DESIGN RIGHT
assignment of, 77
duration of, 77
effect of, 77
introduction of, 76
licences of right, 78–79
licensing, 77

DESIGN RIGHT—*cont.*
  meaning, 76
  must-fit and must-match exceptions, 77
  ownership of, 77
  protection, restrictions on, 76
  qualification for protection, 77
DESIGNS
  document, 76
  duration of protection, 75
  functional, 75
  industrially applied, 75
  legislation covering, 74–75
  meaning, 74, 76
  new law, 76–78
  old law, 74–75
  overlapping rights, 79
  Registered Designs Act, protection
    under, 74–75
  registered, 78
  spare parts exemption, 75
  transitional provisions, 79
  unregistered. *See* DESIGN RIGHT
DRAMATIC WORK
  de minimis principle, 30
  definition, 30
  fixation, requirement of, 40
  originality, requirement of, 39–40
  plays, 30
  unknown authorship, of, 70£
DRAMATISTS
  performances, charging for, 1, 2
DURATION OF COPYRIGHT
  Crown, 67
  early Acts, under, 7, 8
  extended works, 43, 51–52
  films, 43
  general provisions, 43–44
  identifiable personal ownership, 43
  revived, 52
  transitional provisions, 44

EDUCATION
  copying for, 90–91
  educational establishments,
    certification of licensing schemes,
    for, 157

ELECTROCOPYING, 137–138
ELECTRONIC MAIL, 138–139
ELECTRONIC PUBLICATION, 137–138
E-MAIL, 138–139
EMPLOYEE
  works in course of employment, 54–55
EMPLOYER
  author of employee's copyright, as, 16
EUROPEAN AGREEMENT CONCERNING
  PROGRAMME EXCHANGES BY WAY OF
  TELEVISION FILMS, 130
EUROPEAN AGREEMENT FOR THE
  PREVENTION OF BROADCASTS
  TRANSMITTED FROM STATIONS OUTSIDE
  NATIONAL TERRITORIES, 131–132
EUROPEAN AGREEMENT ON THE
  PROTECTION OF TELEVISION
  BROADCASTS, 130–131
EUROPEAN COMMISSION, 10
EUROPEAN UNION
  copyright, exploitation of, 134–134
  harmonisation provisions, 135–136
  law of, 22–23
  Treaty of Rome. *See* TREATY OF ROME

FAIR DEALING
  act constituting, 88
  application of provisions, 88
  criticism or review, use for, 87
  current events, reporting, 87
  guidelines on, 88–89
  meaning, 88
  non-statutory, 89
  research or private study, for purposes
    of, 88
  statutory provisions, 87
  unfair dealing, and, 89
FALSE ATTRIBUTION, 159
FILMS
  definition, 34, 35
  duration of copyright in, 43
  European Agreement concerning
    Programme Exchanges by way of
    Television Films, 130
  infringing performance of, 86
  presumption of authorship, 103–104

FILMS—*cont.*
  rental,
    setting sums for, 157
FOLK SONGS
  recording, 95
FOLKLORE
  copyright in, 70
FOREIGN WORKS
  denial of copyright to, 84
FRANCE
  author's rights in, 16

GERMANY
  author's rights in, 16
GRAPHIC WORK
  definition, 32
  typeface, as, 34
GREGORY REPORT, 8, 151–152

IMPORTATION
  printed copies, of, 107–108
INFORMATION TECHNOLOGY
  computer programs. *See* COMPUTER
    PROGRAMS
  databases. *See* DATABASES
  electrocopying, 137–138
  electronic mail, 138–139
  electronic publication, 137–138
  E-mail, 138–139
  international treaties, 144–145
  non-E.U. countries, 144
INFRINGEMENT
  actions for, 98–100
  commencement of proceedings, 100
  criminal proceedings, 105–106
  exceptions,
    anonymous and pseudonymous
      works, 94
    artist, works copied by, 95
    broadcasts or cable programmes, in
      relation to, 97
    charitable purposes, use of
      recordings for, 96
    educational copying, 90–92
    fair dealing, 87–89. *See also* FAIR
      DEALING

INFRINGEMENT—*cont.*
  films, 96
  folk songs, recording, 95
  generally, 87
  incidental inclusion, 90
  libraries and archivists, copying by,
    91–93. *See also* ARCHIVISTS;
    LIBRARIANS
  public administration, in course of,
    94
  public display, artistic works on, 95
  public lending of copies of works, 96
  public reading and recitation, 94–95
  scientific abstracts, 95
  statutory provisions, 33
  time-shifting, 49, 97
  presumptions in action for, 103–104
  primary, 85
  public performance, by, 86
  remedies,
    account of profits, 99
    Anton Piller orders, 100
    damages, 100
    delivery up, 100–101
    exclusive licensee, open to, 102–103
    injunctions, 99
    limitation of, 90
    plaintiff, options open to, 98–99
  secondary, 85–87
  unfair dealing, 89
INFRINGING COPY
  articles designed or adapted to make,
    86
  definition, 85
  delivery up of, 100–101
  importation, restriction on, 107–108
  importing, 86
  seizure of, 99
INFRINGING GOODS
  U.K. courts, jurisdiction of, 27
INTERNATIONAL CONVENTION FOR THE
  PROTECTION OF PERFORMERS,
  PRODUCERS OF PHONOGRAMS AND
  BROADCASTING ORGANISATIONS (ROME
  CONVENTION)
  basic principle of, 128

INTERNATIONAL CONVENTION FOR THE PROTECTION OF PERFORMERS, PRODUCERS OF PHONOGRAMS AND BROADCASTING ORGANISATIONS (ROME CONVENTION)—*cont.*
film producers, not covering, 128
membership, 129
neighbouring rights, 127
phonograms, protection of, 132–133
INTERNATIONAL ORGANISATIONS
copyright vesting in, 70
works under control of, 84
ISLE OF MAN
Copyright, Designs and Patents Act 1988 extended to, 80

JURISDICTION
Copyright Tribunal, of. *See* COPYRIGHT TRIBUNAL
U.K. courts, of, 26–27

LETTERS
ownership of copyright in, 54
LETTERS PATENT, 2
LIBRARIANS
copying by,
articles, periodicals and parts of works of, 93
other libraries, supply of copies to, 92–93
replacement of works for, 93
unpublished works of, 93
LIBRARIES
copying by, 92–93
deposit of books in, 71
lending of copies by, 93–94
LICENCE
binding nature of, 101–102
nature of, 101
non-exclusive, 101–102
plaintiff, exclusive licensee as, 101–102
right, of, 103
LICENSING
collective. *See* COLLECTIVE LICENSING
design right, of, 77

LITERARY WORKS
de minimis principle, 29
definition, 27–28
fixation, requirement of, 40
institutional copying, 89
literary, meaning, 27
originality, requirement of, 39–40
spoken words as, 28
unknown authorship, of, 70

MACAULAY, LORD, 8
MORAL RIGHTS
author, to be identified as, 56, 59
Berne Convention, rights in, 57
code, introduction of, 15–16, 56
commencement, 63
copyright as, 15–16
derogatory treatment, right to object to, 60–61
disclosure, right of, 62
disposition of, 62–63
duration of, 62
economic rights, and, 56
false attribution, right against, 59
infringement, 62
joint ownership, 62
law, incorporated into, 57
paternity, right of, 59–60
privacy, limited right of, 62
purpose of, 57–58
scope of, 56, 57–58
types of, 56
U.K., introduction in, 58
WIPO performances, 52, 60
MUSICAL WORKS
definition, 30
fixation, requirement of, 40–41
mechanical recording rights, collective licensing of, 149
music, meaning, 30
originality, requirement of, 39–40
unknown authorship, of, 70

OFFENCES
companies, by, 106–107

OFFENCES—*cont.*
  copyright, 105–106
  search warrants, issue of, 106
ORIGINALITY
  presumption of, 104–105
  requirement of, 39–40
OWNERSHIP OF COPYRIGHT
  basic provision, 53
  employment exception, 54–55
  joint and collective works of, 53–54
  letters, in, 55
  presumption of, 104–105
  reversionary interest, 55

PARLIAMENTARY COPYRIGHT
  consents, addresses for, 69
  ephemeral nature of, 68
  generally, 66–67
  other legislative bodies, extension to, 67
  practice, in, 68–69
  subsistence of, 67
  unpublished works, provisions
    applying to, 68
PASSING OFF
  paternity right, and, 59
  tort of, 166
PERFORMERS' RIGHTS
  conditions for protecting, 161
  creation of, 159
  exceptions, 160–161
  exclusive recording contract, person
    with, 160
  historically, 159–160
  infringement of, 161
  performance, definition, 159–160
  property rights, 160
  statutory protection, 9
PETER PAN
  continuing copyright in, 72
  royalty, determining, 154
PHONOGRAMS
  Convention for the Protection of
    Producers of Phonograms against
    Unauthorised Duplication of their
    Phonograms, 132–133
  definition, 132

PHOTOCOPYING
  licences for, 89, 156–157
PHOTOGRAPH
  definition, 33
  owner of, 15
PLAYS
  literary and dramatic work, as, 30
PROPERTY
  copyright as right of, 14–15
PSEUDONYMOUS WORKS
  copyright in, 44
  infringement, exceptions to, 94
PUBLIC ADMINISTRATION
  infringement, exceptions to, 94
PUBLIC LENDING RIGHT
  administration of, 163
  annual payments, 163
  eligibility for, 163
  introduction of, 163
  transmission of, 163
PUBLIC PERFORMANCE
  definition, 159–160
  equipment used for, 87
  illicit recordings, 160
  infringing, 86
  meaning, 48
  restricted act, as, 48
  rights in,
    historically, 159–160
    performer's. *See* PERFORMERS' RIGHTS
    recording. *See* RECORDING RIGHTS
    types of, 157–158
PUBLIC READING AND RECITATION
  infringement, exceptions to, 94–95
PUBLICATION
  definition, 46
  first, presumption of, 104–105
  meaning, 45
  public, issuing copies to, 46–47
  right, 51
PUBLISHERS
  encouragement of, 17

RECORDING RIGHTS
  creation of, 159
  illicit recordings, 160

RECORDING RIGHTS—*cont.*
infringement, remedies for, 161
recording, meaning, 160
RENTAL
setting sums for, 157
REPROGRAPHIC COPYING
licences, 156–157
REPUBLIC OF IRELAND
copyright protection in, 83
RESTRAINT OF TRADE
common law doctrine of, 21
RESTRICTED ACTS
adaptation of work, making, 50
adaptations, in relation to, 50
assignment, 45
broadcasting, 49
bundle of rights, as part of, 44–45
copying, 45
lending work to public, 47
licensing, 45
list of, 45
performance in public, 48
public, issuing copies to, 45
publication right, 51
renting work to public, 47
REVIVED COPYRIGHT, 51–52
ROYALTIES
Convention for the Avoidance of
    Double Taxation on Copyright
    Royalties, 134

SATELLITE TRANSMISSIONS
Brussels Convention on the Protection
    of Satellite Transmissions, 133
SCIENTIFIC ABSTRACTS
infringement, exceptions to, 95
SCULPTURE
concept of, 32
SEARCH WARRANTS
issue of, 106
SOUND RECORDINGS
blanket licensing, 133
broadcasts, included in, 158
cable programme service, inclusion in,
    73

SOUND RECORDINGS—*cont.*
charitable purposes, use for, 96
definition, 34
duration of copyright in, 43–44
infringing performance of, 86
mechanical reproduction right, 45
presumption of authorship, 103–104
protection of, 34
rental,
    setting sums for, 157
SPARE PARTS
designs, exemption for, 77
STAR CHAMBER
abolition, 4
Decrees of, 3, 4
STATIONERS' COMPANY
copies, petition for protection of, 5
copyright of, 3, 4
perpetual copyright, loss of, 6
Statute of Anne, 4–7
STATUTES. *See also* COPYRIGHT ACT 1911,
    etc.
case law interpreting, 21
Statute of Anne, 4–7, 11

TALFOURD, MR SARJEANT, 8
TAXATION
Convention for the Avoidance of
    Double Taxation on Copyright
    Royalties, 134
TRADE MARKS
copyright work, as, 166
fraudulent application and use of, 72
infringement, 166
registration, 165
TREATIES
enforcement of, 22
TREATY OF ROME. *See also* EUROPEAN
COMMUNITY
copyright, exploitation of, 134–135
harmonisation provisions, 135
TRIPs AGREEMENT, 126–127
TYPEFACES, 133–134
artistic work, as, 34
protection of, 29

Typographical arrangements
  duration of copyright in, 43
  meaning, 38
  published editions, in, 38

Universal Copyright Convention
  developing countries, relaxations in
    favour of, 124–126
  minimum obligatory requirements, 122
  Paris revision, 122, 125–126
  parties to, 123–124
  purposes of, 122
  service performed by, 123
Universities
  copyright, 70
  deposit of books in, 5, 6
Unpublished works
  bequest of copyright by will, 66
  copyright in, 7
  duration of copyright in, 42, 43
  librarians and archivists, copying by, 93

Vienna Agreement for the Protection
  of Typefaces and their
  International Deposit, 133–134

WIPO performances and Phonograms
  Treaty, 58, 60, 127, 129
Wireless telegraphy
  definition, 35
Works. See also Artistic works, etc.
  categories protected, 27–40
  fixation, requirement of, 40
  foreign, denial of copyright to, 75
  originality, requirement of, 39–40
  protection,
    capable of, 26
    heads of, 27
    qualification for,
      absence of, 41
      authorship, by, 41
      country of origin, by, 41
      permanence of, 41–42